Think Again!

Innovative Approaches to the Business of Law

Jeffrey L. Nischwitz

Commitment to Quality: The Law Practice Management Section is committed to quality in our publications. Our authors are experienced practitioners in their fields. Prior to publication, the contents of all our books are rigorously reviewed by experts to ensure the highest quality product and presentation. Because we are committed to serving our readers' needs, we welcome your feedback on how we can improve future editions of this book.

Cover design by Andrew Alcala, ABA Publishing.

Library of Congress Cataloging-in-Publication Data

Nischwitz, Jeffrey L.
Think again! : innovative approaches to the business of law / by Jeffrey L. Nischwitz. – 1st ed.
p. cm.
Includes index.
ISBN 1-59031-737-8
1. Law offices–United States. I. American Bar Association. Section of Law Practice Management. II. Title.

KF318.N57 2007
340.068–dc22

2006035496

Discounts are available for books ordered in bulk. Special consideration is given to state bars, CLE programs, and other bar-related organizations. Inquire at Book Publishing, American Bar Association, 321 North Clark Street, Chicago, Illinois 60610.

Contents

About the Author

Jeff Nischwitz is a lawyer, entrepreneur, relationship builder, and business builder who has a reputation as a high-impact speaker, consultant, advisor, trainer, coach, and writer. He helps professionals and business owners to enhance their success through leadership, entrepreneurial thinking, empowered teams, great client experiences, and proven relationship building and business development strategies and tactics. After graduating from Ohio Northern University with a B.S. in Business Administration (summa cum laude), he went on to the Ohio State College of Law, where he received his Juris Doctor degree (summa cum laude), was a member of the Order of the Coif, and was a member of the *Ohio State Law Journal.*

Jeff began his legal career with a major Cleveland, Ohio, law firm where he was elected partner before deciding to take the entrepreneurial leap by starting his own law firm. He was a founding shareholder and later the Chair of Nischwitz, Pembridge & Chriszt, a leading business law firm in northeast Ohio. His prior experiences as a partner in a large Cleveland law firm, building his own solo law practice, and building and leading an entrepreneurial business law firm provide him with a diverse and practical perspective on the business of law firms. During his seventeen years of practicing law and, ultimately, leading his own firm, he clearly saw many of the shortcomings of and challenges with the traditional law firm business model; this was the foundation for his founding a consulting and training business focused on professionals, as well as for writing this book.

After his successful legal and law-firm building career, Jeff has built several successful businesses and helped entrepreneurs and owners build their businesses into profit powerhouses. He is passionate about making a difference in people's lives by helping them to achieve their business and personal goals. He has a keen sense of what it takes to improve bottom line results and profits, and his experience in working with businesses across a wide range of industries and on every aspect of a business, from advertising to leadership to sales, allows him to offer practical and proven ideas and strategies to improve any business. He is recognized for his unique ability to "see" business challenges with a "different eye" or perspective that allows him to identify innovative solutions and enhanced opportunities.

Jeff is well known in the business community for his leadership abilities, creativity, innovation, and energy. He has an established reputation for building strong relationships and using those relationships to help others enhance their own personal and professional success. He is a frequent speaker and presenter on various business topics including Building Businesses, Leadership, Networking, Sales and Marketing, Entrepreneurship, Relationship Building, Business Development, Team Building, Business Planning, Personal Development, and Goal Setting. He has owned several businesses, all focused on helping grow and improve businesses and people, including the Professional Business Institute, which offers seminars, workshops, training, and consulting for professional service providers focused on business issues, including law firm leadership, team development, business development, client service, and relationship-building strategies and tactics.

In addition to his business endeavors, Jeff is involved with numerous business and nonprofit organizations and initiatives as part of his personal commitment to being a strong and supporting member of his community and the region. In addition to numerous business organizations, he is on the Board of E CITY, a nonprofit organization that teaches low-income students business and entrepreneurship skills as a path to escaping the cycle of poverty and empowering them to achieve their goals. He was also actively involved in the launch of a new charter school in the Cleveland area, the Entrepreneurship Preparatory School, in August, 2006, and he is on the Board of Harvard Avenue Community School; his involvement in these schools is all a part of his passion for improving urban education and making a difference in young people's lives.

Jeff currently lives in Westlake, Ohio, with his wife Diane and their two sons, Eric and Kyle.

Acknowledgments

I have talked and thought about writing a book since I was a teenager, but the idea of writing a book has been almost all-consuming over the past several years. Perhaps like many would-be authors, I thought about it a lot and talked about it a little, but I never took any tangible steps to making it a reality. Several years ago I developed a workshop and seminar program for lawyers (for continuing legal education credits) that was variously titled "Business of Law," "Building a Law Business," "Building a Great Law Firm," and "Law Business Solutions." I developed this program because, after experiencing and observing the business of law in a wide range of firms and talking to lawyers across an even wider range of firms and experiences, I saw a need that was missing . . . the need to share with lawyers the power of thinking and acting like business people and entrepreneurs when it came to their law firms and law practices.

I knew from personal experience that we were never trained in the business side of law, whether in law school or once we started practicing. I also saw few if any workshops and seminars for lawyers that focused on the essentials of building and running a law business, including the critical skills needed to attract, secure, and retain clients—the life blood of any law firm. As I started to deliver the workshops and seminars, the feedback was consistent and positive. The attendees had been waiting for someone to bring these types of ideas and perspectives to them, and they were excited to be able to invest some of their valuable time working on the business side of their firms and practices. They all knew that they were not giving the "business side" of the law enough or the right attention, and they welcomed these workshops, seminars, and discussions with open arms. As one senior partner-attendee put it, "The Business of Law program was outstanding. This was the first time I have heard someone that truly understands the business side of the practice of law. This was the best program I've ever heard on how to build a great law firm. Mr. Nischwitz really gets it."

As I was in the midst of delivering these workshops and seminars, the idea of writing a book kept coming back to me, and I finally realized that this book—*Think Again!*—was the book that I was meant to write. Not knowing how to begin, I took the only path I knew—I just started writing, working largely from the ideas, concepts, and perspectives that I had developed for the workshops. Perhaps like most first-time authors, it took much more time than I ever imagined, but with the support and encouragement of many people, I was able to complete it.

Many thanks go to my wife, Diane, who encouraged my writing and allowed me those many hours banging away on the laptop. I must also thank my two sons, Eric and Kyle, who allowed me to be the writer from time to time even though it cut into "being Dad time." I give a big thanks to Pattie Entenok, who transcribed much of the book that I had dictated, despite the challenges of trying to get everything I was saying as I got excited during my dictation. Certainly, I must also thank my parents, who always let me know that I could do anything that I wanted to do, encouraged me to write when I was young, and, ultimately, had a big hand in my decision to pursue a legal career. Thanks also goes to the many friends who supported and encouraged me throughout the writing process and especially during the search for a publisher. The publisher search can often be slow and discouraging, but many friends continued to encourage me to push forward and to never give up.

I must also thank Eric Valentine, an agent in New York, who was the first "professional" to see my book. Eric got the book in front of a publisher and helped move the book along deep into the process. While that publisher ultimately passed on the book, Eric's thoughts on the book and my writing were invaluable in convincing me to be diligent in my search for a publisher and to not give up. Finally, I must, of course, thank the Law Practice Management Section of the American Bar Association. Many people at the ABA were supportive and worked hard to make this book's publication a reality. I especially want to thank Beverly Loder at the ABA, who made it her mission to see that this book was published. Despite many obstacles, Beverly was convinced that this book and its "unique voice" needed to be published, and she made it a reality. I also want to thank all of the people involved with this project from the Law Practice Management Section for their invaluable advice, creativity, and input in making the book that you are about to read the best that it can be.

As with many other authors, this book was a personal mission for me, and I have been thrilled with the journey from writing, to editing, to securing a publisher, to final publication. It has been all that I ever imagined and more, and certainly more challenging than I ever imagined. In the end, I believe that this book was meant to be published, and many people and events came together to make my dream a reality in synchronistic ways. Some people have said that I was inspired in writing this book, but I believe that I was inspired *by* writing it. My ultimate wish is that each of you finds this book to be a resource and tool that you can use to improve your law business and to make it everything that it should be.

Jeff Nischwitz

PART I

The Journey Begins

1 It's Not a Joking Matter

We've all heard the hundreds of lawyer jokes that have made their way around the profession and the Internet. There are so many lawyer jokes and they are so predictable that we can see them coming from miles away. One series of these jokes starts the same way: "How many lawyers does it take to . . . ?" And the answers are sometimes funny and often downright obnoxious. Frankly, most lawyers have gotten more than a little bit tired of hearing all of the lawyer jokes, although the truth is that we've brought much of this on ourselves by the way that we've acted and conducted ourselves with clients and the general public. When you go out of your way to argue that you are different than everyone else, then you'll typically become the target of jokes, criticism, and more.

At the risk of turning you against me at the outset, let me start off with this question: How many lawyers does it take to build a great law business? Do you give up? The answer is ONE . . . who thinks and acts like an entrepreneur and a businessperson. If you think this is a bad joke, you are right . . . it's actually not funny at all. Actually, it's pretty scary because the reality in this answer highlights what is probably the biggest challenge and risk for lawyers and law firms, especially in a business environment where competition is getting tougher and clients are getting smarter and more demanding every day. These business realities have put (or are in the process of putting) law firms at risk . . . at risk of working and operating with a mind-set and approach that no longer fits.

This book addresses the many ways that lawyers can improve their results by thinking and acting like entrepreneurs, and it all starts with embracing the fact that a law

▼▼▼▼▼

Yes, your delivery of legal services is a profession, but how your firm operates, develops business, and delivers client service are business issues that are vital to your business success.

firm (no matter how big or small) is a business and should be run like a business.

Today's business reality is that success in the practice of law requires business solutions, and what follows are ideas, strategies, and tactics to help you take your legal career and law firm to new heights of business success!

For many of you, reading this book will be a challenge. It may push you outside your comfort zone . . . it is supposed to do so. A common theme throughout this book will be that you have to do things differently to get different results. As the saying goes, "If you always do what you've always done, you will always get what you've always got." This certainly is a catchy phrase, but more importantly, it is absolutely true. In fact, the business realities surrounding the practice of law are such that if you continue doing what you've always done, *you'll be falling further and further behind every day.* The business world is rapidly changing and the practice of law is a very real part of those changes. We are in an information economy where the world is flattening every day.

Every day your clients and prospects see and hear of opportunities to get things faster and cheaper from alternative sources, which include the Internet and off-shoring of services (including legal services). If you think that these changes are not your problem or that they will not impact you, then think again. Your clients are getting smarter every day and they are getting more and more demanding . . . they demand not only quality, but more importantly value from everyone that they do business with . . . and that includes you, their lawyer.

If you are happy with your current results and prospects for the future, then you can put this book down, but you'll be the only lawyer who is not affected by the recent competitive and business climate changes, as well as the changes that will be there tomorrow and in the future. But if you want different and better results for you, your firm, *and your clients,* then I invite you to read on with an open mind. This book is about *thinking differently* about the business of law and *acting differently* as you conduct the business of law. The future of law firms will be more about being different than being better. One caveat: If you start to have the reaction that you already know something (or that it is nothing new), then ask yourself if you are already doing it. If not, then ask yourself why you are not already doing it. Many of the ideas in this book are not new, but if you are not already doing them, then keep reading. You may discover a process, a system, or even the right motivation to start implementing these ideas that you have known about for a long time, but for some reason just have not acted upon.

It is a new playing field when it comes to the business of law, and my goal is to share with you some different ways to look at your law business and to share some ideas, approaches, or different perspectives that can make you and your firm more businesslike and more successful. I look forward to sharing this journey with you.

The Entrepreneurial Lawyer

2

While law firms are different in many ways, they all share common goals. Every law firm must

1. Secure more clients;
2. Operate "like a business;"
3. Deliver excellent legal services in the most cost-effective means possible; and
4. Differentiate itself.

From these common goals, it becomes clear that lawyers can improve their results by thinking and acting like entrepreneurs.

▼▼▼▼▼

Success in the business of law generally follows when lawyers think like entrepreneurs, but deliver like professionals.

Too often, lawyers do not see this distinction (between their law business and the practice of law) and, as a result, they make poor business decisions. For many reasons, including ego and institutionally created habits, lawyers continually want to distinguish and differentiate themselves from the rest of the business world by referring to themselves as "professionals." They will often say things like "the practice of law is a profession, not a business" or "our business is different because it is a profession."

Some of this comes from the public's negative perception of lawyers (i.e., lawyers are sharks, dishonest, unethical, and so on), which creates a defensive attitude among lawyers. The legal education system also contributes to this disconnect between the "practice" or the "profession" and the business realities for lawyers. Law schools do not offer many courses on the business aspects of being a lawyer. Instead, the focus is on substantive legal topics and developing the students' legal minds (the ability to think, reason, and interpret logically—in the immortal words of Professor Kingsfield, "to think like a lawyer"). Lawyers are trying so hard to elevate themselves and the profession that they not only forget that they are "in business," but spend their time working hard to "prove" that they are not a business . . . and this is one of the biggest challenges (albeit self-created) facing lawyers today.

Make no mistake about it—the practice of law certainly is a profession, and a noble profession indeed. It is a profession with a long and distinguished history of helping people, and lawyers have always played an important role not only in the development of the law, but in interpreting and using the law to make positive change in the world. Unfortunately, the perception of lawyers has suffered in the eyes of our clients. Without a doubt, our first priority as lawyers is to serve our clients . . . to put our clients' needs and interests first and to zealously represent those interests. But while serving our clients' interests we can and must recognize and understand the business aspects of our profession. We can make a living without being greedy, and success in the business of law ultimately comes down to our ability to do much more than simply be good lawyers. There are many business challenges for lawyers, and if we fail to address and overcome those challenges, our ability to continue in our profession and to serve our clients will be at risk.

One of the significant challenges for lawyers is the billable hour concept, which is actually a fairly recent phenomenon. The billable hour did not become the commonly accepted method of charging for legal services until the late 1950s and early 1960s. Prior to that time, the most common methods were fixed fees, flat fees, retainers, "eyeball" estimates, and contingent fees. Certainly, charging by the hour has hurt lawyers in two critical respects. First, it has caused lawyers to be viewed by clients as necessary expenses, not as value-added advisors. Since lawyers are paid by the hour, not by the value they deliver, it is easy for clients to have this view. Thus, clients always want to know whether they are "on the clock" when talking to their lawyers, and they are hesitant to call their lawyers for advice *before* problems occur. This ultimately causes client service to suffer, since the clients feel that their lawyers are not looking out for their best interests, but rather are focused on "running the meter."

Second, lawyers have also come to see themselves and their value based on the billable hour. Their self-perceived value is directly related to their billable rate. They are not valuable to the firm unless they are billing time. Thus, things that they "know" they should do (e.g., business development activities and client service activities) are not done because they are "too busy" billing time. For example, one of the easiest proven ways to enhance your relationship with your clients and to simultaneously increase per-client revenue is to periodically meet with existing clients, but off the clock. Lawyers, in general, do not do this because they are too busy, because the time is not billable, and because (unlike billable time) it is not viewed as productive or valuable.

Whether this view comes from the bottom up (from the lawyers) or the top down (from firm management), the cause is ultimately the same—these nonbillable activities are not viewed as productive or contributing to the firm's bottom line. In fact, these may be the most productive ways for lawyers to spend their time and may be the most effective means for firms to enhance their revenues. Even if the billable hour remains the norm, lawyers have to change their culture to recognize the great value of investing their time in clients and in business development. This change can then make it easier for lawyers to do the things they know they need to do, but that they are not consistently doing now.

When it comes to business development, the playing field has changed. The "old school" could best be described as the "good old boy" or "country club" method of business development. The model was simple—join a country club, play golf, make friends, and get clients. That model, however, developed in a much less competitive environment for legal services and before clients became more sophisticated and demanding consumers of legal services. Under this model, if a business owner knew you and played golf with you, you got their legal work, plain and simple.

In the business development arena, lawyers have been slow to recognize that the market has changed and, thus, that the business development methods must also change.

In today's competitive environment, lawyers must build relationships with clients and prospective clients based on three key elements: rapport, competence, and value. Ten or fifteen years ago, lawyer-client relationships were built and maintained largely based on the rapport element, but today's clients (many of which are newer businesses) are looking for and demanding more. In addition to liking their lawyer (rapport), they want to make sure that their lawyer is competent (even if many clients are not capable of judging our competence), and they want to perceive that their lawyer is adding value to them and their business. They want to make sure that all of their decisions are good business decisions, including the selection of their lawyers. Business owners are used to making business decisions with respect to their other vendor and consultant relationships based on their ability to differentiate themselves in the marketplace and to demonstrate how they will add value to the client.

As in all sales scenarios, consumers of legal services are looking for the same things in making their "buy" decisions: How can this person or firm save me money, make me money, or simplify my life? These are the basic reasons that anyone buys anything, including legal services. Lawyers now face the challenge of being required to show prospective clients "the money" in terms of money saved, money made, or life simplified.

At the end of the movie *Patton,* General Bradley (Karl Malden) tells General Patton (George C. Scott) that being a good soldier no longer is going to be good enough, that generals will have to be diplomats, politicians, and so on. General Patton (an "old school" general) responded by saying "God help us." Lawyers and law firms face a similar challenge today. It is no longer enough to be just a good lawyer . . . lawyers need to be great managers, great client-service providers, great communicators, great marketers, and great salespeople. Diplomas from Ivy League law schools, top class rankings, and great training may create great legal technicians, but that is no longer enough. Clients are demanding more and lawyers must change how they think and how they act to meet these increasing demands.

Fundamentally, *Think Again!* is about change:

- Changing how you look at the practice of law;
- Changing how you think about and interact with clients;
- Changing your approach to delivering client service (and client experiences);
- Changing your concept of value and the value of your services; and
- Changing how you go about building your law business.

It has often been said that "change is good," and this is more and more true every day in the business of law. While change for the sake of change is never a good thing, the business realities with and surrounding the business of law are driving the need for innovative and forward-thinking approaches for lawyers and law firms. Innovation and different thinking has been driving success in many industries over the past several years and will continue to do so in the future. Now it's time for lawyers to use innovative thinking, approaches, and tactics to build great law practices and law firms. So, if you think that the old ways of practicing law are good enough, then *Think Again!*

PART II

Business Solutions for Lawyers

3 A Rose by Any Other Name

Is the practice of law a business or a profession? You would think the answer would be easy, but it is much more complicated than it appears. This book is about treating your law firm or law practice as a business, about functioning as a businessperson (or entrepreneur) rather than just as a lawyer, and about making better business (and more businesslike) decisions. Every time you try to differentiate the practice of law from a business, you are putting up a thick wall against change, improvements, and enhanced results. If you want to build a great law business (whether as a solo practitioner or as a 400-lawyer law firm), it is vital that you start at the beginning and embrace the concept that the practice of law is, in fact, a business.

Let's assume that every lawyer really does want to have a more successful law practice or law firm. Let's also assume that we are all ready to acknowledge that our law practice or law firm is, in fact, a business. While some lawyers would argue that it is a business like no other business, there are not that many differences between the business of law and any other service business. Every business delivers something, whether a product or service. For lawyers, the "product" that they deliver is legal services (we will talk later about what lawyers really should be delivering). Accountants deliver accounting services, physicians deliver medical services, consultants deliver consulting services, and IT firms deliver IT services. To put it simply, every service business comes down to three basics:

1. Get clients
2. Service clients
3. Keep clients

This is true for every service business, including lawyers and law firms.

Let's break it down to basics. Every service business can be broken down into two basic parts: (1) someone must sell the services; and (2) someone must deliver the services. In fact, the only other element of a service business is someone to provide all of the operations and administrative functions related to a service business (i.e., answering phones, preparing documents, billing, collections, paying bills, and so on). No matter how large or wide ranging a service business may grow, it still comes down to selling services and delivering services. If you do not sell the legal services, the business will not succeed. If you do not deliver the legal services, the business will fail.

Let's talk briefly about that age-old debate about which is more important—bringing in clients or delivering legal services. It is like the chicken-and-the-egg riddle. Without clients, there are no legal services to perform, but if you bring in clients, someone has to perform the services. Actually, this is not a true chicken-and-the-egg situation. The reality is that there are never legal services to provide unless and until there are clients in the door.

> ▼▼▼▼▼
>
> If you have a law firm of great lawyers, but no rainmakers, how long will you be in business?

Without superior marketing, selling, and business development skills, how long will your law business stay in business? If you are uncertain about which is more important (especially in a firm that does not get its business from advertising), then consider this situation: You learn that two of the lawyers in your firm have tragically passed away. One is a top-notch and skilled lawyer who provides great client service. The other is your top rainmaker, who provides very few legal services but brings in many clients. Which loss causes you the greatest concern (or fear) about the future of the firm? Enough said.

Once we take a hard look at what the business of law is (and is not), we discover that the supposed differences are more imagined than real (sometimes conveniently imagined so that we can avoid making hard business decisions or operating in a more businesslike way). We also discover that the perceived differences are the result of outside influences from sources apparently designed to separate the practice of law from the business world. Instead of continually trying to differentiate the business of law from other businesses, law firms need to embrace their status as real businesses and start thinking and acting like true businesses. This is essential for any firm to make the transition from the mere practice of law to building a successful and enduring law business . . . and every lawyer needs to be a good and smart businessperson to build a practice or a firm that not only survives but thrives.

Three Fundamental Truths

4

Everyone is always looking for easy answers, easy solutions, and quick fixes. Lawyers are especially focused on finding "silver bullets" when it comes to their business. They are always looking for one great idea, one simple solution, or the easy answer to improving their law business, but there is no such thing. There are no easy answers, no quick solutions, no quick fixes, and no "silver bullets," but there are *three fundamental truths* that apply when it comes to the business side of the practice of law. When it comes to growing and improving your law business, you *must* change:

1. How you think
2. How you act
3. What you do

Simple truths? Yes. Easy to implement? Not necessarily, but they are fundamental truths. Changing the results in your law business requires that you change all these.

The first and most important step is to change how you think, and much of this book focuses on this critical subject. Throughout this book we will be exploring different ways to look at your law business and the functions you perform in that law business, including management, administration, hiring, employees (professional and staff), client service, and business development. In the end, how you think determines how you act, which determines your results. You may think this concept (how you think) to be too "soft" and not logical, but it is the foundation for making critical changes in your law business and your results. Even if you plan new actions, those actions will not happen and you will not achieve the results you desire without first changing how you think about your law business. If you have doubts, then "listen" to your clients.

Let's consider an example of how clients expect you to think and act like a businessperson, rather than simply as a lawyer. Recently, I came across an article written by a former lawyer who had left the practice of law to run his own business. The subject of the article was his company's law firm—specifically, the firm's practice of sending everything via expedited mail. The firm had been doing some intellectual property work and, when the "official" documentation had been received from the governmental agency, the firm sent the documentation to the client via overnight mail at a cost of approximately $10. The problem? The client had not asked to receive it via overnight mail, it was not late, and it was not time sensitive—in other words, there was no reason for it to be sent via overnight mail. Now, you might be thinking that the law firm did this as a method of enhanced client service, but that was most definitely *not* how the client saw it.

The client's questions: "Are you charging me $10 to send me something via overnight mail that could have been sent via regular mail? If so, then I have a problem with that."—or—"If you are not charging me for overnight mail, then why would you make such a bad business decision to unnecessarily incur additional overhead costs (which ultimately has a negative impact on client fees and service)?" This client was questioning whether his lawyers think like businesspeople or, worse, whether they are bad businesspeople, and all over what seems like a little thing—a $10 overnight mail package. However, it is just such little differences in how you think that can make or break your success.

There is a concept in the business and personal development world called BE—DO—HAVE, which embodies a simple concept—changing the way you think is the critical first step to achieving different results. Many people want to *have* different or better results, but they never *do* things that they must in order to achieve different results. Instead, they rely on luck or hope, neither of which are business strategies nor likely to be successful. Some people understand that they cannot immediately jump to having different or better results, and they focus on doing different things, but they are unlikely to achieve their goals because (despite their best laid plans) they never *do* what they intended. The shortcoming is that they never learned how to think differently or to *be* something different before attempting to change their

▼▼▼▼▼

Doing is also a vital part of achieving different and better results. While businesspeople (lawyers and others) often talk about doing something different, their actions typically fall short of what was needed to achieve the desired results.

actions. The *be* of BE—DO—HAVE is all about changing how you think. When it comes to the business of law, it means that you must *be*come a strong businessperson (and start to think like a businessperson and entrepreneur) in order to *do* the right things that will allow you to *have* the type of law business and the results that you desire.

We will talk later about the vital role of planning, but even the best plan is absolutely worthless if it is never implemented. Ultimately, no matter how great the plan or strategy, it is utterly worthless unless or until it is implemented. No action equals no results, yet many of us continue to operate under the misguided belief that a great plan or a great idea has value, even if it is not implemented. The following principle is an example of a different way that you need to think in order to improve your law business: "Every idea and every plan is utterly worthless until implemented." Let me say that again: "Every plan and every idea is totally without value unless and until it is implemented."

We often make the excuse (to justify our failure to act) that the plan or idea still has value because we hope to implement it in the future. This type of thinking is the kiss of death to the idea because it makes it too easy to continually postpone and delay acting on it. If we convince ourselves that an idea has value in and of itself, then it is all too easy to let ourselves off the hook when we fail to implement the idea. Once we "understand" that all of our plans and ideas are worthless until we implement them, then we will stop making excuses and we will start taking action.

Sometime ago I came across a little story that demonstrates that action, not planning, is the key to success:

> There were three birds sitting on a fence. Two of them decided to fly away. How many birds were left on the fence?

I am sure that most of you got the correct answer—there are still three birds sitting on the fence. Why? Because deciding to do something is not the same as doing something. In business, sitting on the fence and developing new ideas will still leave you sitting on the same fence with the same view of the world. If you want a different and better law business with different results, you need to spread your wings and fly in some direction. In the final analysis, the direction you fly is much less important than the act of taking flight and getting moving in some direction.

Finally, improvements and growth require different action. As we said before, "If you always do what you have always done, you will always get what you have always got." Cute? Certainly. Profound? Absolutely! You cannot and will not achieve different results unless you change what you do and how you do it. If you want to improve client service, your firm must do something different. Client service will not improve simply by talking or thinking about it. Client service will only change if you change what you are doing. Clients are not going to change their perspective of your firm unless you change that perspective, and changes in perspective are born from different actions.

Well, certainly you could rely on hope or luck to change your results, which means continuing to do the same things the same way that you have always done them and then hoping that things will improve. As it has been said many times, "hope is not a strategy." Personally, I do not want my professional and business life to be determined by luck. Yes, sometimes luck plays a role, but most of the time perceived luck is really results achieved through planning, preparation, and different thinking. One definition of luck is when preparedness meets opportunity, but you can also create new opportunities simply by doing things differently.

If you are reading this book, you want to grow and improve your firm and you want different or better results in your law business. While we will be covering different ways to attain these improvements and enhance results, it all begins with thinking differently, taking action, and doing something different. But it all starts with *being* a businessperson and not just a lawyer.

5 What Does a Yellow Light Mean?

If you have seen the television series *Taxi,* and especially if you were a *Taxi* fan, you will remember the episode where "Reverend" Jim Ignatowski went for his driver's test. Let me set the scene for you. Jim was an odd character who never seemed to have any significant grasp on reality. It was discovered that Jim was driving without a hack's license, and Jim was told that he had to get a license to continue as an employee of the Sunshine Cab Company. The "garage gang" went with Jim when he went to take the written license test. After Jim had trouble completing the application, he sat down to take the written portion of the test, with his friends looking on. On the very first question, Jim leaned over and whispered to his friends, "What does a yellow light mean?" One of the gang whispered back "slow down." In what became a classic television scene, Jim responded by repeating his question, albeit much slower: "Whaaaat doooeees aaaa yeeellooowww liiight meeeaaan?" When one of his friends again responded "slow down," Jim continued to repeat the same question—"What does a yellow light mean?"—ever slower and slower and slower. As you might guess, the garage gang became more and more frustrated with Jim, while laughing hysterically.

You are probably wondering what this *Taxi* episode has to do with the business of law. Actually, it has everything to do with the business of law. People are always looking for a quick path to different results. There are no quick fixes, but there is a notable exception, and it comes directly from this *Taxi* episode. Pay very close attention because this may be the most important point that you can take away from this book.

In fact, it is probably the most significant concept that any lawyer can use and implement to improve client service, client development, and business results. Simply put, if you want to attract better clients, to deliver better client service, to have better client relationships, and to improve your business development results, you must *SLOW DOWN!*

This concept—Slow Down—came to me when I was meeting with a young partner as we were exploring ways to improve his business development skills. One of the best sources of ideas, skills, and mentoring is other rainmakers in the firm, but most rainmakers tend not to help or work with the other lawyers on how to become rainmakers because they are focused on (and compensated for) their own business development results. I learned that the young partner had not had the benefit of mentoring from the rainmaker in the firm, but I asked him to identify the top rainmaker for me. He immediately did so, which is easy to do in most firms. Nearly everyone can tell you who brings in the most business. I then asked what the firm's top rainmaker did differently when it came to working with clients and client relationships. He told me that this top rainmaker really did not do anything different, *but* he did have a "different style."

The young partner then shared with me the following example of a meeting involving a client, this young partner, and the rainmaker:

> We were meeting with this client who described to us the facts relating to a business issue that he was facing. Within a very short time, I 'knew' the answer to his question and knew exactly what legal advice he needed for this situation. However, the rainmaker continued to ask the client questions and more questions. To me, none of these questions were necessary because the answer to the client's situation was already clear. In fact, the advice we ultimately gave the client was the same advice that I had come up with early in the conversation. While my style is more to the point, the rainmaker's "style" is to ask lots of questions, sort of wander around in the discussion and to take time in reaching a conclusion.

What he had described to me was not a different style, but actually a better and more effective approach to clients, client relationships, and business development. The rainmaker was a top rainmaker for a reason, and this "different style" was probably the main reason.

The young partner wanted just enough information to know the right answer and was in a hurry to tell the client what to do. In contrast, the rainmaker not only wanted to make sure that he fully understood the issue (including the client's goals and objectives), but wanted the client to be part of the decision-making process. When the young partner had described this scenario to me, I told him that I did not think it was a "different style," but rather a completely different objective.

The young partner wanted to quickly and efficiently tell the client what to do—to give the client the right advice. The rainmaker, however, was not in a hurry, took his time, and wanted to make sure that the client was part of the process, understood all of the issues, and in reality, reached the conclusion himself. The fact is that clients will willingly pay for value, will want to work with the lawyer, will have a great service experience, and will recommend and refer the lawyer *if* the client feels that he or she is part of the process, is involved in the decision-making, and knows for himself or herself that it is a good decision, rather than just being "told what to do."

Whether the decisions are personal or business, the lawyer's ultimate goal should be to help clients make good (actually better) decisions. The operative word is "help," which requires that the lawyer involve the client in the evaluation, assessment, and decision process. Unless a client makes it clear that he or she wants to be told what to do, your role as the legal advisor is to walk them through the issues, ask many questions (the right questions), show the client why a particular path is good or bad (and ideally, show the client alternative paths), and help the client (with your advice) to make a good decision. This process (not a "different style") is a critical ingredient to providing great client service, building strong client relations, and creating a client base that not only tolerates you, but will proactively recommend, refer, and "sell" you to others . . . and it all starts with Slowing Down.

> ▼▼▼▼▼
>
> Lawyers erroneously believe that it is their job to tell clients what to do, but that is not the case at all. In truth, the lawyer's true role is to help clients make good decisions for themselves.

A real enemy of this type of outstanding service is the preoccupation with the billable hour. Too often, lawyers do not believe that they are being productive unless they are billing time, which also means being as efficient as possible. This results in ignoring the client and focusing on speed and quantity, rather than on understanding and quality. Lawyers are so busy that they miss the opportunities before them to slow down and spend time building relationships with their clients. A senior partner in a law firm shared this experience with me:

> A lawyer in my office came to me at the conclusion of a project and asked me what he should do with the completed work product. I told him that he should go to the client's office and hand deliver it. While there he should take the opportunity to get a quick tour of the office and get to know more about the business. At a minimum, it was important to hand deliver this to the client because it was a significant project involving significant fees, and this personal touch was important to the client service aspect of the engagement. Shortly thereafter, I asked the lawyer what he had done and he told me that he had mailed the work product to the client. When I asked him why, he said he was "too busy" to hand deliver it.

Too often lawyers are "too busy" to do what is best for the client, to do what the client really wants, to take an approach that demonstrates a strong commitment to the client, to add the personal touch, and to focus on truly outstanding client service, rather than just getting the work done as quickly and efficiently as possible.

This was a missed opportunity, which was missed because of the focus on efficiency and on all the "stuff" that goes into practicing law. Ultimately, slowing down may not be the most efficient method, but it is the most effective and productive—for the lawyer, the firm, and the client.

Wait a minute, you say, "clients are already hesitant to call us and always want to know if we are 'on the clock,' so certainly they don't want us to slow down our efforts. They want us to be fast and efficient. They want us to be quick, because quick translates into lower bills." This argument seems logical, but it comes from the perspective that you, as the lawyer, are nothing more than a vendor and an expense. You are right. Clients want their vendors, service providers, and "necessary expenses" to be quick about it. Why? Because they do not see vendors, "necessary expenses," and service providers as adding value, but as costs of doing business that they want to keep as low as possible.

None of you wants to be a mere vendor or "necessary expense." You want to be a valued and trusted advisor, but that starts with you believing that you are a valuable advisor and that you provide valuable advice to your clients. You also have to treat your clients the way a trusted and valued advisor would treat them. You need to focus on the value of your services, not the stuff of your services. You need to focus your clients on value, not time. You need to remind your clients about the value that you have provided to them through your advice, counseling, and legal services. Instead of talking about billable time and tenths (or quarters) of an hour, talk about results, savings, and profits. As the client (played by Cuba Gooding, Jr.) said in the film *Jerry Maguire,* "Show me the money!" That is precisely what your clients want and what you need to show them.

> ▼▼▼▼▼
>
> Simply put, if clients do not see your value, then they will question whether or not you are on the clock and they will want you to "be quick about it."

Whether it is legal services, accounting services, consulting services, payroll services, copiers, telephones, or any business product or service, the motivation for the buying is always one of three things: (1) the desire to make money; (2) the desire to save money (or reduce risk); and/or (3) the desire to simplify things (to make it easier for the buyer). Regarding a lawyer, clients and prospects are asking themselves the same questions when it comes to hiring you, continuing to retain your services, or "firing" you. They may not ask them out loud, but be assured that they are going to hire you or work with you if they *perceive* that you can make them money, save them money (or reduce risk), and/or you can somehow simplify their lives. Many people have some sense of this concept (on what motivates people to do business with one person or another), but they make the mistake of assuming that all people have the same motivations. Typically, they will assume that making money is the top priority, but for the person they are dealing with, it is not.

We will talk more about asking questions later, but this is an area where asking questions is so vital to success in building strong and productive client relationships. The mere asking of questions alone can help build the relationship and, by asking the right questions and really listening to the answers, you can discover the prospective client's or existing client's true and most important motives and interests. You can then focus your efforts and attention on what the client wants and needs, rather than on what you think they should want or need. Ultimately, none of this will happen (and you will never discover the person's priorities and motives) unless you Slow Down!

Why *Slow Down?* Slowing down will help you to be a better lawyer. Slowing down will help your clients see you as a trusted advisor and valuable resource, rather than a vendor or a mere expense. Slowing down will create clients who will happily pay for your services because they see the value. Slowing down will help you create great client experiences. Slowing down will show your clients that you care about them. Slowing down will help build longer and better client relationships. Most important, slowing down will deliver clients who will actively and energetically recommend and refer you to others. These are the types of clients and client relationships that you all want and, ultimately, are what you need in order to build a strong law business. It all starts with an answer to a simple question: What does a yellow light mean? Slow down!

The Trouble with Lawyers!

6

Do lawyers have trouble working within the business of law? Yes, many or most do. Do lawyers have unique and different challenges from other businesses? Yes, there are some challenges that are unique or particularly acute for lawyers, but they also face some of the same challenges as other businesses, whether service or product based. In the final analysis, this book is mostly about the challenges that lawyers face in building, running, and growing a successful and profitable law business, but for now let's focus our attention on two key areas where lawyers seem to regularly and continuously make business missteps.

The Trouble with Strategic Planning

The first law firm challenge is strategic planning. Certainly, strategic planning is a shortcoming for many businesses, but law firms actually have a wider range of challenges with strategic planning than other businesses. In most businesses, the strategic planning challenge is that there is none. Businesses (and many law firms) go about their business with no idea of where they are heading, why they are heading there, or how to get there. Sound familiar?

We should all know by now that strategic planning is like having a map on a trip, especially before the advent of superhighways and highway signs. If you were getting ready to set out on a cross-country trip, you would want to at least look at a map so that you would know where you were going and how to get there the fastest. In business, a strategic plan serves not only as a map (helping you to travel toward your destination in the most cost-effective, efficient, and profitable means possible), but it also helps define your destination and why you are heading there. Without this type of strategic planning, you do not know where you are going with your business and, thus, you will never know when you arrive. You may be going in the wrong direction. At a minimum, your journey will certainly be wasteful (in time and money), inefficient, and less profitable than it should be, and frankly you are more than likely to get lost and never arrive anywhere near where you had hoped to go with your business. Remember, hope is *not* a strategy!

This book is not intended to be about strategic planning and it certainly is not designed to provide the framework for a detailed strategic plan. However, it is my intention to help you to start to see the "why" and value of strategic planning. Strategic planning is the method and the process by which you *decide* where you want to go, what you want your law business to be and "look like," the goals that you have for your firm, a long-term vision for the law business, and ultimately, what course you will plot to take your business where you want it to be. Unfortunately, strategic planning is overlooked or ignored for some fairly simple perceived reasons: no time, no perceived value, and the "we're a law firm, not a business" mindset.

Like so many law firm challenges, time concerns, constraints, and biases rear their ugly heads all too often. In a business where the key players in the firm (the professionals) are not only encouraged, but expected, to deliver the legal services, being busy and not having time for the "business of law" is an all-too-common refrain. When your business and profit model typically depends (to one degree or another) on how many hours you bill, then it is very easy for lawyers to put aside everything (including strategic planning) in favor of billing time and servicing clients. While many businesses fail to engage in strategic planning because they say that they do not have time for it, in most businesses (and especially in product-based businesses) their time is not taken up with the delivery of the "product."

If you talk to the president of a manufacturing business, you will often hear that he or she does not have time for strategic planning, but you know that the president is usually not busy operating the machinery and producing the goods or working in the shipping department. In many non-law businesses the leaders' time is taken up with running and operating the business. While the time demands may be real, they are arguably not as directly related to the client or customer. I do not want to create any false walls here, but if you do not do your legal work, the client is not serviced and you will not get paid. However, while it is certainly important for a non-law business leader to handle human resources issues, the failure to spend time on a human resources issue usually does not result in a customer not receiving services or products, at least not directly.

So yes, every business has time demands, but lawyers (and some other service providers) have a somewhat more difficult challenge when it comes to "making time" for strategic planning. In its simplest terms, whether you are a solo practitioner (a clear example) or a 400-lawyer law firm, lawyers by nature tend to serve too many functions all at once. We typically do not have the luxury of doing only one thing, although great law firms are developed when lawyers are able to more consistently and effectively focus on their strengths and leave the rest for others. This is a key ingredient in one of the greatest business concepts that exists—leverage—which is more than just hiring associates to do the work.

Great law businesses most often develop because the lawyers (or at least the leaders) understand that successful and profitable businesses are just that—real and functional businesses—rather than just an assemblage of professionals billing time. A critical ingredient for building a "real business" is implementing businesslike systems and engaging in businesslike practices, such as strategic planning. While you may be busy practicing law, if you are "too busy" for strategic planning then you are not likely to arrive at any desired destination with your law business.

> ▼▼▼▼▼
>
> On the "positive" side, without a strategic plan you probably have no idea where you are heading or where you want to go, and you will not be aware that you are lost!

One other quick note on balancing time demands versus the need for strategic planning. Too many people convince themselves that strategic planning involves expending hundreds of precious hours in meetings, conducting research, and drafting a voluminous strategic plan. While strategic planning does require an investment of time (note the use of the word "investment"), it does not necessarily have to be excessive or overwhelming. Likewise, the value of a strategic plan is not judged by the number of pages or its weight. The greatest value of strategic planning is the process itself. While it is vital to capture the information, ideas, and visions articulated and the course that was plotted, the form of the strategic plan is nowhere near as important as its substance.

In addition, you must always structure your strategic planning efforts based on the goal or the need. For example, every business should have at least a rudimentary strategic plan that defines what the firm is today, what it wants to be in the future, and how it will get there. However, this type of strategic plan is primarily for internal use and growth, not for external usage. In contrast, if you are seeking bank funding, then the banks may want something more concrete and substantial to satisfy their loan requirements. Just remember that the scope and form of your strategic planning depends on its purpose and intended use, but no matter what, be certain to "make time" to develop a strategic road map for your law business.

Now let's talk about the other side of strategic planning for lawyers—the side that is somewhat unique compared to other businesses. Namely, "too much" strategic planning with little or no tactical planning, follow-through, and implementation. Even the most profound strategic plan is worthless if it is never implemented, is not completely implemented, or like many strategic plans, simply gathers dust on a shelf. Why is this challenge somewhat unique (or different) for law firms? Because law firms (especially larger law firms) are more likely to have some form of strategic planning process in place—often called an annual retreat—but that process is not designed to proceed to implementation for lack of a tactical plan and a system designed to assure implementation. While many businesses fail to engage in any strategic planning, law firms will often engage in the strategic planning process but will not take the next necessary steps toward making that plan a reality.

Law firms are famous for annual retreats (often held in another city—and usually in a warm climate) where the partners or shareholders discuss the future of the firm. While these retreats sometimes fall short of true strategic planning (and much of the attendees' precious time is spent just talking about the firm or complaining about what is bothering them), many times the key ingredients for a strategic plan are developed but the plans die on the vine due to lack of attention (or even sunlight when these strategic plans are thrown into a drawer never to be seen again). Just as with the birds on the fence, having a plan is not the same as implementing a plan. While you cannot implement what you do not have, do not pat yourself on the back because you have a plan. If you never implement it, it is actually worse than not having a strategic plan because you wasted all of the time, energy, and money spent developing it.

In addition to having a strategic plan and vision, you need a tactical plan for how that strategic plan will be implemented. You must chart a detailed course in this tactical plan with clearly articulated schedules, responsibilities, assignments, and goals. Like so many things, this all starts with changing how you look at your law business and how you function in it. If you do not genuinely change how you think about your

▼▼▼▼▼

You must build a system of accountability and create (and support) a system that allows the right people to do what must be done to make the plan a reality.

law business, then even the best laid plans will never become a reality. Without that fundamental paradigm shift in your thinking (which recognizes the value and need for things like strategic planning, tactical planning, goals, and accountability), then most lawyers will quickly move back to their comfort zones and that which they know best—the practice of law. Many law firms talk the "business talk," but walking that walk takes more . . . much more.

Too Much Internal Focus

A second law firm challenge is the excessive internal focus, rather than external (or client) focus. It is typical for law firms to talk about client service while overlooking it or ignoring it in terms of real change and genuine focus on improving service. Review any law firm's marketing materials or Web site and you will almost certainly find references to that firm's focus on client service, on providing excellent client service, on understanding their client's needs, on partnering with clients, etc. However, if you ask most of these firms to describe exactly what they do differently, they cannot tell you anything specific. It is all generalities and claims that cannot be proved by any objective methods. In other words, law firms talk the "client service talk," but they rarely walk the walk of excellent client service. While client service itself comes down to the delivery of legal services, it starts with having a truly client-focused culture within your law firm.

One of the best examples (as in most revealing) of how lawyers and law firms are *not* client focused is the fact that lawyers evaluate themselves, and the law firm evaluates the lawyers, by the value they add to the firm (not to the clients). Let me say that again. Lawyers are judged by the value they add to the firm and the firm judges the lawyers by the value they add to the firm. Thus, the focus is internal within the law firm, rather than external and focused on the clients. Before you slam this book shut in disgust and start forming your arguments on how your particular firm is externally focused, consider the fact that in most firms (and certainly in firms that bill by the hour) the billable hour is the heart and soul of the firm's business and revenue stream. While lawyers are certainly expected to provide quality legal services, the law firm's focus is on billable hour requirements, goals, expectations, and so on.

In most firms, the revenue focus is on the age-old concept of "rate times billable hours." When law firms gather for year-end assessments or planning for the next year, the focus is often on how many billable hours are needed (at a projected average billable hour collected) to achieve the firm's financial needs or goals. Similarly, most compensation systems are focused (either exclusively or in significant part) on dollars collected for each lawyer's billable hours and for "their" clients.

All of this is internally focused, not client focused. While it may occur, I have never heard of a law firm planning its future and growth and talking about improved client service as the path to success. Rather, the focus is typically on billable hours, new clients, cross-marketing, billable rates, cutting costs, and so on—all things that are about the firm, rather than the service the firm delivers to its clients. Certainly, non-law businesses focus on sales and revenues as the means to achieving their business and financial goals; however, non-law businesses (at least the good and very successful ones) spend significant amounts of time and attention on client service. Not only do non-law businesses focus on client service, but they create systems that exist solely for the benefit of clients. Once created, non-law businesses continually refine and improve these systems knowing that, ultimately, client service is an integral part of their business success.

While law firms may believe this, typically their actions and decisions do not show an external or client service focus. While developing a system to consistently deliver outstanding service to clients might not be easy, it all starts with the decision to focus on clients as the essence of law firm success. While the delivery system and implementation may take time, law firms can and should decide to be client focused and to have a client-centric culture as the first and vital step on the path to great client service.

Another clear example of how law firms are internally focused, rather than externally or client focused, is spiraling associate salaries. Some of you are reading and saying that these higher associate salaries are client focused because they allow the firm to attract and hire the best lawyers, but this is not a true correlation. First, the high salaries only attract the best law students, not the best lawyers. It takes time and experience to identify and determine the best lawyers, and hiring the best law students may help in this process, but it is no guarantee. Second, rarely are clients interested in the law schools attended or grade point averages achieved by young associates. Clients are looking for and expect quality legal advice, not highly compensated new associates. So do not try to take the easy route by claiming that higher associate salaries are client focused. At best, that is an excuse that will not stand up to review.

In fact, rapidly escalating associate salaries cause a variety of repercussions, all of which are ultimately (or certainly potentially) detrimental to clients and client service. It is readily acknowledged that new associates in most firms do not become profitable for several years and that, during those first several years, they cost the firm money. With that in mind, higher salaries translate into ever greater losses for the firm in those early years. And how do law firms deal with higher costs such as increased salaries? With increased billable hour rates and/or increased billable hour requirements or expectations. Certainly, increased billable hour rates are not a client benefit. Likewise, increased billable hour requirements carry several potentially damaging side effects for clients. Whether it occurs or not, increased billable hour requirements can lead to excessive billing because of the enhanced pressure on the lawyers. Similarly, increased hourly rates or billable hour requirements will often result in more disagreements with clients over bills and/or a greater percentage of write-offs.

In short, there is nothing about increasing associate salaries that actually benefits clients and client service. For those of you who have a contrary argument to make, consider this question: When law firms decide to increase associate salaries, do they do so after carefully evaluating and determining that the increase will benefit clients and improve client service? Likely not. Unfortunately, clients and client service are generally not the motivation behind increased associate salaries.

If you have lingering doubts about the internal focus of law firms, consider this insight that was recently shared with me by a business owner. We were talking about lawyers and legal marketing, and this business owner mentioned a recent television ad that he had seen. At the end of the ad a lawyer looked into the camera and with a very serious look said, "We're serious about the law." Sound good? Not according to this business owner. His perspective (the only one that matters) was this: "I don't care if they are serious about the law. I only want to know if they are serious about me and helping me with my problems." He then added, "Why is it that lawyers are always so concerned about themselves instead of worrying about us clients?" Isn't that interesting! This excessive (if not exclusive) internal focus is a law firm challenge that must be corrected if lawyers and their law firms want to build solid and sustainable law businesses. Without this critical shift in focus, law firms will be at risk far into the future.

> ▼▼▼▼▼
>
> Unfortunately, law firms have developed a habit of focusing on themselves (an internal focus) rather than on clients and client service (an external focus). As a result, clients do not feel that their lawyers really care about them, their problems, or their businesses.

Certainly, there are other business challenges for lawyers such as poor or slow decision making, difficulties in differentiating themselves from other lawyers, and the reluctance to admit that they are and must be salespeople, and we will be exploring these challenges and some solutions throughout the rest of this book. All of these areas need to be addressed by law firms to create a more profitable and efficient operating structure. For now, remember that successful law firms must think, function, and operate like any other business. Without undertaking this fundamental and critical first step, lawyers and law firms are destined to continue to be "just okay" when it comes to the business of law, and "okay" should not be good enough for any of you!

7 A Penny for Your Thoughts . . . and Advice!

What would you say to a client who came to your office and asked for your legal advice and started off by saying "a penny for your legal advice." Hopefully, all of you would say "no way" and tell the client that your advice is worth much more than a penny. Okay, that was an easy question, but it becomes harder as the amount goes up. For example, imagine that your rate is $200 an hour, but a prospective client says that is "too high" and "I can go to another firm at a rate of $150 an hour." In fact, that prospective client is saying to you "I am interested in your advice and your services, but I think that they are only worth $150." In Chapter 18, we will discuss client perspectives on the value of your services (including client perspectives on hourly rates), but for now let's focus on your own perception of your value to clients.

How Much Are You Worth?

Let's try an exercise. In the box below write down a dollar figure that represents what you believe is the value of an hour of your time. Do not spend too much time thinking about it or pondering the ramifications, but write down your immediate reaction to the question of what an hour of your time is worth. Do not turn the page until you have written down a number in the box.

AN HOUR OF MY TIME IS WORTH $__________

If you are like most lawyers, the number you wrote down is frighteningly close to your billable hourly rate. The good news is that you are in good company. Many lawyers equate their value to their hourly rate and, frankly, can only conceive of their value in terms of their hourly rate. The bad news is that most of you are undervaluing your time if you are looking at your hourly rate, but that means there is plenty of opportunity to increase and expand your own perception of your value.

Why do we tend to see the value of our time as a function of our hourly billable rate? Because (if we bill by the hour) that is what we focus on nearly every minute of every day. Our entire focus is on rate times billable hours, the standard law firm revenue model. From day one we are told that the path to success is billing hours, that it is vital to bill as much time as possible and that it is critical to be as efficient as possible every day (in other words, to bill as many hours as you can during your workday). This is described as the law firm path to success, but we never hear about value and we never talk about value to the client. No wonder the profession is viewed as mere vendors and expenses, rather than as valued advisors.

Let's look at an example that demonstrates how reference to our hourly rate significantly undervalues our time. Assume that you spend a total of ten (10) hours to bring either a new client or a new matter into the firm. Then let's assume that the new client or new matter (in the first year only) generates an additional $10,000 in fees for the law firm. Doing some simple math we find that the value of that business development time was $1,000 an hour. What if the fees the first year had been $50,000? That is an hourly rate of $5,000 an hour. We can all do various calculations, but the inevitable conclusion is that when it comes to business and client development, there is no limit to the value of our time. In effect, the value of our time is almost infinite. The purpose of this discussion is not to start arguing the issue of which is more valuable—billing time (doing the work) or bringing in the business (making the rain)—but to focus on the fact that the value of your time is something totally different from your hourly rate.

Another example of how your hourly rate significantly undervalues your time is when you consider the value you deliver to your clients. Unfortunately, your clients often are not aware of the real value that you have provided to them, so it is up to you to educate them. I was recently conducting a business development workshop with a group of partners,

▼▼▼▼▼

When it comes to business development, you are using your time to create and build relationships, to create opportunities, and to create business from those relationships. Even as lawyers, when we are *creating* we can build and develop incredible value far beyond our time expended.

and I asked one of them this question: "What is the most money you ever saved for a client in a single transaction?" He answered that he had saved a client $500,000 as a result of certain business tax advice, for which they had billed the client approximately $50,000. Thus, the value to the client was ten times higher than the classic "rate times billable hours."

Whether or not you choose to bill clients according to the value delivered, the value is there for all to see, but first you have to see and recognize it and then you must take steps to make sure that your clients also see it. Certainly, the reverse can also be true—that the real value of your services rendered to a client falls short of your regular hourly rates—but the underlying principle is the same: your value is something separate and apart from your hourly billable rate and, many times, the true value of your time far exceeds your regular billable rate.

If you want to build a successful law business or to become a rainmaker, you have to throw away the old idea that values your time based on your billable rate. You have to start seeing the value that you can create that far exceeds whatever your hourly rate might be. At a minimum, success in the business of law requires that you start to see the real value of what you do for your clients.

We Are Worth What We Think We Are Worth

As a starting point, you have to strongly believe that you are worth the hourly rate that you are charging your clients. I am often asked, "How do I get clients to stop thinking of me as an expense?" The answer is simple: stop thinking of yourself as an expense and stop acting like an expense. You may think this solution is overly simplistic, but clients perceive you as an expense because you act like an expense. When I asked a lawyer to give me a list of things that differentiated his firm from other firms, one of the supposed differences was that his firm billed in tenths of an hour, rather than quarters of an hour. If that is what makes your firm different (how you bill your time), are you an expense or are you a value-added advisor? If you spend your time trying to justify and prove the reasonableness

▼▼▼▼▼

There certainly will be a percentage of clients who will view you as an expense no matter what you do and no matter how you view yourself. For those clients, you still have a decision to make—do you want them as clients? Believe it or not, you get to choose your clients, and if you choose clients who cannot see you as anything other than an expense, then you must live with that choice.

of your hourly rate to clients, are you talking like an expense or as a value-added advisor? If you hesitate to talk openly about fees and hourly rates, are you an expense or are you a value-added advisor? Whether you are viewed and treated as an expense or as a value-added advisor is up to you, not your clients.

Many advisors and consultants in other industries have already discovered the truth about how you value your time and the impact it has on the quality of clients you attract and on the growth of your business. Most business advisors either charge hourly rates much higher than standard hourly billing rates for lawyers or charge for their services on some type of fixed or flat fee (where the effective hourly rate can be in the thousands of dollars per hour), yet they continue to attract and retain quality clients and build profitable businesses. The following is a summary of an experience that was related to me in the last year or so:

> A business advisor (who had developed a reputation for helping family-owned businesses) was charging approximately $500 per hour for his consulting services. However, he was working too hard and wanted to work less. With the goal of having fewer clients, he decided to increase his hourly rate to approximately $1,000 per hour. The result—his consulting business dramatically *increased!* Despite the fact that he had doubled his hourly rate, he had more clients and more people who wanted his services.

Why? Because people will gladly pay for perceived value *and* many people associate value and quality with hourly rates. In other words, many people do believe that you get what you pay for and, therefore, the higher the hourly rate, the more valuable the advisor. With that thought in mind, why are we so worried about our hourly rate and always trying to sell ourselves as the lower cost (and therefore supposed better value)?

Consider one more example:

> I recently was speaking with the president of a sales coaching and training company, and he shared with me a recent marketing program for his company (including Web casts and commercials). The relevant part of the advertisement went like this: "Hi, I'm John Jones with Sales Coaching Company. We're famous for our expensive and in-depth sales development and training programs."

"What is he doing?," you might ask. Why is he advertising his business as "expensive"? It's because he is selling his services on value, not on price.

Do not kid yourself. If you are telling clients and prospects that you are a great value because of your low hourly rates, then you are not really selling value. You are selling lower price which, for most of you, is not where you want or need to be. You should be selling value . . . period! As a business owner recently shared with me, "If you're selling on price, get into another business." Selling on price is not where you want to be, and it is not a tactic that will help build and grow a successful law business in the long term. Even if your hourly rate is below market, if you market and sell based on your low price, you will always attract clients who are looking for a low price, rather than a relationship or a value-added advisor.

Another question that I often get is, "How do I deal with questions about hourly rates in the initial meeting with a prospective client?" Once again, the answer is fairly straightforward—deal with it before the question is asked, rather than trying or hoping to avoid it. You all know the scenario . . . we are in a meeting with a prospective new client and rather than making fees and hourly rates part of the agenda, we play the "I hope" game. In other words:

> I hope that they don't ask about hourly rates, fees, projections, or budgets. I hope we can get through this meeting without fees and hourly rates being discussed. "I hope" that they will just sign the fee agreement without ever asking or even reading about the rates and fees. Best case scenario, they won't read the fee agreement relative to rates and fees until after our meeting, so I won't have to talk about it or answer questions about it. Boy, I hope they don't ask.

An exaggeration, right? Not by much. Many lawyers have admitted to me that this is how they approach client meetings and the topic of rates and fees. They are afraid of the topic, and they hope it does not come up. They hope that they will be hired without ever having to discuss rates and fees.

What is the reason for this reluctance (even fear) to openly discuss fees? Usually it indicates that the lawyer has doubts about the value of his time and does not firmly believe that he or she is worth that hourly rate. When lawyers are faced with fees and rates questions they either become defensive or start talking about how it varies and it depends on different things or they start talking about blended rates, project staffing, and so on. If you do not believe you are worth what you are going to charge that client, why should the client believe that you are worth it? Ultimately, it is your responsibility and obligation to demonstrate to that client that you are worth what you say you are worth. That starts with you believing it and confidently showing your client that you are worth it!

> ▼▼▼▼▼
>
> If you believe that you are worth $200 dollars an hour, then you should take the initiative and make rates and fees a topic of the initial meeting. When asked about your hourly rate, you should look the client in the eye and confidently state your rate.

Talking the Value Talk

Many lawyers have told me that the value of their time "depends." Sometimes the value of their services far exceeds their hourly rate, and other times the value of their services is far below their hourly rate. For example, one lawyer described for me a scenario where he had provided critical tax advice that saved a client approximately $100,000. That was a valuable service rendered, yet he may have billed the client only $5,000, $10,000, or even $25,000 for those services. In that case, the lawyer was certain that not only were his services worth his hourly rate, but the value that he delivered to the client far exceeded rate times billable hours. Does that mean that he should have billed the client more? The answer is maybe. We will cover alternative fee arrangements in Chapter 23, but it also depends on the arrangement with the client. However, even if the client is charged only for the agreed hourly rate times billable hours, it is the lawyer's responsibility to make sure that the client knows and understands the *value* of the services. Too often, clients do not or cannot figure that out for themselves. It is up to you to talk to them in terms of value rather than rate times billable hours.

Talking the "value talk" with your clients (from start to finish) is vital to having your clients see you as adding value, rather than as just an expense. Remember, prospective clients and existing clients "buy" to make money, save money, reduce risk, or simplify, so you must focus your "value talk" on these areas from the beginning. Value talk should take place when you are starting the engagement, during the engagement (especially right before sending your bill for services), at the end of every year, and at the end of the engagement. There is no such thing as reminding your clients of your value too often, but you certainly can fail to talk value enough. Clients do not always see your value, so it is up to you to show your value to them. Clients sometimes forget the value that you've provided during the engagement, and it is up to you to remind them (especially at billing time) because clients will often forget by the end of the engagement. If you do not remind them of your great value at the end of the engagement, then they may "walk away" without knowing (or remembering) just how valuable your advice, counseling, and services were. What a shame! You may have provided great value, but the engagement ends with the client not having a clear understanding of

> ▼▼▼▼▼
>
> We all know that we cannot control or guarantee results, yet results are often what clients focus on (unless we do a great job of educating, preparing, and creating our own value expectations for the client).

that value and, therefore, the client will not be ready or willing to spread the word to others.

Talking the "value talk" before the engagement begins is a great way of laying the foundation for what is to come and for creating the right expectations with the client. Even if we do a great job of educating on value at the beginning, clients can easily forget all of that throughout the course of the engagement. With all the "stuff" that goes on during the course of the representation (and remembering that clients are dealing with their own issues during the representation), it is not surprising that clients might forget the value justifications for retaining you. Do not let them forget. Remind them at every opportunity (especially when you are sending out a bill) and at least once a year. You can do this in a meeting, by telephone, or even in a letter, but do not be shy about reminding clients of what value they should expect and what value they receive.

One practice area that does a great job of "value talk" is estate planning. Before being engaged, the estate planning lawyer shares various scenarios, and it usually goes something like this:

> This is what (dollar amount) you have now. If you do nothing, this is what you will have later. If you choose Option A, this is what you will have later. If you choose Option B, this is what you will have later.

After laying out all the options, the lawyer asks the clients which option they want to pursue and, of course, the clients typically choose an option that gives them the most value based on the relative risks. Then and only then the estate planning lawyer tells the clients what amount they must "invest" for the chosen option, and most of the time the clients never question it at all . . . because they have already been shown the value that they are getting in return for their investment. Then, once the necessary documents are prepared and ready for signature, the estate planning lawyer "reminds" the clients of the value achieved by the chosen strategy, which of course comes right before the clients are billed for the services.

▼▼▼▼▼

The use of the word "invest" or "investment" is intentional and strategic. "Cost" is how someone views expenses. "Investments" relate to value and expected returns on that investment. This need not be about winning and losing (or guaranteed results), but it is about creating an expectation that your client is investing in you to achieve a valuable return from your advice.

Yes, estate planning is an easy practice area for showing real dollar value and for "dollarizing" that value, but value is a state of mind, as much as objective dollars. It is up to you to make sure that your clients know (every step of the way) that you are there to add value to them or their business. It is kind of like the old mantra in speaking: Tell them what you are going to tell them. Tell them. Tell them what you told them. The same applies to "value talk." Tell them what value to expect, show them the value when it is provided, and constantly remind them of your value. This is the path to being a value-added advisor and not just a "necessary expense."

What about the other scenario? Perhaps you were not as efficient as you could have been and the fees incurred are higher than what you believe to be the real value of your services. Perhaps you went down a path that proved to be a mistake on your part, and therefore billing the client for the full amount of those fees would exceed the value of your services. Do you bill the client less? Do you not bill the client for some or all of your services? Ultimately, that is a decision that needs to be made, but that is exactly what you have to consider. If you want to be a valued resource and trusted advisor, there may be times that you need to bill your clients according to the value that they received (especially when the value is less than your standard hourly rate). Many of you may be jumping up and down and screaming, "No, no, no, we can't do that. That is just part of the practice of law—the uncertainties of the practice of law—and those are burdens that should be borne by the client." Interesting perspective, isn't it—the perspective that clients (not you and the firm) should bear the costs of your mistakes or inefficiencies? Is that really the type of lawyer that you want to be and, if so, what types of clients will you have if that is your client service model?

If you think that what I am suggesting is extreme or unreasonable, then consider this example. For various reasons you spend the equivalent of $10,000 of legal time that you reasonably believe should have taken only $5,000 of legal time (either by inefficiencies, mistakes, poor staffing, and so on). You go ahead and bill the client the full $10,000 and hope that no one objects, but what you are really saying is this: "Dear Client. We made some mistakes on your matter that resulted in the fees being twice as high as they should have been. However, we are choosing to bill you the full amount in the hope that you will not discover our inefficiencies and our mistakes." Is that really the type of lawyer that you want to be?

▼▼▼▼▼

Some firms deal with this situation by billing the full amount but they are prepared to "cut" the bill if the client objects. In the end, this is not a client-centric solution. You are hoping that the client does not notice, does not object, or does not question the bill, but you are willing to make adjustments only if the client raises an objection. This approach is focused on the law firm, not the clients.

These are tough decisions, but they are the types of decisions that can determine whether you are a mere expense or a value-added resource with great client relationships and clients who not only trust and respect you, but will gladly pay for your valuable advice and refer you to others. The choice is yours. Are you a client-focused law firm or not?

What does having a client-focused (or client-centric) firm mean in your day-to-day practice? It means that you have to think about everything that you do for a client in terms of the value to the client. You need to "put the client hat on" whenever it comes to what you do, when you do it, how you do it, and how much you bill for your efforts. You need to make every decision as if the client was sitting in the room with you and hearing every thought, justification, and argument. The excuse that the clients do not know everything you are doing, deciding, and saying is just that—an excuse—and it means that you have put your interests ahead of the client's. Being a truly client-focused lawyer means that you have to slow down and do more than just track and bill your time. If you want to be a trusted advisor, then you need to function like a trusted advisor. Clients know the difference, but you have to show them that difference!

8 Decisions, Decisions!

So many decisions to make, and so little time. Every day in the practice of law is filled with decisions and judgments that must be made. In fact, the essence of practicing law requires us to review and evaluate facts, research and consider applicable law, assess risks, understand goals, determine client needs and interests, ponder and analyze all of the foregoing, and then decide on a course of action . . . and often right now! For those of you who are thinking that we, as lawyers, do not decide anything (that clients ultimately make the decisions based on our advice), you need to think again.

Yes, clients ultimately should decide what to do based on our advice, but the reality is that we can, should, and must make decisions throughout the process of representing clients. Most of us do make those decisions and we make them fairly quickly. Why? Because we do not have time to delay these types of decisions. There always seems to be a time deadline of some type that pushes us forward and forces us to make decisions quickly. If you have had any success in the practice of law, then you are likely very well skilled at making relatively quick decisions and judgments when it comes to the practice of law—the activities relating to representing clients and giving legal advice.

Unfortunately, many lawyers are not so skilled at making decisions when it comes to the business of law, are slow to decide (or never decide), and waste thousands, tens of thousands, or even hundreds of thousands of dollars when it comes to their "business of law" decisions. Not only does poor decision making (or no decision making) waste dollars for a law firm, but the lost opportunity costs are even higher. If you want to enhance your firm's profits, one business success key is to make more decisions. In other words, stop worrying about making better decisions, and instead focus your energies on making quicker decisions.

Anatomy of Decision Making

Three aspects of decision making significantly impact your firm's bottom line (either positively or negatively): (1) deciding what to do; (2) not deciding; and (3) how you make decisions. The first—deciding what to do—is really an element related to planning, but it bears some consideration under the topic of decision making. The reality is that everyone wastes time in minutes, not hours. This is not hard to believe if you just give it some thought. Consider the last time you felt that you had wasted a considerable amount of time. For example, you were going about your daily work schedule, you looked at your watch and realized that three hours had passed and you did not feel that you had accomplished anything. You felt that you had wasted several hours. If you think about what you did during that time, you'll quickly see that you did not waste hours, but rather you wasted minutes (many minutes), and the cumulative result was that you wasted hours.

You would think that we would know and understand this concept, since most lawyers track their time in minutes. Most of you at some point in your career (and maybe even now) track your time in six-minute increments—the infamous tenth of an hour. If you talk to anyone in business and talk about tenths of an hour, they will look at you as if you have two heads. They will wonder "what in the world are tenths of an hour?" As lawyers we are certainly capable of understanding that time is very valuable (especially minutes), and we are trained to become almost fanatically focused on how we spend every minute. Yet, most of us fail to grasp the concept that we waste time by the minute, not the hour.

▼▼▼▼▼

There are three things you do with your time: (1) you *spend* your time doing things, usually without thinking about how you are spending your time or how you should be spending your time; (2) you *use* your time—thus the saying, "use your time wisely;" and (3) you *invest* your time. While there is much talk about time management, the path to greater effectiveness, productivity, and profitability lies in how you *invest* your time. Nearly everything that you do should be viewed as an investment of your time . . . either a wise investment or a poor investment. Too many people focus their energy on what things cost, without ever considering their time investment. If you want to enhance your personal and business success, focus on how you are "investing" your time.

Consider these types of responses that you have given or that you have had others give when it comes to how time is spent:

- "Don't worry. It will take me only five or ten minutes."
- "I can't understand where the time went today. I worked hard all day. I talked to a couple of people during the day, but that was for only ten or fifteen minutes (each)."
- "I have only three or four personal calls a day and they are usually less than five minutes."

Are you starting to get the picture? Whether it is your time or the time of any member of your law firm team, time is slipping away and being wasted *by the minute*. For most of you, in some fashion, time is money. For all of those wasted minutes, which add up to wasted hours, days, and weeks, dollars went out the door, whether as additional cost or as lost opportunities. Whether it is cost or lost opportunities, wasted time costs you money—specifically, profits.

One of the main time (and profit) bandits is failing to plan, which means that you do not know what to do at any particular point in time. Without a daily plan (a prioritized daily plan) that you can quickly scan before deciding what you need to do next, you end up wasting your time in the "what next" dilemma. You are sitting at your desk working on a particular project or matter. You finish and are ready to move on, but what do you work on next? Many times we do not know what we should or will work on next. Instead, we waste time figuring out what to do next. This lack of planning is particularly harmful when it comes to making telephone calls and business development efforts. If we haven't already decided who we need to call (and in what order), we're less likely to make the calls and certainly are very likely not to make the most important calls first. Likewise, when we're facing a desk full of work and do not have a plan for our business development efforts, it is much easier to do billable work than to invest time on business development. Why? Because we hadn't decided in advance what to do next.

I was recently speaking with a lawyer (formerly with a large corporate law firm) who had gone in-house to become general counsel. We started talking about business development and lawyers, and here is what he had to say:

> You know, I really like doing all of the client development stuff. Getting out there and meeting people and building relationships was much more fun and even more beneficial for the firm, but I was expected to spend most of my time doing the legal work. It would have been great if I could have just focused all my time on business development, but the reality was that I had to primarily be the person delivering the legal services. Like most lawyers, my legal work was never completely caught up. I always had legal work to do, so it was easy for me to go through a day, a week,

or even weeks being a lawyer and then realize that I had not done any business development work.

Surprised by this story? Of course not, because most of you can probably describe a similar scenario and pattern in your law business life. The biggest reason for this failure to undertake business development efforts is the lack of an easy-to-access plan and a reasonable goal for your business development efforts. The good news is that having a plan and a goal is also the easiest way to consistently do what you want to do and need to do when it comes to business development.

The next decision-making topic is not deciding. As practicing lawyers, we generally do not have the luxury of not deciding when it comes to doing the legal work and representing our clients. Whether client driven, opposing counsel driven, calendar driven, or court driven, we usually cannot get away with not deciding when it comes to practicing law. Admittedly, there are times when we do fail to decide and we regret the consequences. In some cases your failure or delay in deciding can hurt you and your client, but on the business side of law, the big damage flows from not deciding (or delaying decisions).

> ▼▼▼▼▼
>
> Deciding what to do first and next . . . in advance . . . will pay huge dividends in the form of increased efficiency, productivity, quality of work, and results! Not planning, not knowing what to do, not deciding what to do, and not deciding what is most important will cost you money both in lost dollars and lost opportunities, all of which will negatively impact your firm's bottom line and yours.

Consider the following: "What hurts us most is that we fail to realize and remember that failing to make a decision is a decision. And it is almost always the wrong decision!" If you think about this, you will quickly realize that it is not only accurate, but profound. In nearly every case when we fail to make a decision, we are actually making a decision . . . and it will almost always turn out to be a bad one. Yes, there will be rare occasions when we fail to make a decision and it fortuitiously (with the benefit of blind luck) works out to our advantage (or at least we think it is to our advantage). But is that really how you want to run your business or even your law practice, relying on blind luck for your success? Most of us want to control our destiny, want to control our future, and want to, to the extent possible, control our results. Ultimately, we cannot control our results, but we absolutely can control (and must control) our decision making.

One "example" of a non-decision being beneficial that lawyers always want to share involves underperforming employees. The lawyer and/or the law firm want to move this person out, but everyone delays because it is unpleasant, because they need to "paper the employee file," or they are concerned about a discrimination claim. Suddenly (and via a perceived stroke of good luck), the employee announces that he or she is leaving the firm. Everyone breathes a sigh of relief and believes that this non-decision worked out for the best. In fact, nothing could be further from the truth. We will talk more about the vital role that great employees play in any law firm business, but we fail to realize how much not making a decision to fire an underperforming employee costs the firm up until the time that the employee made the decision for us. An underperforming employee not only holds you and the law business back, but literally sucks productivity and profits out of your business.

Let's consider this scenario. You have an employee who is not doing the job, yet you continue to pay him or her *as if he or she is doing the job.* So, instead of having the right person in place to not only do the job but enhance the job and the firm's performance, you have someone who is holding you and the firm back. At the same time, every employee knows and sees that this underperforming employee is being tolerated. Are these other employees then motivated and inspired to put in their best effort? Of course not, because you and the firm have "told them" (with your non-decision) that it is not only okay to be mediocre, but it is okay and acceptable to underperform and not do your job. What do you think this does to the firm's overall productivity and profitability? As a result, there's a good chance that some of your best employees will become mediocre (or worse) and stay that way because you failed to make a decision that needed to be made. And some of your best people may leave because of your non-decision. So, before you start to consider your "good luck" when an underperforming employee leaves, consider all the damage that was done and the dollars that were lost while you were not making a decision.

If you want to enhance your business results, you need to make more and quicker decisions. This is a statement that typically gets quick and adament objections from lawyers. They tell me that quick decisions are bad decisions, that our role as lawyers is to make perfect decisions, and that making perfect (or the very best) decisions requires time, careful consideration, full evaluation, in-depth assessment, and deliberate analysis. They tell me that you cannot rush decisions when it comes to being a lawyer. Well, I must respectfully disagree . . . at least regarding the vast majority of the decisions that lawyers must make.

First, there is no such thing as a perfect decision. Put that goal out of your head right now. If you are spending your time trying to make perfect decisions, then you are wasting your time. When representing our clients, our job is to provide the best possible advice under the circumstances and based on our training and experience. Typically our goal is (or should be) to help our clients make better decisions based on our advice and counsel.

The search for perfect decisions is one that will ultimately lead you down a path of proscrastination and analysis paralysis that will hurt your clients, your firm, and your bottom line.

Second, the reality in the practice of law is that you are regularly making decisions quickly and without being 100 percent certain of the answer. We all know that there is rarely a question for which the answer can be given with absolute, 100 percent certainty. That is the nature of the law, whether it be litigation, business transactions, estate planning, or any other practice area—we as lawyers live and work in a constant shade of gray. Many times our value to a client is what we can do with that gray area for the benefit of that client. Do not confuse avoiding malpractice (the giving of objectively bad advice) with the impossible search for perfect decisions. You must always fulfill your professional and ethical obligations; however, there is no obligation to make perfect decisions. They simply do not exist in reality.

All of you can remember situations (maybe even within the last 24 hours) where another lawyer or a client provided you with some facts and said, "What do you think?" Most of you are in a position to (and do) answer these types questions on the spot based on your experience, training, and knowledge. There are certain times that you may indicate a need to do further research or assessment, but most of the time you provide your judgments, thoughts, and answers based on your wide range of experience, including instincts. So, not only is there no perfect decision, but we are all skilled and practiced in making decisions (on the practice side of the law) without 100 percent certainty, without long, painful, and wasteful analysis, and confident that we are making good decisions. Our search should be for good advice and good decisions, not perfection at the cost of timeliness.

How Big Is the Decision?

▼▼▼▼▼

It is vital to understand and recognize the true significance of various decisions. In other words, it is vital to recognize that some decisions are more important than others (with greater or lesser risks and rewards) and that you must be judicious in assessing the value and importance of decisions.

Too often (particularly on the business side of law) we waste time on what appears to be big or important decisions, when the importance of the decision pales in comparision to the time and money wasted (and opportunities lost) in making that supposedly critical decision. One of my favorite examples relates to the purchase or lease of office equipment such as a copy machine. When I had my own law firm the purchase or lease of a copier "appeared" to be significant because the cost was approximately $25,000. It was a seemingly large investment, which appeared to justify spending significant time making the best decision. In reality, this was not and is not a big decision. More specifically, it was not a $25,000 decision.

Ultimately, the most important question was whether we needed a new copier and, if so, what features did we need that would be of value to our firm and to our clients. This is not a question relating to costs, but rather a question of functionality, firm needs, client needs, and determining what type or level of copier would best fulfill those needs and requirements. It turns out that, for the functions that we needed, the price range for the copiers was between $23,000 and $28,000. In other words, financially this was really a $5,000 decision (the difference between the copier prices), not a $25,000 decision. Many business decisions for law firms fall into this category. Unnecessary time is spent and wasted on what is perceived as a big or important decision, but by focusing on the right numbers, you find that the decision is not as big or as significant as you imagined.

You should also note that many decisions relating to the business of your firm need to be delegated and relegated to the experts, rather than to the lawyers (including the managing partner). In the copier example, lawyers are generally not the experts who should be evaluating copier needs, copier functions, or copier costs. That is not what they know best and, therefore, involving lawyers in that process is a monumental misallocation and misdirection of valuable resources. We will talk more about the power of delegation and empowerment, but law firm decision making is a critical area where effective delegation and empowerment can not only avoid a waste of time, but can actually pay positive dividends for the firm as a business.

When I first started my own firm (with other partners), we operated as a democracy. For the first year we were involved in virtually every decision—big or small—relating to the business of the law firm. One of the reasons was that we did not know any better. Another reason was that, for a time, we liked the idea of making those business decisions. It seemed like a natural extension of our desire to have our own firm and to control our own destiny. Eventually, the "glamour" of making all of these decisions wore off, and we realized that we were wasting time and money having all of us involved in every decision.

▼▼▼▼▼

The key to remember is that you must be diligent in properly assessing the importance of each decision and, with respect to most of the decisions that need to be made regarding the business of the law firm, decisions need to be made quickly and implemented and then you move on. The fact is that the cost of delay is usually more damaging than the risk of a bad decision.

The next step in the evolution was to reserve democracy (and our collective involvement) for only the most important decisions, but we had to go through a lot of trial and error to learn which were really important decisions and which were not. With respect to what were agreed to be less important decisions, we delegated responsibility for different areas of the firm to different people. It certainly wasted less time and made us more productive, but ultimately it was not the answer. Lawyers are busy with many things, especially in a smaller law firm. Lawyers not only have to deliver the legal services and maintain the client relationships, but they have to build new relationships, work on bringing in new business, and help administer the operations of the firm. Typically, administration and operations were the low priority. In addition, people's schedules are all different. As a result, even day-to-day decisions were delayed when a single shareholder had responsibility for that decision (or for presenting the information to the collective owners for a decision). It was better than the "democracy," but decisions still did not get made fast enough and time and resources were wasted (and opportunities lost) because of an inefficient decision making system.

Ultimately, we determined that most decisions needed to be put in the hands of one person. Now, this one person might not necessarily be the person who did the research and the analysis to support the decisions, but having decision making authority in one person proved to be the most effective for the business. Most businesses operate this way. While authority is delegated to the experts in each area, and someone in each of those areas is empowered to make decisions, the buck stops somewhere. Decisions can and should be made when they need to be made, not when various people are available to be involved in that decision. Having a single decision maker is truly the most profitable, effective, and productive method for managing any business, including a law firm.

Once again, this does not necessarily mean that there is one person at the top who makes all of the decisions. It means that in the areas of expertise, there is a go-to person who makes decisions. Parameters are created, goals are outlined, and objectives are determined, but ultimately there are decision makers with accountability and responsibility for making most of the decisions. That is the most effective method of operating any business, whether it is a law firm, a manufacturer, a distributor, or some other service business.

One area that is particularly damaging to a law firm is the excessive use of committees in making decisions. Contrary to most businesses, law firms have tended to rely on committees to run the business and to make decisions, which has resulted in slow decisions, non-decisions, and the painful waste of valuable professional time (in terms of billable hours and lost opportunities) because of the use of committees, especially for the wrong decisions. Most decisions do not require the time and attention that are given to them, and it is important to reserve valuable time and resources for only the most important decisions. The reality is that leadership and decision making by committee is inefficient and generally wasteful of valuable firm resources.

Law firms have a somewhat unique challenge—there are typically multiple owners (shareholders or partners), while many privately held businesses have a single owner or only a couple of owners. This creates an urge to have all of the owners involved in all of the decisions. Good business practice dictates that you not go down this path. It may be a challenge to get all of the owners to buy into this system, but you can show its value by:

- Focusing on the efficiencies created by quicker and better decision making;
- Understanding the time and resources that are wasted and lost by ineffective decision making; and
- Identifying and clarifying how opportunities for growth and enhanced profits are being missed or lost every time decisions are delayed, not made, or involve more people than are needed.

In the end, it is in the financial best interest of every owner to create an effective and efficient decision making process, not only in the "how-tos" of decision making, but also in the philosophy of decision making. In most cases, more decisions (not better decisions) will help enhance your business.

Going with Your Gut

You may say that "going with your gut" is a great concept but "it does not apply to law firms. The things that we do are too important and our business is so different from other businesses that we need to spend more time making (if not perfect) excellent decisions." As we discussed earlier, continuing to see the business of law as different than every other business will not only hold back your firm, but it can have a negative impact on your financial results. In addition, the reality is that the business or practice of law is not significantly more important than most businesses. For every business that you could name where the practice of law arguably has a more significant impact (or potential risk associated with bad decisions), there are dozens of businesses and industries where the products or services that they provide have a significantly greater impact than (or at least an equal impact to) the practice of law. Let's look at an example.

We may disagree, but there certainly is a strong argument that the military is engaged in important business with respect to not only the nation but also the citizens of this nation. Colin Powell, military leader and former secretary of state, has this philosophy on decision making:

> Use the formula P = 40 to 70, in which P stands for the probability of success and the numbers indicate the percentage of information acquired. Once the information is in the 40 to 70 range, *go with your gut.**

Powell's advice is don't take action if you have only enough information to give you less than a 40 percent chance of being right, but don't wait until you have enough facts to be 100 percent sure, because by then it is almost always too late. . . . Procrastination in the name of reducing risk actually increases risk.**

Isn't that interesting! The former Chairman of the Joint Chiefs of Staff believes that it is critical to "go with your gut" when it comes to decision making. Unfortunately, many of us do not heed this advice. Instead, we waste valuable time, resources, and opportunities while trying to attain a comfort level that a decision is as near perfect as it can be. While we engage in this analysis paralysis, time, money, and resources are wasted, and opportunities are missed or overlooked because the focus was on trying to make a great decision when all that was needed was a decision.

If you want to improve your law firm business, particularly the results, you need to commit yourself to making more decisions and faster decisions, rather than making great decisions. Admittedly, these are concepts that were not taught in law school and, frankly, are generally not taught in business school: go with your gut—trust your instincts—make more and faster decisions. When you get that "bad feeling," you need to go with your gut and sometimes that means walking away (even from a perceived opportunity). To learn more about how we make these subconscious decisions, I encourage you to read *Blink,* by Malcolm Gladwell. While they might not be taught, these are the "business rules of law" that you must embrace to change and improve your business results. Ultimately, it is the quantity of the decisions that matter most, not the quality of the decisions.

▼▼▼▼▼

There is one other "business rule of law" that you must remember: If it feels wrong or bad, it probably is. This is similar to the "go with your gut" concept, but it is even more specific and applicable to people, situations, and clients where you get this feeling that something does not make sense or feel good—that "bad feeling." All too often you ignore that feeling and go with your head (analysis, evaluation, and often, dollars).

**The Leadership Secrets of Colin Powell,* Oren Harari (McGraw-Hill 2002) at 260 [quoting from *Quotations from Chairman Powell:* A Leadership Primer, Oren Harari, *reprinted from* Management Review (American Management Assocation, December, 1996)].

***Id.*

Being Right Can Be Wrong!

9

Many of you may be skeptical of this concept—that being right can be wrong—but when it comes to working with clients, many lawyers provide answers too often and too early . . . which is "wrong" when it comes to building and maintaining great client relationships. There is the all-too-common perception that lawyers are "deal killers" and spend all of their time telling clients what they did wrong, what they cannot do, why something will not work, and the "right answer" under the law. For most clients, this is *not* what they want. Instead, they want to know what they *can* do, how they can do it, and what is best for them. They want help in making good business decisions. Clients (especially business owners and executives) want their lawyers to be business advisors, not just lawyers.

Most lawyers also want to be true advisors, yet in practice we do not advise, we tell. We do not create, we shoot down. We do not provide legal advice, we recite the law. We do not help clients succeed; we tell them why their plan or course of action will not succeed. The difference is monumental, since clients who perceive you as a value-added advisor will willingly and happily pay for that advice, will consistently come back for more advice, and will enthusiastically endorse and refer you to others. This is how law firms grow and become successful.

Like many things, this concept has been developing in my mind for many years. When I was an associate at a large law firm, a partner said something like the following to me: "Why do you keep telling me what won't work? All you do is keep telling me what won't work, what's wrong with the approach or the argument, and what we cannot do." I responded, "That is my job. Your job is to come up with ideas, approaches, and strategies, and my role is to tell you the flaws and whether or not the ideas will work." At the time, I was certain that it was my role to find the flaws, while the partner was the creative one, the idea person. My role was to take a critical look at the partner's ideas and strategies to see if they worked under the law. In hindsight, that probably was my role. Someone (in this case, me as the associate) had to play the role of looking for flaws in ideas and approaches. In any business, it is important to have people serving in that role. Often, the best and most successful ideas have been created and developed, but then tested by having people "take shots" at the ideas. The result is generally a better approach, a better strategy, a better idea. Unfortunately, most lawyers spend their time in the role of "deal killer," idea trasher, and the "let me tell you why it won't work" person.

▼▼▼▼▼

This way of thinking (always looking for what will not work, why it will not work, and why it cannot work) is drilled into us in law school.

Law school taught us to be logical, analytical, and to think critically. Unfortunately, this often translates into being critical and looking only for flaws, not solutions. In an early scene in the movie *Paper Chase,* Professor Kingsfield says, "You come in here with a brain full of mush and you leave thinking like a lawyer." To the detriment of clients and client service, most of us did learn how to "think like lawyers," which means focusing on what cannot be done, what will not work, and what is wrong with a strategy, rather than on solutions that *will* work. While there may have been some opportunities to be creative, there were not many of those opportunities in law school. Like most of you, I was trained to find flaws and holes in arguments. In the classroom, students were not only permitted but encouraged to identify the flaws in other students' arguments. Certainly, these skills are valuable in the *practice of law,* since we do need to be able to assess and evaluate sometimes complicated facts, using applicable law, and determine a course of action. However, for many lawyers this has become the only approach used in their day-to-day practice, especially when it comes to working with and advising clients.

Some of you may be saying, "Wait a minute. My job is to protect my clients and to make sure that they do not do something that they shouldn't do. That means that I must tell them what to do and make sure that clients do not do something wrong or stupid." Ultimately, you are right in that you do have an obligation to make sure that clients conduct themselves or their businesses in accordance with the law. The flaw in that argument, however, is twofold. First, we all know that the law is often more gray than black and white, which means that a variety of factors need to be taken into consideration beyond the objective facts and the law. Second, there is a dramatic difference in *how* we advise our clients versus the "*what*" of advising clients.

Most often lawyers have a reputation for being deal killers, naysayers, and the masters of "no" because of *how* we advise clients, rather than from the advice we give clients. In part, this relates to a concept we have already discussed—slowing down when it comes to working with and advising clients.

Let's consider a practical example. You are in a meeting with an existing client, or even a prospective client, and they tell you that they are planning on starting a new business or somehow getting involved in a new venture. They briefly outline the facts and then tell you that they are planning on creating a general partnership to operate this new venture. Certainly, there is a place and a role for general partnerships, but we all know that there are some significant risks and downsides to a general partnership as a legal entity (particularly in the area of partner liability). For that reason, there are many reasons why other legal entities (single member LLCs, limited partnerships, C corporations, Sub-S corporations, and so on) are often better choices and at least require consideration. Let's even assume that the client has said something in their factual description that tells you that almost certainly a general partnership is the wrong entity choice. So, you are confident that a general partnership is the wrong choice, and it is certainly your obligation to communicate this to the client. How do you do it?

There are three different approaches to this situation. First, once the client has finished their overview, you say something like this: "From what you have just told me, the general partnership is probably not the way to go and probably does not make sense in this situation. It involves much more risk and liability exposure than you want, and there are many other legal entities that will be better for this situation." Short, efficient, to the point, and probably right, but is it the best course of action for you as a client advisor?

Second, you could say something like this: "I have a pretty good idea of what you are trying to accomplish, but I need a little bit more information. I am not sure that a general partnership is the right way to go, but let me ask you some more questions before we talk about what is the best approach." Again, this is relatively short, efficient, and to the point, and it involves asking the client some more questions and making sure that you have all of the information before you tell the client that the general partnership is the wrong choice.

While the message is a little less direct, from the client's perspective this is not much different than the first approach. You have basically told the client that you think that they are wrong, but you need to ask them a few more questions before you can be certain that they are wrong. While perhaps legally correct, neither is the right approach in terms of having your client see you as a valued advisor, rather than a deal killer who is always in a hurry to tell them that they are wrong or what they cannot do.

The third approach involves using questions that will not only help your client know, see, and understand the pros and cons of a particular course of action, but will also allow the client to be an integral part of the decision-making process and, ultimately, to reach their own conclusions on a beneficial course of action. This is very similar to the concept we discussed regarding slowing down and not being in such a hurry to tell clients what to do, but rather allowing them to achieve better decisions based upon your advice. Even if you are right, if you are continually telling clients what to do, how to do it, that their ideas are wrong, or that your ideas are better, most clients will naturally view you as negative, as someone who serves only to shoot down ideas and tells them only what they cannot do rather than what they can do. Even if you are providing them with alternatives (even better alternatives or options), the client's perception (which is all that really matters) is that you are negative and focused only on what cannot be done rather than on what can be done.

▼▼▼▼▼

No one likes to be told that they are wrong. No one likes to be told (directly or indirectly) that their idea or concept was bad or even ill-advised.

People (and especially people in business) like creativity, like to try new things, like to be aggressive, and like to find the best way to do things. Sometimes that means pushing the envelope to the limits of what can be done. When people create and "push the envelope" but are met with negativity and roadblocks from their lawyer, they tend to have a negative experience and a negative view of their lawyer.

I am not suggesting that you start allowing clients to do things that do not make sense, that are fraught with risk and liability, or that are not legal, but how you communicate with clients will go a long way toward establishing yourself as a trusted advisor, counselor, and resource, while negating the often present view of lawyers as deal killers. Let's take a look at the prior example and see how you could reach the same result but do so in a positive, supportive, and interactive manner.

Instead of immediately telling the client that a general partnership is probably not a good idea (and enlightening them on a better idea), and without even asking questions that are really for the purpose of confirming your belief that the client is wrong, start out with questions that are near and dear to the client's heart. "Why are you doing this? Tell me about the opportunity? This sounds very exciting. Can you tell me more about the opportunity, the expectations, the goals, and so on?" In other words, pump them up—tell them it sounds like a terrific opportunity. Tell them that it is creative and cutting edge. Basically, encourage and support their ideas, their goals, their aspirations, and their insights. Then start asking questions that will help you better assess the proper legal entity, but frame the questions to help the client start to see some of the shortcomings of their suggested approach.

For example, start asking questions about risk exposure and liability. Start asking about their "partners" in the enterprise. Ask them all of the questions that you would typically ask someone in assessing which legal entity makes the most sense, but do it with questions that are focused on the client's interests and needs, rather than walking them through questions like some kind of "choice of entity" handbook.

This may seem like a distinction without a difference, but believe me, the difference is very real and the impact will be significant. Nearly every client wants an advisor who supports them and encourages them. If you treat your clients as if you are just there to watch their backs, they will treat you the same way—as someone who is just there to watch their backs. They will tolerate you as a necessary evil, rather than as a professional advisor who can help them make better decisions and help them to be more successful. The "advice" may be the same, but how it is delivered will make all the difference in whether you have clients who view you as a necessary expense or you have long-term client relationships with people who willingly and actively seek you out as a resource to help them to be more successful.

If you do not want to be a mere vendor, stop acting like one. If you want to be an advisor who helps clients make better decisions and supports them in their creative endeavors, then do that for your clients.

A key ingredient in showing your client that you are interested in what they are doing and that you want to help them succeed is to make sure that their goals are always a topic of discussion. You cannot and should not assume that you know what they want or need or what their concerns and challenges are. You need to ask so that you can give them advice that fits them, rather than providing textbook legal analysis. One objection that clients have is that they are given what is stated to be the "correct" legal advice, without any consideration of the factual or business realities that are involved. This is a perfect example of where being "right" can be very "wrong" if your goal is to provide valuable legal advice and counseling to your clients. Think about times in the past when you have advised a client on a particular question or issue, and the client's response was something to the effect that, "Well, that's all well and good, but it's not very practical for this situation."

For example, you advise a business client that they should have employment agreements with all of their employees and a written policy handbook, including an affirmative "at will employment" statement. This would generally be sound advice in any state where the at will employment doctrine applies, but the reality in your state may be that the employer cannot unilaterally force employment agreements on existing employees without the giving of some new consideration. You then give the client good advice (that they need to come up with a program of additional consideration for the employment agreement). Yet the client tells you about all the practical impediments to such a program. If your only response is "that is the law," then you are falling very short of what that client wants and deserves.

Clients want you to understand their business (including business realities) and to provide advice that takes these realities into consideration. First of all, this requires that you have some understanding of their business. Second, this requires that you periodically and consistently ask them questions about their business and update yourself on their business. Third, this requires that you at least at some time visit their business so that you can see it in action and better understand what they do and how they do it. Finally, this requires that you understand your client's goals, needs, wishes, aspirations, and plans. Without this information, your advice cannot be what the client wants and needs.

One area where this is particularly applicable is in litigation. Every lawyer knows that there is more to litigation than winning and losing. By its nature, litigation is unpredictable, fraught with risks, and presents challenges in controlling and even accurately assessing costs. In addition to costs, litigation involves time and diverts time, energy, attention, and money away from other business opportunities. Therefore, advising clients on litigation matters requires that you fully understand not only the facts and the issues, but how these issues relate to the business, to the owner, to business goals and plans, to desires or concerns regarding precedential value in the company, and risk and liability exposure. Everyone knows that litigation is unpredictable, and if your advice does not take into account every angle and perspective, then you are not providing quality legal advice. It may pass the test to avoid a malpractice claim, but you are not fulfilling your role as an advisor if you fail to account for all of the realities at stake.

We all know that many business cases settle not over the issue of dollars, but over the issue of time. When the business or business owner fully understands the time and distraction that will be involved in proceeding, this is often the motivation for settling on perhaps less favorable terms so that the business and the owner can focus their valuable time, energy, and resources on positive business opportunities, rather than on fighting a litigation fight where the results will be uncertain. If you are advising your litigation clients only on the merits of their claims and the likelihood of success or failure, then you are doing them a disservice. They want and expect more.

Great law firms (and great lawyers) advise their clients with 360-degree legal advice, not simply facts-and-issues legal advice.

If you do not want to be viewed as a deal killer, stop killing deals. If you do not want your clients to see you as negative and always telling them what they cannot do, then stop telling them what they cannot do. Instead, show them what they can or should do. There is a difference, not only to the client but for you in how you deliver the message. The biggest difference is in the results that you will achieve for your clients, with your clients, and in the client relationships that are cultivated because you advised clients from their side of the table, rather than sitting on the other side of the table and telling them what they cannot do. Make your advice practical given all of the circumstances, rather than simply providing clients with technically correct legal advice.

We said at the beginning that most legal advice is measured (particularly by clients) in the *how* rather than the *what* of your legal advice. Clients who view their lawyers as mere lawyers will treat them like lawyers, pay them like lawyers, and not refer them. Clients who perceive their lawyers as interested "partners" focused on helping them make great decisions and enhancing their success will view and treat them as such, will pay them as an advisor, and will willingly and enthusiastically refer them to others. Never forget that *how* you advise your clients is a major factor in the growth and success of your firm.

10 *Who Is Driving Your Bus?*[1]

The bus is your law firm and someone must be in the driver's seat steering the bus and making sure that the bus is headed in the right direction, that the bus is always in good working order (and capable of operating at optimum effectiveness), that every person is in the right seat, and that everyone knows their role on the bus. Unfortunately, most law firms have no driver (at least not a single driver), which results in the firm either going nowhere, getting lost, or (even worse) going in reverse. Nearly every business (whether it has a single owner/employee or hundreds of employees) needs three role players—leaders, managers, and producers—and these three roles are particularly critical for law firms. This basic business structure is integral to building a law business that can consistently, efficiently, and profitably deliver its services. When law firms have mostly producers, few managers, and ineffective leaders, they are creating an impediment to the development of a business model that can deliver the financial results they desire.

Law Firm Leadership

Let's start with leadership. Can anyone seriously question the importance of having effective leadership? Apparently, law firms generally do not see the critical leadership role that is needed in a law firm. At a minimum, law firm leaders often do not understand what their role should be, and they often spin their wheels and waste time trying to manage (or worse, micromanage) the people and the operations. That is definitely not the role of the leader in a business, so let's look at what role a leader should fill in any law firm.

First and foremost, any leader must be responsible for creating, keeping, and communicating the firm's vision. Where is the firm going? What is it striving to become? Why is it pursuing that path? These are vital questions, and it is the leader's role to make certain that the questions are asked (and answered) and that the firm develops a shared vision and an implementation plan consistent with that vision. Even if the vision is decided upon by committee, ultimately the vision must be carried like a torch by the law firm leader. If your firm does not have a clear vision, then shame on the firm, but the real responsibility for failings related to firm vision lies with the leader.

Who is leading your firm? Who is the person most connected with, in tune with, and focused on the firm's vision? Does your law firm have a leader that everyone can look to for guidance when it comes to the firm's vision and future? If not, then this is priority number one for your firm. If there is such a leader in your firm, then you still must take appropriate steps to assure that this leader is filling the right role.

One role that a law firm leader should not have is overseeing operations! Overseeing operations is a job for some level of manager in the firm and, ideally, these are not lawyers. First, most lawyers know very little about the business operation aspects of a law firm. Practicing law is not good training for operating a law firm, so do not put inexperienced lawyers in the role of overseeing and managing operations. Second, lawyers are your most valuable assets in terms of not only delivering legal services but bringing in new business. Unfortunately, most law firms have lawyers wasting a great deal of valuable time (and opportunities) on managing the firm's operations, but at a minimum, law firm operations absolutely should not be part of the leader's responsibilities.

▼▼▼▼▼

Day-to-day operations are not important enough to have a skilled practitioner or rainmaker spending valuable time on the "stuff" of the practice of law.

What about hiring and personnel? Do you think that these are appropriate responsibilities for the law firm leader? It depends. One vital role for any business leader is to help build the business team, but this relates primarily to high-level team building and development issues. For example, issues relating to the hiring, promoting, and engagement of high-level lawyers (the key drivers within the law firm) are part of the leader's responsibilities. Likewise, the leader must be an integral (if not primary) mover and motivator when it comes to developing a model for the types of people that the law firm wants to have on its team. This includes taking a leadership role in coaching and mentoring the leader's "successors" and others who are the future of the law firm. The leader may also work extensively with others (lawyers or non-lawyers) who are responsible for the firm's day-to-day activities relating to the law firm team. However, the leader cannot and should not be involved in day-to-day issues and problems relating to the law firm team. This is not where the leader can add the most value to the firm and its overall team.

As with many issues relating to law firm leaders, the primary question is whether the particular issue relates to the future of the firm. If the answer is yes, then the firm's leader should be involved. If the answer is no, then the leader probably should not be involved with the issue. It may sound too simple, but in every business the quality of the business' future depends a great deal on the quality of the leader, including that leader's ability to focus solely on the firm's future.

What law firm leaders need to learn, remember, and implement is the concept that their primary role is to focus on opportunities. This includes seeking out opportunities to increase business, to build relationships, to share the firm's vision, to lead by example, and to create a great law firm team. An effective leader is able to create business and growth opportunities both internally (within the law firm) and externally (primarily in the form of business development or developing and maintaining key business or community relationships). Remember, leaders should manage the opportunities, not the operations.

A final area where leaders must excel is in setting an example for the entire firm and its team, particularly by the leaders' actions (not words). Your people are very astute. They may hear your words, but they judge you by your actions, which means living the age-old mantra that "actions speak louder than words." For example, an open-door policy means that your door is always open. Claiming to have an open-door policy, but working with your door closed, are inconsistent messages. Giving motivational speeches about the future of the firm are nice, but the words are lost and forgotten if your people see you looking and sounding worried when you are not "in front" of the team. Remember, your people are always looking to you for leadership and that means that they are always "looking." So make sure that you are walking the talk and doing as you say.

> ▼▼▼▼▼
>
> One key change in thinking that can ignite your firm is to recognize and acknowledge that time is not money. Rather, opportunities are money and it is the opportunities (both today and in the future) that will define the firm's success.

Most important, great leaders lead by how they think, not by what they do. If you want to be a great leader, the first step is to think like a leader and then to act according to that thinking. Most people are looking for someone to follow—they are looking for a leader—but they will not follow just anyone. They will follow a leader who inspires and motivates them, mostly by how he or she thinks. In the immortal words of Henry Ford, "If you think you can or you think you can't, you're right!" This philosophy—that you must believe in yourself and in your business in order to succeed—can mean the difference between mediocrity and great success in any business.

Law Firm Management

Next, let's focus on the critical (but generally overlooked) role of the manager in a law firm. In contrast to the leader's role, the manager *is* responsible for managing the firm's operations, which includes all of the systems, processes, and technology. In larger firms, this particular role is often well defined and effectively performed; however, smaller firms tend to either ignore this important role (wrongly believing that they are too small to need such a manager) or fail to fill it because they believe that they cannot afford to have it filled. In reality, every business needs to have this role filled in some way, since a lack of management necessarily translates into an ineffective, inefficient, and underperforming business.

Another key role for anyone in the operations management role is to focus on monitoring and improving the firm's efficiencies and expenses. This is certainly an important role or function, since the results (if effective) translate into enhanced profits. However, this area is often given too much attention and focus at the expense or exclusion of other vital managerial roles and functions. For example, in most law firms the first (and often only) "officer" other than lawyer members of the management or executive committee is a "chief financial officer"—typically, an accountant tasked to manage, monitor, and oversee the firm's financial operations, but nothing more. Likewise, those firms that have moved toward more nonlawyers in management roles will often hire an accountant with the title of "executive director" or "chief operating officer." While many accountants are capable managers outside the financial arena, many firms with accountants in these roles will move forward narrowly, focusing only on financial operations. This is a critical part of law firm management, but it is only one of many parts, and law firms tend to overemphasize financial operations to the exclusion of other areas such as client service, business development, and professional development.

Another key manager role is providing the necessary tools, training, and mentoring for the producers in the business. In a law firm, the producers are the lawyers, which means that a complete and effective management team should include one or more people who manage the lawyers. This is an aspect of the business of law that is often overlooked or poorly implemented, which leaves the lawyers without the tools, support, and training that they need to be the best they can be for clients and for the firm. Does your firm have someone who manages the lawyers (associates, partners, or shareholders)? When I ask lawyers (especially associates) who manages them, they typically look at me with a look that says, "What are you talking about?" By the way, having the head of a department does not equal having a manager. Managing people is about what you do, not your title.

Lawyers have years of legal education, but that is not the same as training on how to be a lawyer. Lawyers are also required to regularly take continuing legal education courses, but most of these courses focus on areas of substantive law, not better lawyering skills and rarely on better "business lawyering" skills. Rarer still are opportunities for lawyers to learn how to better service clients or how to get more clients. Lawyer-producers (especially younger ones) are hungry for help in how to develop business, but rarely do law firms offer that help beyond an occasional workshop or seminar. This is a managerial failure of omission or misunderstanding, and it generally comes from an ignorance of its value to the firm's business and its clients.

Take a look at your firm. Who is managing and training your lawyers? Do the lawyers (especially the younger lawyers) think and believe that they are being managed and supported? Are there managers in place to lead and mentor the lawyers? If there are lawyers who ostensibly are tasked to offer some level of management for the other lawyers, how much time do they have left for managing after they have satisfied their billable hour requirements? Too often the supposed law firm managers are full-time lawyers who are expected to deliver their quota of billable hours, with their "managing" responsibilities relegated to whatever time is left. Unfortunately, and to the detriment of most law firms' bottom line, this role—managing the lawyer/producers—is usually either ignored or poorly performed. This is an area where law firms can have a dramatic and positive impact on their financial performance and on client service, but it will require a commitment to building a true business model to make sure that the firm not only has designated managers, but that those managers have the skills, support, and time to properly perform their duties.

Law Firm Producers

So what about the producers in a law firm? Producers exist to do the work—to deliver the legal services. Another producer role for lawyers is to increase the firm's revenue by either increasing business from existing

▼▼▼▼▼

It may seem obvious, but it is worth stating here: There are only two ways to grow a law firm—increase business from existing clients or bring in new clients. There are no other avenues for growth. Unfortunately, some firms miss this point. How do we know? Because many law firms invest little or nothing (in time, training, and dollars) on either of these two areas.

clients or bringing new clients into the firm. In general, law firms do very well with producers—at least in that they have enough lawyers to service clients (although the training and development of these producers often falls short of what is necessary). Certainly, there are things that law firms can do better when it comes to their lawyer-producers, but law firms typically do their best when it comes to the lawyer-producer side of their business.

So, what is the state of law firms when it comes to these vital business roles? In many law firms (including even solo practices), it looks like this: Too many producers, few if any managers, and little or no leadership. Among the many changes required to improve the business of a law firm, this is one of the most challenging for a variety of reasons. First, it requires a totally different mindset regarding billable hours, which is a major challenge. Second, it requires a willingness to turn over real management to non-lawyers (or at least lawyers who are not primary producers in the firm). Third, it requires a commitment of time and dollars to the process of implementing a new business model. The process of change may be difficult and full of bumps in the road, but the movement to a more businesslike model of operating, managing, and leading the law firm will pay dividends in the form of improved financial performance.

Note

1. The analogy between a business and a bus comes from *Good to Great* by James Collins (HarperCollins 2001). *Good to Great* discusses the key differentiators that propel good companies to greatness. This is a very practical and simple approach to building a great business and a must-read for every businessperson, including lawyers.

11 Goals Set Are Goals Achieved

Planning of any kind is one of the most overlooked and ignored aspects of running a business—law or otherwise—but lawyers are even more likely than others to claim that they are "too busy" to plan. Admittedly, making time to plan can be a greater challenge for lawyers because of the ever-present billable hour demands, but we must change our priorities to recognize the value of planning as a source of revenue enhancement. As has been said repeatedly over the years, "Failing to plan is planning to fail." This is not just a catchy phrase but an insight into a key ingredient for achieving business success. Tactical planning (the creation of specific action plans) will serve as a key tool to help lawyers begin to take new actions and thereby achieve different and better results.

How can you achieve goals if you do not know what they are? Many people in business are reluctant to set and track goals, but law firms are even more hesitant and resistant to goal setting and especially to tracking results. The main reasons are that lawyers in general do not see (or understand) the value of goal setting and, perhaps more important, people do not want to be held accountable. Writing and tracking goals requires that people be accountable for their actions and their results. This accountability represents the pros and the "perceived con" of goal setting.

The "perceived con" is the resistance that we have to being accountable. Yes, it is true that if you have goals, then you will know if you do not achieve those goals. Whether the goals are results oriented (e.g., business development goals for numbers of new clients, new matters, revenues, and so on) or action oriented (e.g., number of networking meetings, number of articles written, number of referral sources meetings, and so on), simply having them creates immediate accountability (at least to yourself), albeit at a minimal level. If you write down your goals (which you should), then the level of accountability is enhanced (as is your likelihood of achieving the goals). The highest level of accountability comes when you not only create written goals but share them with someone else, which now makes you accountable not only to yourself but to that other person. If you want to really accelerate your transition to better results, then in addition to sharing your goals with someone else, ask them to "coach" you and hold you accountable.

Over the years I have worked with several coaches (some official and some unofficial), and I have found one fascinating and recurring theme—no matter how important my goals and plans are and no matter how committed I claim to be, many times I have achieved goals, followed through on my commitments, and stayed on track with my plans solely because I did not want to let my coach down. Human nature is such that we do not like to let people down and, if we have committed to a third party to achieve something, we are likely to follow through so that we can be assured that we can say, "Yes, I did it."

Do not underestimate the power of having someone there to help you make sure that you do what you know you need to do. Having goals makes you accountable and that accountability is a driving force to help us achieve our goals and implement our vision, but this accountability scares many people, which is why accountability is also a "perceived con."

▼▼▼▼▼

It has been shown over and over that people tend to achieve that which they are asked to achieve. If you lower the bar (or have no bar), then that is what you are likely to achieve (underachieve, that is). If you raise the bar (or at least have one), then you are likely to achieve that which you have set out to achieve.

These very same accountability features deliver the biggest and best "pros" of goal setting—accountability (the greater the better) delivers results. At a minimum, your results will far outdistance the results achieved with no goals at all. In fact, goal setting and tracking of goals will almost automatically enhance the firm's results and the results of the lawyers who are also setting individual goals and tracking their personal results. Although experts disagree about the percentage of increase, it is well accepted that the mere process of setting and writing down goals (and tracking them) will enhance your results by at least 10 percent. That is right, just taking the steps of developing written goals and tracking your progress will enhance your results and your firm's results. So, what are you waiting for?

Let's be honest. We all know that setting goals will enhance our results and our success, yet we do not do it. What are we so afraid of? We know that goal setting is good for our business, but we hesitate to do it. Sometimes we are afraid of failing—of falling short of our goals—but that is only because we wrongly believe that not achieving our goals is a failure. Nothing could be further from the truth. We need to change how we look at goal setting and recognize that not setting goals is the only failure—a failure to do what will do the most for our chances of achieving our goals. If we set goals (and fall short), then we need only to evaluate why we fell short and adjust our actions so that we improve our chances of achieving our goals in the future. Goals should be aggressive, and even if we fall short of achieving them our results will far exceed what we would have accomplished without any goals at all.

Finally, when we do set goals we need to make sure that they are aggressive. Frankly, setting easy goals is a waste of time. In working with various businesses, I often hear business owners talk about a desire (or goal) to increase sales by 10 percent or sometimes the very aggressive goal of 15 percent. When I ask them why, they never seem to have an answer, except to say that it "seems like a good number." For some reason, we have fallen into a mediocrity trap of setting goals that are either too low or that are not based on anything (facts, markets, reality, and so on). Interestingly, I have yet to find any book or study that says (or even suggests) that a 10 to 15 percent increase in sales is good or appropriate. For example, if you decide to "go crazy" and set a goal of increasing revenues by 30 percent (instead of only 15 percent), but fall short and increase revenues by only 27 percent, then your results will still far exceed what you would have achieved if you had set an artificially low goal.

In the real world the "rightness" of a goal depends on many facts and circumstances. There is no such thing as a generally accepted goal for annual business growth, no matter what the industry. Even if there are industry standards against which you can compare your results, there is no reason to be limited by any supposed industry standards. Why limit yourself to what others can achieve? The only limits on your success and growth should be the limits of your imagination, initiative, and commitment to turning plans into reality. When it comes to revenue goals, they should be based not on some arbitrary percentage increases, but on a determination of the goals that you and your firm can achieve by following through on the activities (e.g., sales and marketing activities) that are designed and intended to deliver the financial results you desire.

Whenever someone tells me what their goals are (especially results-oriented goals), I always ask them "Why?" If you cannot explain the logic behind the goals (why they make sense and are aggressive under all the circumstances), then they are bad goals. You must also be able to explain how the goals will be achieved by specifying the actions that are intended to deliver the desired results—in other words, you must have a plan and know what activities will achieve the goals and how those activities are designed to achieve them. Instead of just picking numbers, you should reverse the goal-setting process and begin with the activities that you intend to pursue, and then determine the results that such activities should deliver. This is the only way you and your firm can achieve the highest potential, since this approach is limited only by your creativity and commitment to following through with your plans. In the future, forget about 10 or 15 percent and start setting goals that will help you build your firm (or your individual book of business) into what you want it to be.

We Are What the Public Thinks We Are

12

A harsh reality, but absolutely true. Perceptions are the reality when it comes to the consuming public, and all lawyer jokes aside, the public perception of lawyers is, at best, poor. Ask people what they think of lawyers and you will hear a long list of less-than-favorable descriptions: dishonest, sharks, unethical, "always on the clock," willing to do anything for clients (this is not a positive trait), manipulative, egotistical, obnoxious, liars, negative, deal killers. . . . The list goes on and on. Now, before you start objecting and getting defensive, remember how this discussion started. These are the perceptions of many people but certainly not all people. Clearly, these perceptions are not true of the profession as a whole, but every perception is true to the person with that perception. When facing perceptions, you cannot convince the person (or public) otherwise, nor can you change their mind. Your only option is to change those perceptions, one person and one perception at a time.

Some of you may think that your clients do not have these perceptions, and in some ways you are probably right—if they had the worst of these perceptions they would not hire you and continue using you—but the reality is that some of your clients have these or similar perceptions. These perceptions are preventing you from achieving the kind of professional and financial success that you not only want but deserve. The reality is that some people will hire and retain a lawyer (and even pay for legal services) even though they have a less-than-favorable opinion of that lawyer. Some will come back to the lawyer for additional work even when they have a low opinion of them, although this is very rare. However, clients who only tolerate you will definitely not refer you to others, and referrals are the best means for growing your law business. If you want to grow your firm, you need to create the perception that you are more than just a lawyer. You must create in their minds the perception that you are a trusted advisor who adds value.

While changing perceptions requires consistently doing and saying the right things, too often we forget that it is the little things that leave a positive or negative impression (or perception) with people. We often send poor messages to our clients by the way we do business, even if it does not have an immediate or direct impact on them. If you think that client perceptions of their lawyers are not that bad, consider the article in the *New York Times* titled "A Lawyer's Role Must Be Defined, and Also the Fees" (Feb. 24, 2004, Section G, Page 2). The article explores the needs, interests, and desires of small business owners (not tiny, but not large corporations) as it relates to their lawyers. Here are some of the comments from clients and other lawyers:

- "They [the lawyers] tend to fascinate themselves with all sorts of trivial things."
- "[Smaller companies are] more practical and less theoretical. They don't like long contracts, and they like them to be in plain English."
- "[L]aw firms can lose sight of the cost effectiveness of their work and may be driven by the perverse incentives inherent in hourly billing."
- "Lawyers for small companies take on a patronizing role. They will consume as much time as they possibly can and will assume as great a role in a transaction as they can. . . . You find that the whole deal is negotiated and you haven't even seen it."
- "You don't have to hit a flea with a sledgehammer."
- "For some lawyers, the meter is always running. If you want to talk about your kids or your vacation, don't do it with your attorney."
- "An attorney, to me, is like an expensive pen. It's a tool. You should negotiate the business points yourself. They should document what you've negotiated."

▼▼▼▼▼

As we all know, excluding the lawyer from the client's business negotiations is generally a recipe for disaster, since clients do not understand the legal or perhaps the tax implications of what they are negotiating, and it is always difficult to try to "undo" something that the client has already negotiated. It is usually best for the lawyers to be involved very early in the process, *but* the clients often do not see any value in this and only see additional cost. It is our job to help them to see *that value.*

Is this true or partially true? Actually, it does not matter whether it is objectively true or not. What matters is that clients and prospective clients have these types of perceptions about lawyers in general and even their own lawyers, and it is up to us to change those perceptions . . . not by telling them so, but by showing them.

We will talk more about perceptions later, but remember these two important points. First, client perceptions (and even public perceptions) are an important part of the attorney-client relationship (positive or negative). While you need not waste your time on public perceptions, these perceptions must be kept in mind as you go about the practice of law and the business of law. Remember, you generally cannot change people's minds, but you can change their perceptions, so your time and effort must be focused on changing perceptions . . . and the only way to change such perceptions is by what you do, not what you say.

Second, clients want their lawyers to be good businesspeople, and they are looking for signs (even little signs) that their lawyers are good businesspeople. *Everything you do* can impact the perception your clients and prospects have of you as a lawyer and as a businessperson, so make sure that you invest time, attention, and money on how you go about your business (from delivery of legal services to billing) and make sure that you are making good business decisions in everything that you do and say.

"I Can Do It Myself" 13

We have all heard this phrase before, but do we ever really listen when we say it or act in accordance with it? This mindset is a significant challenge for most professionals and especially for lawyers. To find (and then fix) the problems in your law firm business, you have to be willing to let others function without excessive oversight. Most lawyers have a strong need and desire to control everything, which is an impediment to their own personal success and certainly to the firm's success. Giving up control and allowing others to fill their respective roles is vital if the firm is to achieve its highest and most profitable business potential.

Since lawyers are typically required to be the primary producers of services—in other words, the delivery arm of the firm—lawyers learn early on that part of their responsibility is to do the work. Unfortunately, this can foster the "I can do it myself" mentality. Another factor that contributes to lawyers adopting (or expanding) the "I can do it myself" approach is the misperception that doing it yourself helps the firm earn more money. While this perspective can sometimes be justified in the short term, in the long term it is in the firm's financial best interests if the lawyers delegate as much work as possible. Assume that a partner has a billable hourly rate of $300, while that of an associate is $150. The shortsighted perspective suggests that the partner should perform all necessary services as long as he or she has time to do the work. Assuming that the matter requires 20 hours of services, if the partner does all the work the total fees are $6,000. If the associate does all the work then the total fees are $3,000. Thus, many lawyers conclude that it is $3,000 "better" for the partner to do all the work, but this is misleading and shortsighted.

First, this approach is certainly not in the client's best interests. The client-centric approach is to have the most appropriate lawyer (in terms of experience, skills, and hourly rate) perform necessary services. The partner should perform only the services that he or she is uniquely qualified to perform, while the associate should perform the rest of the services (as long as the associate is qualified to perform them). Second, if the partner is performing all of the services, there is a greater risk of an unsatisfied or unhappy client and/or a dispute over the bill. This is certainly not a client-focused approach.

Third, and this is a very important example of a different way to look at your law business, if the partner is performing all of the services, then he or she is certainly missing opportunities to develop or nurture client relationships. While the younger associate might also have opportunities to develop relationships, the partner will likely have greater opportunities to build and deliver the relationships that benefit the firm. The difference in perspective is that billing more hours has the potential to increase revenues in the short term, but the growth and success of the law firm will ultimately depend on the opportunities that are created, nurtured, and converted to new business in the future. The old way of thinking says that "time is money," but the business reality is that "opportunities are money."

> ▼▼▼▼▼
>
> There must be certain people in the firm who focus on functions that help grow the business—not what pays the bills. This means having a strong group of lawyers who are focused on "selling" the business, not doing the work.

Billable hour requirements can also push lawyers to try to do it all themselves, since they decide to keep all the work on their plate because of the pressure to meet the firm's requirements. If you focus on this you may be hesitant to delegate to others and, instead, choose to do it all yourself. This would not be a good business decision. It certainly is not in the client's best interests and it is not in the firm's best interests in the long term. A critical point is that the firm must also be accountable for contributing to this pressure. The firm must educate and encourage all of its professionals to perform only those services that are appropriate for their skill and experience levels. Instead of simply looking at billable hours, management should consider the type of work that exists in the firm and whether it is properly allocated among the professionals. Proper allocation and delegation should be rewarded, rather than simply looking at billable hours. This requires a completely different culture and way of thinking in the firm—specifically, a more businesslike approach to the practice of law.

Obviously, delegation and empowerment are critical elements to avoiding the "I can do it myself" trap, which applies both to other professionals and to nonprofessionals in the firm. Every level must delegate as many nonessential functions as possible, recognizing that this type of delegation leads to the long-term financial success and health of the firm.

Here are the key questions for every lawyer to ask every day:

- Is this my job?
- Is this the highest and best use of my time right now?
- Will this activity help me accomplish my goals or the firm's goals?

These types of questions (supported by a firm culture and infrastructure that encourages and rewards appropriate delegation) will result in the best and ultimately most profitable allocation of the firm's most valuable resources—its people. This is also consistent with your obligation to look out for your client's best interests. What a great combination—it is good for the firm and its clients. This is a win-win solution that must be the goal if you want to be trusted advisors and true partners with your clients.

I hope you can already see that the "I can do it myself" approach is not healthy for your firm or for your clients. If not, you may be thinking that there are valid reasons for doing a wider range of the work. If that is the case, then you probably would say or think something like this:

> It's not that I have to do it myself. It's just that if I do it myself I know that it's done, that it's done right, and I can take it off the to-do list.

Sorry to disappoint, but this is exactly what the "I can do it myself" mentality is. It is about trying to control the situation and being convinced that you are the only person who can do the work the right way. In most cases this is either not true (others can do the work just as well) or the work does not need to be done by the most qualified (or overqualified) person. These are the types of judgments you need to make every day and make in a more businesslike and client-focused manner. Are you focused on performing the legal work or on building relationships? Legal work pays the light bills, but building relationships is the path to growth and success. Effective delegation is a critical step that will allow you to focus and invest more of your time on relationships. In the end, dumping the "I can do it myself" mentality will enhance the firm's financial success, build more and better client relationships, and deliver outstanding client service. This is the path to building a great law firm.

14 Teamwork Works . . . Even for Lawyers

Some of you are reading this chapter title talking about teamwork and thinking "blah, blah, blah. Nice concept, but it has no practical application." Well, nothing could be further from the truth. Your people will make or break the success of your law firm. It starts with hiring the best people, giving your people the right training and support, and compensating your people according to their abilities and contributions (as opposed to years of experience, and so on). Law firms have made a bad habit of setting the bar way too low when it comes to their people, professional and otherwise, the results of which are law firm performances that fall below expectations and certainly far below their potential. As James Collins asserted in *Good to Great* (HarperCollins, 2001), people are not your most important asset—the *right* people are your most important asset—and it is about time that law firms started focusing on getting the *right* people on their law business bus.

The right people are vital ingredients for the growth and success of your business, but the wrong people not only will limit your success but can actually drag your business down (even to the point of failure). This "people truth" is equally true for law firms, yet they typically do a poor job when it comes to their people—professional and nonprofessional. The failings with professionals usually relate to how they are hired, a lack of training (the right training), and a lack of understanding of (or concern about) the working environment that the firm has created. The failings with nonprofessionals are similar, but typically flow from the firm's view that nonprofessionals are just necessary evils—with the firm failing to recognize the significant impact that the right people can have on the firm's business success. Law firms need to recognize how valuable all of their people are and change how they think and act with respect to personnel. It is easy to talk about how important your people are, but your people only know what they see in your actions. They know whether they are respected and valued, and your firm's success depends on showing your people that they are respected and valued.

Before we talk about some specific areas where law firms need to improve their team development, it is important to first focus on one vital but often overlooked aspect of team building. While most firms do not invest enough time and money on improving their people and creating a truly people-centric workplace, they at least know that they have employees and, to varying degrees, spend some time and thought on their people. What lawyers often fail to see, however, is that they depend on (or at least should depend on) numerous teams beyond their firm employees. For any law firm or even an individual lawyer, your team is a vital part of your leverage, and this applies to all the teams that are there to help and support you. The most obvious, of course, are your employees, which we will call your "work team," but what about your relationship team, your networking team, your mentoring team, your personal team, your family team, and so on.

In every part of your life, a team is part of your leverage, and success in business typically requires that you invest and nurture all of these teams; it is critical that you realize that success often follows those individuals and firms that build great teams around themselves. The list goes on and on, but the quantity of the teams is not important. Rather, the quality of the teams (which is totally dependent on the quality of the team members and your investment in them) is the most critical part of building a great and leveraged team. Remember, in every part of your life, your teams allow you to achieve greater success quicker and easier.

> ▼▼▼▼▼
>
> Success teams can allow you to achieve greater earning power, expand your talents and resources, provide you with greater and enhanced connections and networks, allow you to achieve and expand your goals, and provide you with a greater level of success.

Do not make the mistake of discounting this discussion of teamwork and team building as more "touchy-feely" stuff. Great businesses have great teams. If you do not yet have a great team, there's no reason to despair because, remember, teams are built and developed (unless you are the New York Yankees). It takes time and effort not only to assemble the right "players" on your team, but to get the team working together and producing outstanding results. This does not just happen. Every member of the team must be committed to the team and must be prepared to invest in the team and the team's results. As the saying goes, there's no "I" in team.

As noted earlier, one of the biggest failings of law firms when it comes to their people is that their only view of leverage is hiring more people. However, if the only value of "your team" is providing more bodies to perform more work over more hours, you are seriously shortchanging the value of team and the magic of leverage. When people work together, incredible power can be released. In fact, a synergistic team (like-minded, success-oriented, value sharing, and positive team members) is one of the most amazing success tools. One team definition is "two or more people with a common purpose where both hearts and heads are in harmony with one another." When it comes to getting the right people on the bus, you must always be on the lookout for the best people and, when you find them, ask them to join one of your teams (work or otherwise).

Who Do You Want on Your Team?

In creating and building your own success team, what should you be looking for? One of the biggest mistakes made by most businesses is focusing all of their energy on experience, but experience alone is not enough. In fact, attitude is critical and can make or break your team's success. When evaluating a potential team member, ask yourself whether this person has the integrity, the passion, the energy, and the commitment needed to achieve your desired goals. Values are so critical that if a prospective or existing team member does not share your core values, he or she needs to be removed from the team (or should never join your team). It is that simple.

Who should you avoid? Selfish, negative, or egotistical people. Team is about building and working together, and negativity and selfishness prevent the magic of leverage from working. This negativity also tends to spread through the organization like a disease. You want committed team members. You want team members who are always looking for new and different ways to contribute. Perhaps most important, the team members must share common vision, values, and purpose. Team members certainly will not agree on everything. In fact, disagreement can often be a powerful tool for team improvement and success, but there must be alignment on the team's core vision, values, and purpose.

For those of you who are reading this and saying that this sounds great, "but I/we cannot find good people," do not give up so easily. Generally, any businessperson (and that includes lawyers) who says that he or she cannot find "good people" does not know what a "good person" looks like, is not doing anything to find the right people, and is not doing anything to "build" the right people. The right people require an investment and a genuine commitment, not only to getting the right people, but also treating them right. As the very old saying goes, "you reap what you sow," which applies to many things in life and in business, including your people.

As was posited in *Good to Great,* three simple truths apply when it comes to your people: (1) If you begin with "who," rather than "what," you can more easily adapt to a changing world; (2) If you have the right people on the bus, the problem of how to motivate and manage people largely goes away; and (3) If you have the wrong people on the bus, it does not matter how great your direction and vision is, you still will not have a great company—"Great vision without great people is irrelevant."[1] In *Good to Great,* the author expected to find that good-to-great leaders would begin by setting a new vision and strategy. He found instead that good-to-great leaders *first* got the right people on the bus, the wrong people off the bus, and the right people in the right seats.[2] Then they figured out where to drive the bus. *Good to Great* concludes that, with respect to hiring decisions, good-to-great companies place greater weight on "character attributes than on specific educational background, practical skills, specialized knowledge, or work experience."[3] They view skills and work experience as teachable and learnable, but attributes such as "character, work ethic, basic intelligence, dedication to fulfilling commitments, and values" are ingrained.[4]

Is your firm focused on character or skills and work experience when it comes to your people? My guess is that your primary focus is on skills and work experience. Why? Because I have not known many law firms that even talk about hiring for character and even those that "talk about it" have not done the things they need to do in order to find and hire for character. For example, if you claim to hire for character, do you have an employee profile (for professionals and nonprofessionals) that lists the traits you desire? If not, then you probably are not finding them. Likewise, what systems and procedures are in place to attract, identify, and hire people with the desired character traits? Without systems and procedures, you cannot expect to consistently (if at all) find and hire the right people.

My guess is that most of you and your firms focus most of your hiring efforts on skills and experience. Take a look at the advertisements or job descriptions that you use for nonprofessionals. Are they focused on skills and experience (most are) or are they focused on character? If you talk about character traits in your advertisements and job descriptions, what are you doing to follow up on those words to make sure that you actually hire people with those traits? Likewise, take a look at your internal forms (especially your "job application"). Does it have questions about education, prior work experience, and skills? Most likely it does. What questions does it have about prior successes, prior contributions to an employer's business, and values? Probably none. "You reap what you sow" and, when it comes to employees, you usually get exactly what you ask for and look for. If you want the "right" employees, then start looking for them and start asking the "right" questions.

By the way, the foregoing concept applies to both professionals and nonprofessionals. Too many law firms are looking in many of the wrong places, applying the wrong standards, and asking the wrong questions when it comes to hiring professionals. Let's be honest. How are most new lawyers judged? Typically, it is by their grade point average and the perceived quality of their law school. Before you give up on me, I will acknowledge that grades are one (but only one) relevant inquiry for new associates, but there is much more to being a good lawyer than good grades. In fact, I am sure that each of you know many excellent lawyers who were not in the top 10 percent of their class in a top-tier law school. Remember, the concept of law school tiers is a relatively recent phenomenon, which came into existence after many still-practicing lawyers went to law school.

Hiring the top-ranked lawyers from the top-ranked law schools might lower the risk of a hiring "mistake," but there are no guarantees and most clients do not care about where their lawyers went to law school (most would not even know a supposedly good law school from a so-so law school) or about their grade point average. It is only the law firms that are so narrowly focused on grade point averages and law school rankings. As with so many shortcomings in law firms, this narrow focus flows from the fact that grade point averages and law school rankings are relatively objective and "easy" to apply. But like so many things in business and in life, easier does not always equal better.

> ▼▼▼▼▼
>
> It's very interesting when you start to look at how many senior and successful partners in law firms would not be hired today by their current law firm. In fact, most would not even get an interview because their firm does not consider their law school to be of a high enough quality.

One effective strategy is to avoid the mistakes and financial losses inherent in hiring lawyers right out of law school by letting other firms make the mistakes and take the financial losses. They then hire the good lawyers (and now well-trained lawyers) from the firms that have not done the right things to make their associates want to remain. Some lawyers believe that this strategy shows that these firms cannot hire the right people out of law school, but it actually shows a keen understanding of business. These firms know that it is more difficult to judge the "best" right out of law school, including some of the character traits that we outlined above. However, these character traits often get highlighted in the first few years of a young lawyer's career, which makes it much easier for the firm to find the type of lawyers they are looking for and for the lawyers to know what type of firm they are looking for based on experience. Rather than being the "easy way" of hiring lawyers, it may be reflective of a sound business approach to the hiring of professionals.

When it comes to identifying the types of traits that you want in your people, the one overriding trait that you need to look for is people who care—people who care about the organization and its success, and people who care about the quality of their work. Obviously, this may not be an easy trait to identify, and it usually requires that you look for indicators that a prospective employee has the potential to care. In some cases you can discover this trait via the types of questions that you ask about their prior work experience (successes and failures), the type of working environment that they crave, and the types of people that they have liked working with in the past (and why). Pre-hiring assessments (discussed later) are also an excellent tool to use to help determine the "heart" of the people you are interviewing. Yes, that is right, their heart. From my personal experience (mainly as an employer but also as a lawyer working with my assistants), I am convinced that you should *always* hire for heart, not for skills.

Outstanding People Make a Difference

I learned this lesson the hard way many years ago, but fortunately I was able to overcome it and essentially "undo" the mistake. Since striking out on my own, I have been blessed to have outstanding assistants work with me, especially when I was practicing law (more on my outstanding assistants later). When I went from my solo practice to starting my own firm, my assistant came with me to the new firm. She was a terrific assistant and I considered her my right arm. Unfortunately, the time came when she decided to move to another firm, and I panicked. I was convinced that she was irreplaceable, but, of course, that proved not to be the case. Her replacement, Tracy, had a different style, but she proved to be even better. One of the great things about Tracy was that she was constantly looking for ways to help me and the firm. She was never content to just do her job but aggressively sought out ways to do more, whether it meant helping another team member or picking up the ball on things that needed doing in the firm. Tracy was always pushing herself and learning new things and, over time, she became not only an important part of my success but a critical part of the firm.

Some time later Tracy was presented with an incredible opportunity with another business, involving more responsibility and a good deal more money. My partners and I got together to talk about the situation (since none of us wanted Tracy to leave) and made several bad decisions. First, we acknowledged that Tracy would make a terrific office manager for our firm, but concluded that we did not need an office manager yet—that it was too early in our existence and given our firm size. Big mistake. Second, we concluded that we could not match the compensation that Tracy had been offered. Another big mistake. We were thinking about dollars and expenses, rather than focusing on what value Tracy brought to our firm and on investing in Tracy and our firm's success.

As a result of our mistakes, Tracy decided to take the new position and leave us. At her going away party Tracy shared with me that she thought her replacement would work out fine, but then she hit me right between the eyes with this truth: "I am sure that she will work out fine, but *she'll never care as much as I do.*" When she said this to me I realized that it was true—that what made Tracy so special is that she really did care about our firm and our business. At that moment I decided that we needed to do something to get Tracy back. We quickly decided that, while it was a little early in our existence to hire an office manager, Tracy was perfect for the role and that we should have put Tracy in that role now. Fortunately, we were able to bring Tracy back as office manager within a few months, which also included paying Tracy what she was making in her other position. Why? Because we realized that the additional compensation was an investment in ourselves and our business and that we could reasonably expect to get a return on that investment. That is exactly what happened, as Tracy grew into the role and ultimately was responsible for nearly every aspect of our operations and her compensation proved to be small compared to the returns we got on our investment in her.

My experience with Tracy taught me several important business lessons. First, do not let an outstanding employee get away because you think you are not ready for them. If they are the right person for your bus, you should find or create a seat for them. Second, great employees will pay dividends to you and your business. Do not focus on them as an expense, but as an investment with expected returns. Finally, employees who care are worth their weight in gold and you should do everything in your power to get them and to keep them as part of your team.

As noted above, one aspect of employees who "care" is that they care about the quality of their work. I have always found that the best employees are those who rarely require any sort of reprimand when their efforts fall short of expectations. They themselves know it and they feel that they have let you and the organization down without you saying a word.

They are disappointed in themselves when their efforts fall short and often they are harder on themselves than you could ever be. I have always looked for people to be part of my business teams who share the same goal for their performance—excellence. There have been times as a business owner when my fellow partners felt that my standards were too high—that I had very little tolerance for people who were average—but you should never compromise when it comes to your team members. Average is not good enough and you should strive to have every team member committed to excellence. By the way, excellence does not mean perfection, because no one is or can be perfect. It means looking for people who want to be excellent and are continually striving to be excellent. These are the types of team members who genuinely care and who will prove to be the vital foundation for the success of your business.

To those people who suggest that excellence is too high a goal, remember that people tend to achieve what they are asked to achieve. If the standard is average or good, then that is the best you will achieve. If this is the standard you are expecting from your people, then you are lowering the bar and only hurting yourself. Rarely do people achieve significantly more than what they are asked to achieve. Therefore, if you want to build and maintain a great team, you need to raise the bar so that the pursuit of excellence is the standard for everyone. Those people who do not share a passion for excellence will not last in your organization and that is a good thing. The cream will rise to the top, and you will (over time) create a team of people who are all committed to pursuing and achieving excellence. Great businesses build precisely these types of excellent, caring, and committed teams.

▼▼▼▼▼

The pursuit of excellence should always be the goal, and a great team is one where all (or most) of your people are pursuing excellence and, when they fall short, immediately commit to improvement.

I have long been blessed to have outstanding people work as my assistant. As you can gather from the above, Tracy was an outstanding and valuable person in helping me to not only do my job, but to become a successful lawyer and business owner. When she became the office manager, I hired a young man named Jamie. Jamie's style was different from Tracy's style, but he quickly proved that he was a person who cared about my success, about the firm's success, and about his personal performance. He was committed to being excellent in everything he did and he was never satisfied with just doing his job. Instead of waiting for me to tell him how he could help me, he was aggressive in making suggestions and in taking things off my plate so that I could focus my time and energy on what was most important for my practice and for the firm's success. The support of my assistants was one of the most important factors in the success that I achieved as a lawyer and as a business owner.

For those of you who are wondering how do you find someone like Tracy or Jamie, my answer is simple. First, you must go looking for them, know what you are looking for, and insist on excellence (and do not settle for average). Second, great team members are more often built and developed, rather than found. Let me say that again—great team members are developed, not found. Certainly, Tracy and Jamie had potential greatness in them, but they never would have shone unless I allowed them to shine. In fact, Jamie had worked for others in the past but was not considered great. Why? Because he had not been given the opportunity to be himself and step up to a higher level. The biggest factor that I have found in building and developing great employees (and this includes finding out if an employee has what it takes to be great) is the area of responsibility. Most people want and even crave responsibility—the opportunity to make a difference and to add value. Unfortunately, too many times their employers (as a business or as individual managers) refuse to give them that responsibility, so the employees are content just doing their job because that is all they are expected to do (and even allowed to do). Excellent people will excel when you ask them to, expect them to, and allow them to.

Empower Your People

One of the reasons that many employees end up just being mediocre is that employers (individually or as an organization) do not really understand responsibility. They also confuse or fail to understand two critical concepts—delegation and empowerment. The two concepts are similar, but delegation (at least as it is usually understood) is much too narrow and limiting, while empowerment is what the right employees want and is vital in developing great employees. For too many employers, delegation is limited to delegating tasks, which amounts to nothing more than telling employees what to do and how to do it, and then expecting them to do as they were told. Not only does this prevent employees from having any real sense of responsibility and involvement, but it usually makes them feel that you do not trust them to do things on their own.

> ▼▼▼▼▼
>
> If all you do is give employees a list of tasks to fulfill in order to achieve a certain result, they are just doing what they are told and they have no ownership at all.

Instead of delegating tasks, it is important to delegate responsibilities. In other words, share with the employee the goal, the timetable, and some parameters and then leave the details to them. In most cases, the exact method of getting a job done is not important (or it only seems important to you because you want it done "your way"), and there is plenty of benefit to allowing employees to figure things out on their own and finding their own path for completing tasks. This type of empowerment—delegating responsibilities instead of tasks—is the surest path to developing great employees who are engaged and committed to you and to the organization,

This also makes everything easier for you, since you do not have to waste your valuable time messing around with the details of how things get done. Instead, you can delegate responsibility and empower your people to get things done. This does not mean leaving them alone without guidance, but it does mean being willing to let them find their own way most of the time and being willing to let them fail sometimes in the process. These failures will not significantly damage your business but instead are an integral part of building great employees and great teams. You have to believe in your people and give them opportunities to be successful. While this may initially seem a little scary (giving up control), it is ultimately the only true path to building the type of team and team members who will allow you to build the type of law firm that you desire.

Look for Great People

Another vital consideration in building a great law firm team is your hiring process, whether for professionals or nonprofessionals. Who does the screening? Who does the interviewing? Who does the evaluations? Are they experienced? Are they asking the right questions? Many businesses are starting to realize that hiring is much more of a science than an art. Yes, there will always be aspects of hiring that are more like an art (and many times hiring decisions—especially "no" hiring decisions—should be made with the gut), but in today's world businesses are implementing better hiring and evaluation systems and relying on experts (whether inside or outside the organization) for screening, assessing, and even hiring. In many cases this means hiring outside experts to find the right people for your firm. I am not just suggesting the use of headhunters, but the right search firm can help you find the right people or at least improve the chances that you will hire the right person. One aspect of the "right" search firm is that they have an intimate knowledge of your firm and your culture, including knowing the people that the new person will work with most closely.

Smart businesses also use outsiders (or highly skilled and expert insiders) for screening or initial interviewing. These experts then narrow the list of prospects down to a select few, and then only these select few make it to the next stage of the assessment and interviewing process. Note the key word here—the process. Hiring the right people depends on knowing what you are looking for and having a process designed to deliver the best candidates and to enhance the likelihood of finding and hiring the right people. There is no perfect system or process, but having no system or process is a recipe for continuing to hire the wrong people and to miss (or lose) the right people.

▼▼▼▼▼

Too often employees are hired based on their resumes, which primarily focus on their skills, education, and work experience. At some point during the evaluation process, one or more people get a "bad feeling," but candidates are hired despite this gut feeling because of their strong resume. How often does that decision prove to be wrong? When it comes to hiring your people, if it feels wrong it probably is, and you are doing yourself and your business a major disservice if you say "yes" when instinct tells you "no."

I have already mentioned the word "assessment" or "assess," so let's spend a few moments on this important topic. I am referring to assessment tools that exist in the marketplace today for evaluating a wide range of criteria relating to potential new hires. These assessment tools can also be used very effectively with and for existing employees, but this discussion is on using these tools to make better hiring decisions. Many years ago these tests or evaluations might have been known as (and limited to) personality tests, but they have come a long way in even the past 20 years. Many businesses have discovered the science and art of these assessment tools and use them to help them to make better hiring decisions. There is such a wide range of types of assessment tools or tests that we will not try to cover them all here, but there are different tools that assess practical skills (beyond skills like typing speed), people skills, leadership skills, and sales skills. They also assess how people think, work, and solve problems, ideal working environments, and what motivates people.

Many of these assessment tools have advanced to the point that they are much closer to science than art, and they are particularly helpful in identifying the character traits that are so important when looking to hire the right people. Unfortunately, the use of these assessment tools is still very much in its infancy, especially for law firms. The good news, however, is that you can immediately improve your firm's hiring decisions by finding and implementing one or more of these assessment tools. While most businesses do not rely exclusively on these assessment tools to make critical hiring decisions, they do rely on them to screen the candidates down to a small pool of people who are most likely to be best and right for your firm.

Most of these tools also provide you with insight into the types of interview questions to ask each candidate and even suggestions for areas to work on if you decide to hire the person. The best way to describe the role that these assessment tools can play is that they serve as "indicators" of performance in various areas and at many different levels.

So the business question for you is this: When making hiring or advancement decisions in your firm, do you want quantitative information regarding how each person is likely to perform, adapt, contribute, interact, and think? Great businesses consistently use this additional information to help them make better "people decisions," and I encourage you to at least investigate these additional tools that can help you make better "people decisions." Even if you are hesitant or uncertain about such assessment tools, you have very little to lose and everything to gain by making them one part of your hiring and evaluation system.

What Is Your Firm's Culture?

Throughout this book we have talked about the important role that culture plays in building a great law business, whether it is a businesslike culture, a client-centric culture, or a business development culture. One of the most important environments that you need to develop, nurture, and support in your firm is a culture that attracts and keeps the best people. There are many ways to develop and maintain such a culture, which we will explore below, but it is vital to understand that developing a culture requires much more than just "saying so." Many law firms already claim to have such a culture, yet their people would tell a very different story. Their history of losing good people would also tell a different story. And their management would tell a different story in terms of whether they believe that their organization is made up of people committed to working together to create a better and stronger business. Partners often bemoan the fact that they cannot find associates who are willing to "do what it takes" to make the firm successful, which usually means that they do not think that the associates are working hard enough. However, most of these same partners likely were never asked to work as hard as these associates.

At the same time, the associates bemoan the fact that many partners do not work very hard, yet they receive handsome salaries and distributions "at the expense of the associates." Certainly, many associates do not understand the business operations of the firm, including a little thing called overhead. Associates are always calculating their billable rate times their billable hours (usually not considering dollars collected, which is the only thing that really matters) and "seeing" all the profits that they deliver to the firm (even after their own salary). Somehow they forget about things like rent, operating expenses, staff, and even the additional costs associated with their own salaries. So, yes, the associates' perspective may be askew due to a lack of understanding of law firm operations and finances, but who is to blame for that lack of understanding? Most firms (by design) keep their associates uninformed about law firm operations and finances. They intentionally withhold that information from associates yet express frustration when associates develop uninformed opinions.

What is the big secret? Every successful business knows that the best way to build a fully committed and engaged team of people is to make sure that they know what is going on and to get them involved. If you ask a successful business leader the secrets to having a team that is working together to make the business successful, you will invariably hear that their people knew a great deal about the business operations and finances and were involved in developing better ways to operate and grow.

Some time ago I was working with a group of associates on improving their business development skills and efforts, which included having them develop their own personal business development goals and action plans. During this process I discovered that they had no idea what the firm's annual revenues were, which (unfortunately) did not come as a surprise to me. They also had no idea what amount of business the rainmaking partners in the firm generated, so they were being asked to develop personal rainmaking goals in a complete vacuum. This is not productive and makes it more difficult (not easier) for the associates. If the associates know that the top rainmaker in a firm generates $1 million in annual fees and that the average per partner is $75,000, they can do a much more effective job of setting their own personal goals.

Again, why all the secrecy? If you are intentionally hiding information from your people, then what kind of culture are you building—a culture of exclusion where your people feel like mere employees, rather than like important parts of the firm. So one of the key ingredients for developing a culture that attracts and keeps the best people is to include all of your people in information, in decisions, in planning, in brainstorming, in solution finding . . . in everything.

Your people (no matter how good they are) are rarely going to take the first steps in giving themselves 110 percent to the firm. They are looking for signals from the firm (at all levels) that the firm really

▼▼▼▼▼

Remember, building a culture committed to your people is the first and most important step in building a culture where your people are committed to the firm. It absolutely does not and will not work the other way.

believes in its people and will support them in every way to help them become all that they can be. This includes making certain that they have the training and support they need to be their most effective. This includes making certain that you respect them as employees and as people. If you allow them to be pushed around, harassed, and belittled, then *everyone in the firm* will know that you do not care about your people. This is an all-too-common situation in many businesses and especially in law firms. If this type of treatment is tolerated by anyone in your firm, then this becomes your firm's overall culture. You cannot have a culture focused on your people and on getting the best people when you allow such situations to exist.

Why the Right People?

Look at the people on your bus. Are they the right people? Are they in the right seats? If not, it is time to make a change. It may not be a pleasant change or an easy change, but "getting the right people on the bus" is critical not only to your success but to the success of everyone around you. The ultimate litmus test comes down to two questions: First, knowing what you know now, would you still hire this person? Second, if this person announced that they were leaving, would you feel terribly disappointed or secretly relieved? If the answer to these questions is that you would not hire them again and that you would be secretly relieved, it is time for a change. It does not necessarily mean that a person is fired. Rather, an effort should be made to find a different seat on the bus for that person (a different role or a different position). However, if these efforts fail, it is time to get that person off the bus.

One of the most important philosophies to remember when it comes to your people is this . . . *hire slow and fire fast!* Too often, we get this backward and hire too fast and fire way too slow. We have already talked a great deal about the hiring process, but the firing process (especially its speed) is just as vital. Some of you may be thinking that you cannot fire fast because you have to worry about your liability exposure and making sure you have followed all the right procedures and fully documented the employee's failures. I am not suggesting that you ignore procedure or your legal obligations; however, these concerns do not justify the types of delays in making termination decisions that are dragging law firm businesses down. Yes, dragging the business down. If you have an underperforming employee, you must make a change . . . and quickly.

You must keep a sharp eye out for underperforming employees. When you see them, you must take quick action. If that means discovering the reasons for their underperforming, then discover them quickly and get a clear idea of what the problems are. Once identified, you need to quickly take action to either eliminate the problems or resolve them. If they need additional training, then get it for them. If they need a change in how they work with their superiors, then consider such a change. If they need a change in their working environment and such a change is workable, then make the change, but quickly. As suggested above, maybe they are in the wrong role or working with the wrong people, in which case a change in roles or their work group could be beneficial. If so, make the changes quickly. If you do not see an opportunity for improvement or creating the right fit, then you must quickly move them out of the firm. It is that simple. Too often, these decisions are delayed (even when there is no realistic hope of improvement) and these delays can literally kill your team.

Just think about all the negative impacts on your entire firm when you have an underperforming employee. First, you are paying them for a level of performance that they are not delivering. That is wasted money. Second, the entire firm (including all of your good people) will see that you will tolerate poor performance or even average performance. That will become the norm for the organization and even your best people are likely to lower their performance. After all, why should they excel and put in extra effort when average or poor performance is acceptable? Third, there is a significant risk that your best people will leave in search of a firm that demands excellence. Fourth, think of all the time and energy that is wasted and lost forever "dealing with" the problem employee—all of the meetings and discussions about what to do, and all of the lost productivity for everyone who has any contact with the underperforming employee. When you find a problem within your team, it is vital that you remove that problem as quickly as possible. Remember—*hire slow, but fire fast!*

▼▼▼▼▼

I cannot overstate this point—having a poor or underperforming employee in your firm is a cancer that must be removed as quickly as possible. Every day that you delay is killing your firm, and you may never know how much damage was done by this person.

Compensation Equals Performance

The final topic relating to building a great team is compensation, particularly for your nonprofessional staff. In most firms the compensation system is designed (albeit unintentionally) to encourage mediocrity. Why? Because compensation is not merit-based, but rather longevity-based. In too many firms compensation (and other perks such as year-end bonuses and vacations) is based more on seniority than on performance. Here is an example. In most firms the staff's compensation is based (at least in significant part) on years of experience or years of experience with that firm. So, if you were hired with 5 years of experience, your salary was X. If you had 10 years of experience, it was Y (higher than X). Frankly, this is an easy but ridiculous method for determining compensation. The result is invariably that your best people will lower their performance (because they are not paid to be great) or they will leave. Your best people should be your most highly compensated, irrespective of years of experience. If you have someone with one year of experience who comes into your business and proves to be your top employee, then pay them as your top employee. It is that simple.

Failing to appropriately compensate your best people is the surest way to push their performance down or to lose them. If you want great people, then pay them for their performance. For those of you who say this will not work, that people with experience and seniority will leave if they are not the highest compensated, then you do not need them. There will always be good people to do the job and, just as keeping underperforming employees can kill your firm, failing to fairly compensate your best people will also kill your business. It may not happen overnight, but you absolutely cannot build a great team unless your best people are compensated accordingly. This is a critical flaw in most law firms, since too many compensate in some type of lock-step method that assures that mediocrity is compensated equally with excellence. This is a formula for disaster and certainly is not the way to build the type of high-quality team that you need in order to build a great law firm.

When it comes to building a great team of people for your firm, it starts with raising the bar. Demand and insist on excellence from everyone in your organization. Most will rise to the occasion, and those who do not are not the type of people you need to build a great firm. Building a culture of excellence in your business starts with changing how you think about your people. If you treat your people as mere cogs, then they will act as mere cogs. If you reward mediocrity, then you will build a firm filled with mediocre performers. If you treat your people like valuable members of your team, then most will perform like valuable members of your team who are committed to the firm's success.

Building a culture of excellence also requires implementing a screening, hiring, and training system designed to get you the right people—people who care and who are committed to excellence. Remember, you must decide what qualities you want in your people and then develop a hiring process designed to find people with those desired qualities. When it comes to the right qualities, focus on heart first and skills second. You can develop skills, but heart is more often something that is difficult to develop (although how you treat your people and the working environment in your firm can bring out the best in the right people). If you invest in your people—the right people—the result will be a law business that delivers great success for the business and for everyone in the firm.

Notes

1. *Good to Great* at 42 (HarperCollins 2001).
2. *Id.* at 41.
3. *Id.* at 51.
4. *Id.*

15 Teamwork Begins with Compensation

While we're on the topic of teamwork, we cannot ignore the important role that compensation plays (with lawyers) in either promoting a cooperative environment or creating an "every person for himself or herself" mentality. An in-depth review of every conceivable type of compensation system for lawyers is beyond the scope of this book, but I hope we can all agree that the range of varying compensation systems is wide and confusing. When it comes to compensation, law firms certainly have invested a great deal of time (and perhaps thought) creating complicated formulas for compensating lawyers, especially the partners. For now, let's focus our attention on just two basic questions: (1) compensation of associates for business development; and (2) compensation of partners in general.

As we will see, pushing associates to become business developers (with no financial reward) is not conducive to developing a strong business development team. Likewise, if the primary focus of partner compensation is each partner's own business development results, then you are creating and encouraging a "what's in it for me" attitude, and this is not the path to business success. Finally, failing to compensate partners for their efforts to train, support, and mentor other lawyers on business development results is perhaps the biggest missed opportunity for any law firm. So, if you want to improve your firm's financial results, develop a compensation system that promotes and encourages cooperation and teamwork.

Compensation Systems Drive Results . . . or Lack Thereof

Compensation of associates for business development seems to be a "tricky" issue in law firms. If you compensate associates for business development, they will be more likely to focus time, energy, and effort on business development. That is the reality, but very few firms have any direct compensation mechanism for associate business development. Instead, some firms have adopted the "we'll consider it" approach to compensating associate rain. In other words, if you bring in business during the year, we will take that into consideration in determining your bonus or your compensation for the next year. But do these firms really take it into consideration and, if so, is there any way for the associates to know to what extent or what the impact was? Of course not, which means that effectively there is no incentive for the associates to bring in their own business.

Yes, of course, for associates there's always the motivation to be a strong contributor to the success of the firm and the goal of one day becoming a partner, but that is years down the road and uncertain at best. Perhaps, the law firm "thinking" is that they do not want associates to worry about business development until after they become good lawyers, and they fear that compensating associates directly for bringing in business would send a "mixed message." As will be discussed in Chapter 25, law firms are making a big mistake in delaying the process of getting associates involved in business development, so if this is the "reason" that law firms do not directly compensate associates for bringing in business, it is likewise a mistake that is hurting law firms and their futures.

Associates may be younger (typically) than partners and less experienced, but they come to the table with the same internal drives and ways of thinking. Partners do not develop a "what's in it for me" thought process upon achieving partnership—it is fundamental in most people. Associates therefore should be expected to ask "what's in it for them" when it comes to business development efforts. While some forward-thinking associates will invest in business development because of the potential long-term rewards (i.e., partnership), many or most will not spend time on business development unless there is a more immediate motivation to do so. Therefore, if you want your associates to start thinking and acting like rainmakers (which every law firm should), then it is in your best interest to make sure that the associates can clearly see a direct benefit for their efforts and results.

Unfortunately, it would be an overstatement to conclude that every partner compensation program has been well thought out. Some time ago I was told of a partner compensation formula that had approximately 20 different parts, and the lawyer who shared this with me had concluded that the formula was obviously the result of partners simply adding new criteria over the years without any serious consideration of how the formula would work—or even whether it would "work" at all. We can all imagine the partners sitting around the table when a new criterion was proposed and pulling out their calculators to figure out whether the change would hurt them, help them, or be neutral. While this behavior—looking out for yourself—is not unexpected, it exists only where the system (or lack thereof) allows for and promotes a "me first" mindset.

We would love to think and believe that compensation formulas are always the result of careful consideration, evaluation, and assessment of all aspects of the proposed formulas, but we all know of situations where the formulas are either thrown together, pushed through by the most senior partners who have "locked in" their client base, or have never been carefully considered in terms of the results and incentives that they deliver.

To be fair, this "compensate for what you deliver" approach is not new or unique to lawyers. Many sales compensation programs and even employee compensation programs driven (in whole or in part) by personal performance have been used in non-law businesses for years. In fact, some businesses have implemented or expanded these programs even more aggressively during the past several years in a misguided attempt to deal with increased competition and a sluggish economy. Their logic is that if all or a portion of compensation is tied to results, then they can reduce their overhead (and pay only for results) and they can (in theory) motivate their people to deliver better results. Unfortunately, businesses have learned the hard way that this approach has two fundamental flaws.

First, a commission only (or primarily commission) compensation structure fails to create or nurture any company loyalty. Instead, the employees wisely learn that their success will depend on their own efforts and results, notwithstanding the overall performance of the business. They also quickly realize that, if they are good at what they do, they are essentially hired gunslingers who are inclined to "sell their gun" to the highest bidder. This results in the best people leaving to take better offers because they have no loyalty, and this lack of loyalty is fueled by the compensation system. Another manifestation of this is that the incentivized employees are typically reluctant to follow instructions from the company unless those instructions best fit with the compensation system. Business owners and sales managers will often have a difficult time convincing salespeople to sell higher-margin products or sell to specific target markets unless it fits with the compensation system. For this reason, many companies recognize that they must develop a compensation system that balances the goals of incentivizing the employees to deliver certain results with the desire to have the employees committed to the overall success of the business.

Second, many incentivized compensation systems result in not only a lack of loyalty, but also a total lack of team thinking and support. The two biggest "victims" are cross-selling (or up-selling) and client service. If employees are only (or primarily) compensated for their personal business results, then they typically will not work on (or even think about) helping others succeed. They also will focus their energies on results, rather than process. While results are certainly important, this is the same mentality that often keeps lawyers from "slowing down" and investing time with existing clients. They either do not see the potential returns (perhaps not always immediate) from this investment in client service and relationships, or they are uncomfortable with the risk of the time delay on the returns. In other words, they want to pursue those opportunities that are most likely to yield quick results, not necessarily the best or right results for the firm. As a result, businesses are now seeing the flaws in these "eat what you kill" compensation systems, the biggest flaw being that these systems are major impediments to firm growth and overall success.

Frankly, none of this is a shocking revelation for us. What law firms have found (and continue to find) is that, if lawyers are not compensated for their efforts on behalf of the firm "team," they are less likely to make those efforts. That should be no surprise. As much as we would all like to think that people are naturally team players, everyone (including your clients, by the way) wants to know "what's in it for them." That is not selfish—it is human nature. In fact, it is rare indeed to find people who will act unselfishly in the face of a rewards and compensation system focused solely (or significantly) on individual contribution. After reading the previous chapter (compensate your best accordingly), you may be thinking that my ideas here are contradictory. However, they are actually complementary. As we discussed in the last chapter, to develop and keep great people, they must be rewarded in tangible ways for their efforts and you cannot build an effective team of quality people if you compensate underachievers (or even average achievers) the same or better than high achievers. At the same time, if your people are incentivized with no element of contribution to the team, then it is unreasonable to expect that they will focus their efforts on working together and on firm success (versus individual success). People (including lawyers) just do not think that way.

Let's consider a couple of examples. Every lawyer knows that the best source of new business is existing clients, but do they work with other professionals on cross-marketing initiatives or similar programs? In most firms the answer is no and in almost every case the reason is simple—there is nothing in it for both lawyers to help each other cross-market. In all too many firms the compensation system is structured to encourage the "my clients" approach and mindset, which results in opportunities being missed, ignored, or even consciously avoided. I have heard of many instances where partners have gone out of their way to keep certain business of existing clients away from their own firm because they did not want to create the possibility that another partner could claim some "credit" for the client or the work.

In some firms not only do the partners not work together on business development, but they actually take affirmative steps to keep other partners away from "their clients." This is not only a shame, but it has a devastating negative impact on the firm's financial results.

That is a fundamental problem with most law firm compensation formulas. There are no cooperative incentives, there is no opportunity for lawyers to "share" some form of credit (whether it depends on the type of work, the role played (delivery, relationship management, or origination) or other factors) and/or various contributions are not equally rated in the formula. Even though cross-marketing is still the single and best source of new business for any law firm, many compensation systems actually discourage lawyers from working together and, instead, encourage one lawyer to seek out (at a higher cost in terms of time and dollars) his or her "own clients." By the way, in nearly every case the result is *not* that the "original" lawyer gets full credit for the work that comes in the door. Rather, and to the financial detriment of *everyone in the firm,* most of the work *never comes in the door.* Boy, is that a shame!

One of the biggest flaws in compensation systems is a structure that basically gives the first lawyer full credit for everything that client ever does with the firm, with no opportunities for anyone in the future to share in the financial rewards related to that client. We all have seen repeated situations where some lawyer from "way back when" is listed as the origination lawyer for a client (and receives all the financial benefit under the compensation system), despite the fact that the lawyer has no ongoing role with the client (and in many cases the client does not even know who that lawyer is). There is something seriously wrong with a compensation system when the clients are asking "who is that" when told that a certain lawyer is responsible for the account, for billings, and so on. Obviously, this is not a client-centric approach if clients are confused about whom they are working with and whom the client believes is most responsible for their business being with (and remaining at) the firm. This "once my client, always my client" attitude works as an effective bar against any cooperative marketing and business development efforts, all to the detriment of the firm and, ultimately, every lawyer in the firm.

Recently, a younger associate in a law firm shared this assessment with me. It seems that his firm's compensation system provides that, if a lawyer (partner or otherwise) establishes a referral source relationship with another business (for example, another law firm or an accounting firm), then every referral from that other business is fully credited to the original lawyer. Think about this. If I form a relationship with an accountant in an accounting firm (and identify the accountant as a referral source), every piece of new business referred from *any accountant* in that accounting firm is credited to me, even if I never speak to, communicate with, or do anything else to build or maintain a relationship with any of the other accountants in that firm. This does not make sense. Of course, none of the other lawyers are going to work on developing any relationships within that accounting firm, since there is no incentive to do so. Instead, they must try to "win the race" to develop a strong relationship with someone in another referral source business.

All of this hurts everyone in the firm, including the lawyers who "won the race" to be the first with a relationship in a referral source business. We all know and recognize that personal relationships are the most effective means to develop new clients or business, whether they are direct business relationships or referral relationships. Even if a lawyer has a great relationship with one person in a referral source business, it is unlikely that the lawyer will build equally strong relationships with others in that business. The result is that the firm will never come near to achieving the most potential from this referral source business, all because one lawyer was "anointed" to be the lawyer responsible for that business. At the same time, the other lawyers who are essentially forced to go out and find their "own" referral source business will never come near to optimizing the opportunities with that business. Why? Because they too cannot possibly have effective relationships with everyone within that business. This is a compensation feature that essentially assures that the firm (and the individual rainmakers) will consistently and repeatedly underperform, with countless opportunities being left on the table and likely picked up by other firms. While this seems so very clear to us, it is either overlooked or ignored in many firms.

Partners as Mentors

One area in a law firm where the incentives typically fall far short is in compensating partners for working with and mentoring associates or younger partners on their business development efforts. Rainmakers know what to do and how to do it, but rarely do they spend much time working with the younger lawyers. Admittedly, some do not see a need—they mistakenly believe that everyone should already know what to do and how to do it, when the opposite is true. Lawyers are looking for someone to tell them what to do, to show them how to do it, and to mentor them along the way. In most cases, rainmakers do not work with others in the firm on business development for a simple reason—they do not get compensated for doing it. They may share in some way in the firm's overall improved performance from this business, but they are busy with their clients, their work, and their business development efforts.

▼▼▼▼▼

As pointed out earlier, the best and most potentially effective tool for improving business development efforts and results in any law firm is its existing rainmakers.

As I have heard before, "I just do not have the time or incentive to help others." How unfortunate! The firm's best source of improved results is not implemented because the compensation system does not value such efforts. This is a big mistake and, frankly, overlooks the quickest way for a firm to improve its business development results with little additional expense. It is simply a matter of reallocating dollars to lawyers who help other lawyers become better at business development. What a great investment for a law firm to make in itself and its people!

In addition to a lack of financial incentive for partners to train and mentor younger lawyers, another reason that law firms fall short in this area is that they do not think it is important or they do not really think about it at all. That may sound incredible, but it is an all-too-common situation, particularly in small and medium-size firms. While the situation can still occur in larger firms, the impact is not usually as extreme as in smaller firms. While the incidence of larger firms that simply "go out of business" has increased in recent years, larger firms are typically in a better position to overcome (in the long term) a significant reduction in business revenues, although the result may be a significant layoff of staff and professionals. In many small and medium size firms, there is either a lack of understanding or simply a failure to address the reality that the long-term future of the firm depends on many of the younger lawyers developing into effective rainmakers. This is a reality that many firms have not yet faced, especially firms that are in their first generation.

Some time ago I was meeting with a senior partner in a law firm with approximately eight partners and the same number of associates. This partner freely acknowledged that neither he nor the firm had done much of anything to develop their associates or young partners into effective business developers. He also told me that three of the eight partners brought in a significant percentage of the firm's business each year. Certainly, this is not at all an unusual situation in a firm of that size. I then asked this lawyer about his retirement (several of the partners were 55 and older), and he told me that the firm did not have any significant retirement plan, but that he was not concerned (financially) about his ability to retire.

I then asked him the more important question: What did he expect to happen (and what did he want to have happen) when he and the other senior partners retired (probably in close proximity to each other)? Specifically, did he want the firm to continue after his retirement and the retirement of some of his fellow senior partners? He indicated that he wanted the firm to continue, but I confronted him with the harsh reality that unless several of their younger lawyers developed into effective business developers, the likelihood is that the firm would cease to exist shortly after the retirement of the top rainmakers. If the top partners have all of the relationships, most of the clients are likely to leave once their relationship contact leaves and, without any training and development, the younger lawyers simply will not be able to sustain the ongoing needs of the firm. In response, the partner looked at me and said, "You know, I never even thought about that, but you are probably right."

This is a reality that many partners have never even considered, especially in first-generation law firms. Those firms have never faced the reality of partners leaving or retiring, and they have always assumed (mistakenly) that because the business is thriving now, it will continue to thrive in the future. But this assumption is not supported by the facts. As we will talk about more later in the book, the reality is that most effective business developers are built, not born. You can certainly take the right steps to enhance the likelihood that the people you hire have the right skills and mindsets to be potential rainmakers, but rarely do people just "become" rainmakers.

> ▼▼▼▼▼
>
> There is no reason to assume that even the most well-established firm will continue to thrive—or even exist—unless the firm takes the necessary steps to assure that it will have a significant number of effective business developers in the future.

Most lawyers must be shown the skills, attitudes, and thinking processes of rainmakers, they need to be trained and supported in their development, and they need to be mentored. And this does not happen overnight, which is why it is so important for firms to invest time, attention, and money in associates earlier rather than later in their careers. Without taking these steps, every firm is at risk, and ultimately, the survival of the firm is at risk without a commitment to building a team of business developers.

Another particularly troubling and damaging compensation concept arises when partners retire or otherwise leave the firm (and are no longer practicing law). At one large law firm there was a major rainmaker who was beginning to approach the later years of his practice and, rather than waiting until he retired, he and the firm developed a careful plan for transitioning clients from the rainmaker to other partners in the firm. This included allocating some credit to the newly responsible partners with respect to revenues derived from these clients. This is a great example of a team and forward-looking approach to business development and to client service. It was a win-win for everyone, and it worked because the system (or the rainmaker) recognized that working together benefits everyone, as opposed to creating a system where one lawyer wins and another loses (when, in reality, the entire firm loses).

In sharp contrast is a compensation or "credit" system that provides that origination credit for a client goes into the firm's "general" category or pool when an originating partner leaves the firm (but the client remains). In this scenario, no one at the firm is motivated to service the client, to build any relationships, or to cross-market the firm, because the system itself has decreed that there is no value to anyone at the firm with respect to this client. To be honest, it would not necessarily be a horrible result if every client was a firm client, but if there is any aspect of the compensation system that rewards lawyers for bringing in business, it makes no sense to arbitrarily dump clients of retiring partners into some general pool where no one is motivated to enhance the relationship with and results from that client. It just makes no business sense, yet these programs exist all too frequently.

What Behaviors Are You Compensating?

While we cannot evaluate every type of compensation formula, it helps to consider (at least generally) what messages are sent depending on where you place greater emphasis in your formula and system. Without getting into percentages, if lawyers are financially rewarded primarily for billable hours, then those lawyers will almost certainly spend their time thinking about billable hours and doing the work. It is simply human nature. You cannot expect people to act contrary to their best interests. While partners technically have the opportunity to share in the firm's net profits, in many firms it is only a very small group of partners that are true profit-sharing partners (with most partners ultimately compensated on some combination of salary and compensation formula). Next, we will look at the benefits to a law firm when it has a compensation system that provides upside opportunities for everyone based on the firm's overall success. If your compensation system emphasizes deliverables or billable hours, nearly all of your lawyers will focus the vast majority of their time, thought, and energy on doing the work, with business development left for their few spare moments of thought and time. What do you think their business development results will be if it is only an afterthought? The lawyer and the firm will get "afterthought" type results.

Likewise, if the compensation system primarily rewards business development, then the lawyers (like all people) will tend to invest their limited time and resources on business development. When given a choice, they will invest their time on relationship building and business development activities because these are the activities that are most likely to bring them personal rewards. Again, this is not selfish, but merely human nature and a fact of life in any business. Every law firm needs rainmakers and providers, and as is always argued, a firm cannot exist without both. However, no law firm (that is right, *no* firm) can survive if it has only providers. While a firm that only brings in business, but never delivers the services, will also fail, which are easier to find—good lawyers to deliver the services or good rainmakers who can build the law firm? Admit it—we all know the answer. I am not suggesting that the compensation system should therefore be weighted extensively or exclusively on business development, but there must be a significant incentive for business development. Without it, your firm is doomed to failure—or at least to mediocrity.

Likewise, if your compensation system (as it relates to business development) is more heavily weighted on doing the work that you bring in, then you risk developing an environment that is too "self" focused—to the detriment of the firm's overall business. For example, if lawyers are more heavily compensated for bringing in work that they themselves deliver, then they have very little motivation to keep their eyes and ears open for opportunities to bring in business that they cannot or will not deliver. Certainly, any compensation incentive may cause lawyers to think about other business opportunities, but will a lawyer actually invest valuable time, thought, and energy on new business or cross-marketing opportunities if the "real money" comes from bringing in work that they perform themselves? The answer is generally no. Once again, the practice of law is heavily dependent on the lawyers doing the work as well as bringing in the work, which means that a lawyer's time is highly sought after.

In theory, lawyers in this scenario would "fill their own plate" and then feel free to focus on bringing in business that they cannot perform (either due to lack of time or lack of experience in an area). However, the reality of law firm life is that our plates are rarely perfectly or predictably "full." Instead, our work flow is a moving target, which means that it is almost impossible to determine when your plate is or will be full and then (and only then) to seek out business development opportunities that would fall outside your plate. The real world just does not work that way. Therefore, if lawyers are highly compensated for bringing in work and doing their own work, then you can virtually be assured that many opportunities are being

▼▼▼▼▼

When faced with the choice, most lawyers will invest their time where it is likely to provide them with the most (and most immediate) benefit.

missed and that your firms' business development results will never achieve anywhere near their potential.

So what is the answer? While it may not be simple, the key to an effective compensation system is three-fold. First, the balance between credit for delivery and rainmaking must be carefully considered, and the system must find a fair balance between the two. If you are thinking that a 50-50 balance or at least something close to it is what I am suggesting, then you are correct. Law firms most often fail due to insufficient revenues, not a lack of lawyers to do the work. While you may have heard of a firm folding or failing because of a catastrophic malpractice case against it, have you ever heard of a firm failing or folding because it could not hire enough lawyers to do the work? I doubt it. Yes, law firms have failed or folded due to mismanagement, including other things like overhead or growing too fast in people and/or space. But we all know that when law firms fail (or fail to be excellent for the law firm team in terms of financial rewards) it is most often because the firm has not done a good enough job of bringing in business.

This is the business reality that law firms inherently know but must objectively confront when building and implementing a compensation system. And by the way, the fact that the compensation system has worked for the past 50 years does not mean that it should be expected to work today. The market for legal services has changed and is continuing to change, and law firms must recognize these changes and develop a compensation system that will work for the overall success of the law firm of today.

Second, opportunities must be built into any compensation system that allow for and reward cross-marketing and cooperative efforts among the lawyers. If your compensation system is strictly a "that's my client" system, then you are certainly missing out on many opportunities to grow your client base and your revenues. People are hard-wired toward self-interest, and it is not a bad way of thinking. It just requires that you plan for this way of thinking and develop a compensation system that truly encourages cooperation.

> ▼▼▼▼▼
>
> Remember, lawyers (like all people) will focus their time, effort, and energy on that which is most likely to benefit them. Rarely do you find people who will invest their valuable time on efforts that exclusively or even primarily benefit another individual in the firm.

The ways to accomplish this are myriad, but it all comes down to making sure that there is something in it for everyone to work together in identifying new business opportunities, in bringing in new business, and on identifying and seizing the many cross-marketing opportunities that exist. I have heard it said before that if a law firm was able to effectively nurture its existing client relationships and cross-market the appropriate opportunities, the firm would never need another new client (other than to allow for natural attrition). That is how valuable existing relationships are for any firm, and it is vital that you build a compensation system that motivates everyone to work together within that system for the greater success of all.

Finally, the only way to develop a true team approach to your law business is to include (to some significant degree) the firm's overall success in your compensation system. With the exception of partners who directly share in law firm profits (which is not the focus of this discussion), I rarely see compensation systems that reward professionals not only for their success, but for the firm's success. It is rare, in part, because so many compensation systems are entrenched and typically very "self" focused, which makes it even more difficult to change the system to one where individual success alone is not enough. Imagine if you had a compensation system that appropriately incentivized the professionals to bring in business and to work together in doing so, but one in which their financial rewards also depended on the firm's financial success. What incredible power of teamwork and pulling together would be released by your firm! Every professional would focus on the firm's success first and foremost, knowing that they win if the firm wins. This is an environment where great things can happen within a law firm, but it is certainly not an easy concept for a group of individuals to embrace . . . despite the enormous upside for the firm and each professional if they work together.

In simple terms, create a system where each lawyer achieves their desired financial goals by meeting or exceeding their individual goals *and* by the firm achieving its financial goals. This creates a true firm-centric focus and commitment from all of the lawyers. Everyone is responsible for everyone else's and the firm's goals. If someone sees that another lawyer is struggling to achieve their goals, then other lawyers will be motivated to offer assistance. This creates a true team environment where all the lawyers are motivated and incentivized (collectively) to work together on everything from identifying and bringing in new clients, identifying and delivering on cross-marketing opportunities, delivering the legal services and—surprise, surprise—client service. This type of compensation and incentive system is the only way to assure that everyone has "skin in the game" and puts the firm's success ahead of individual success.

Obviously, this is not for everyone, but if you want to build and nurture teamwork and cooperation in your business development efforts, then this last ingredient—including the firm's overall success in some significant way in the compensation system—is critical. Without it you will have a difficult time reaping the fullest potential from the opportunities that exist for the future of your law firm.

16 Power of Your Staff

If you ask most law firms what they have done recently to improve their business development results you will typically hear answers such as:

- We just started a new advertising program in a local business publication;
- We have asked our lawyers to start doing more client entertainment;
- Some of our lawyers are focusing more on business lunches; and
- Several of our lawyers have recently been presenters at continuing legal education seminars.

Unfortunately, these are typical law firm business development "initiatives."

Rarely do you hear about:

- Creating a business development culture;
- Training and developing the lawyers on business development skills;
- Creating business development systems;
- Goal setting, testing, and measuring;
- Mentoring; and
- A systemized approach to cross-selling.

These are the types of efforts and investments that will ultimately drive your business development results, but one thing that you almost never hear from law firms when it comes to business development is that they have made a focused and committed investment in the most underutilized tool in law firm marketing and business development—their staff.

For most law firms, the nonprofessional staff are seen as only necessary evils and expenses. Certainly, they provide a valuable service by taking care of the "little stuff," while the lawyers take care of the "important" work, but this approach results in significant missed opportunities. If properly identified, trained, empowered, and supported, your staff will prove to be one of your most effective marketing and business development resources.

We are *not* talking about:

- Having staff type up drafts of your Web site content or marketing pieces;
- Training staff to be pleasant on the telephone (although this is certainly an important part of client relations and business development); and
- Having a more effective and productive staff that allows lawyers to be more effective and productive, thereby freeing up more time for business development efforts (although this is a vital contribution from your staff).

We are talking about recognizing that your staff should be an integral part of your business development efforts, including your client service system. Even more so than your technical skills and abilities, the right staff person, with the right training and support, can be one of the most important ingredients for turning your clients into raving fans . . . and raving fans (not just satisfied clients) are the key to enhancing your financial results and your overall success.

Too many firms, however, mistakenly separate great client service from business development results, but the two go hand in hand. Your firm must develop and implement the right mindsets, skills, tactics, strategies, and systems to enhance your new client business development results, and the quality of your client experience results will have a profound impact (positively or negatively) on your business development results with existing clients (i.e., the extent to which you enhance your business with an existing client, maintain the status quo, or lose client business). When you overlook the connection between client service and business development, you tend to view client service efforts as something that you should do or ought to do, rather than as the foundation of your business development efforts.

▼▼▼▼▼

While the conclusion is obvious, many of us forget (or at least forget to act on) the fact that great client service results in more clients, more business, and long-term client relationships.

Business development relating to existing clients is not just about cross-selling or up-selling, but also about creating such high-quality relationships with your clients (in significant part based on the level of their client experience) that your clients become consistent and valuable sources of referrals of new business. Client service is not just something to think about, but it is one of the key ingredients to an effective business development culture.

Just as critical to building a client-centric culture is the need to develop and nurture a business development culture in your firm. There are two fundamental pieces: (1) making business development a top-of-mind subject that permeates nearly all of the firm's decisions, processes, and systems (business development cannot be something that you think about and work on just some of the time); and (2) building a culture that recognizes that every single person in the firm is a part of your "sales team." From the managing partner, to the executive committee, to the partners, to the associates, to the office manager, to the paralegals, to the administrative assistants, to the accounting department, to the receptionist, to the custodial personnel—*everyone* is a part of the sales team and has the potential to have either a positive or a negative impact on your business development results . . . and your financial results.

Take a look at the people in your firm and try to identify a person or role who has absolutely no client contact. Contact could be face-to-face, by telephone, in writing, or even in passing conversations. While we would like to believe that clients will judge us by the best foot that we put forward (and the people whom we put directly in front of the clients), clients are people, and people tend to judge organizations by the lowest common denominator, not the dressed up "face of the firm." Look at how your team members answer the phone, how they converse with a client or business contact on the phone, how they look and talk to them around the office, how your accounting department deals with clients, and how well your people maintain the appearance of your offices. All of these things can have an impact on client service and your business development results and, in fact, they should be designed to have a positive impact in both areas.

In my business travels (to law firms and other businesses), I often see assistants reading a book or a magazine at their desk. You will probably think that I am a taskmaster for saying this, but that should not happen. Even if that person is on a break or even a lunch break, the clients or other people who see them do not know whether they are on a break and whether what they are doing is "on their own time." Frankly, some clients and other visitors may not have any reaction, but some will and almost all of those reactions will be negative. If this person does not have enough to do, then that reflects poorly on the firm's management and operations. Does this mean that the firm or the individual lawyers are not doing an effective job with this employee? Does this mean that the firm itself does not have enough business? Is the firm filled with people who do not work hard and who waste their time? Obviously, none of these conclusions are going to help your reputation in the eyes of your clients and other business guests. Even worse, some of these conclusions could result in failing to get a client, losing a client, or not realizing the full potential value from your relationship.

We can all agree, I hope, that there are potential problems when your team members read books or magazines during business hours, at least in open areas where visitors can see them. However, many firms will prohibit this type of conduct, without explaining the reasons behind it, which are the most important pieces of information. Your people need to understand that they are an important part of the client experience and the firm's business development efforts. Most people want to be an integral part of something, and your quality people will rise to the occasion and embrace their enhanced role as part of the business development "team." Frankly, people who see no value or benefit in being an important part of the business development team may not be right for your firm.

▼▼▼▼▼

If you get the right and best people, you can begin to build and expand an incredible network of people who are all committed to doing the right things and the best things to enhance the firm's results.

This is all about creating that business development culture in your firm. As we already discussed, having well-trained and empowered people assisting your lawyers will make them more productive, which translates into more billable time, more marketing time, and more time to invest in building and maintaining those most valuable client relationships. But this is only one piece of the puzzle whereby your assistants (not "secretaries") can be invaluable in your business development efforts, particularly as they relate to client services.

We have already talked about the concept of empowerment, but one of the most important areas (and also the scariest) for you to empower your assistant relates to client communication and interaction. Yes, it can be a little scary, but the results are incredible. One of my greatest business development assets proved to be my assistants, once I supported them in being a more direct link and source of information for clients. Rather than insisting that I be the only person who communicated with clients (either in outgoing or incoming calls), I encouraged my assistants to have regular communication with clients. The fact is that probably eight out of ten times the phone call to the client or from the client did not require or need my special skills as a lawyer. And the clients did not care whether they talked to me or not. You may believe that your clients insist on talking to you, and while that may appear to be true, only a very small percentage of your clients will actually insist on communicating only with you. They appear to insist on talking only to you because you have allowed them to conclude that that is how they should communicate.

Most clients will accept whatever communication system you establish as long as they see the benefits of it, whether those benefits are stated or seen in action. If a client is forced to communicate with an assistant who has no idea about anything and is not empowered to have any intelligent conversation with that client (in other words, can only say things like "I don't know, but I can find out" or "let me take a message and [lawyer's name] will get back to you"), then clients are not going to feel cared about and are not going to feel that they are properly serviced and treated. However, if your assistant can answer their questions or can demonstrate that they know what is going on with that client and, even if they do not have the answers, can go get the answers for them, clients will respond favorably. Most clients do not care whether they talk to you, but they do care whether they get the type of service they expect.

A couple of years after I left the active practice of law I met with a former client and his business partner. During the meeting, and without any encouragement, my former client said to his business partner something like, "Jeff's old law firm is the greatest. I would refer anyone to Jeff's old law firm. They did the greatest job of client service ever." Of course, I was compelled to ask why he thought and felt so highly about our firm, to which he responded that we were easy to work with, we always kept him informed, he always knew what was going on, and it was very easy for him to check in and get answers to his questions. Notice that he said nothing about our technical expertise, our experience, or the results in the matter. In fact, this client was less than happy with the ultimate results in a particular arbitration matter, but he was a raving fan of our client service.

I then asked him how he felt about his communication with my assistant, Jamie, while we were working with him, to which he responded that he loved working with Jamie and that, in fact, he often preferred to talk with Jamie. He said that eight out of ten times his communications were with Jamie and that this was just fine, if not better than communicating with me: "Jamie always knew the answers to my questions [often without having to check with you], and even if he did not have an answer, he could get it for me quickly. I always felt important." This is not an unusual experience. Most clients want you to do what you do best, and how they get information and how it is communicated is not important. What is important is the fact that it is timely and consistently communicated.

I had empowered Jamie to be a resource for clients. I had empowered Jamie to be, in most cases, a primary contact point with clients. I made sure that Jamie knew what was going on and empowered and permitted him to communicate with clients on an open basis. If a client called to find out the status of a certain project, Jamie was permitted to relate that status, and he usually knew the status. This was all about

▼▼▼▼▼

Some firms have adopted a policy whereby they commit to answer phone calls within 24 hours, which many lawyers (including me) believe is very difficult to do. However, it is a very doable standard if you rely on your valuable assistants to be a part of that communication and response process.

making certain that Jamie actually functioned as an integral part of our client service team.

One important part of making your assistants and the rest of your team an engaged part of your business development team is the simple act of introducing them to clients. Whether that introduction is over the phone or in person, it is important that your clients know your staff, that your staff knows your clients, and that your staff is treated as an important part of the team. Introducing them makes them an important part of the team. When I met with clients in my office I would make every effort to introduce them, in person, to my assistant and say something like, "This is my assistant Jamie. I wanted to make sure that you met each other because I am sure that you will be communicating a great deal while we are working together. I depend heavily upon Jamie in working with clients, and you can expect to be in regular communication with him throughout the time that we are working together. If you ever have a question or need information, please feel free to contact Jamie directly, since we want to make sure that you get what you need as quickly as possible."

With this simple but purposeful introduction and explanation I have communicated two powerful messages. To Jamie, I have made it clear that I trust him, that I rely on him, that he is important to me, and that he is important to the firm. To the client, I have communicated that I trust Jamie, that he is and will be a valuable resource during our working relationship, and that we are focused on doing the right things to assure that the client's experience with us is great. These simple steps can make all the difference in the world between merely having a satisfied client and developing a long-term relationship with a raving fan. Satisfied clients sometimes pay the bills—raving fans build great law firms.

Remember, your nonprofessional team not only can be, but should be, an integral part of your client service system and your business development efforts. Rather than merely sustaining a staff of helpers, bigger and better results for your firm will follow if you hire the right people, engage them in the process, empower them to be representatives of the firm with clients and others, and demonstrate to them that they are an important part of your business team. *Everyone* in your business should and must be a part of your business development team. This is essential if you want to have a true client-centric and business development culture. Without these two synergistic cultures in place, a law firm is not only going to fail to achieve its highest potential, but it will always remain at significant risk of being unable to continue as a viable and profitable business. Build the culture, build the team, and let your team work together to provide a great client experience and great business results for your firm.

17 Marketing the Invisible—The Law Firm Challenge

Let's be very clear on this message: What your clients do not know can kill your law firm! Yes, that is right, kill your firm! Despite this reality few firms directly confront the reality that the services they sell and deliver are intangible and, ultimately, invisible. Invisible because clients cannot see, feel, or touch the services that are provided. In addition, such "invisible" services generally cannot be judged objectively (except of course if they are judged on results and, since lawyers cannot control results, this is a dangerous place to be). As the old saying goes, "We don't know what we don't know," and this concept is perfectly applicable when it comes to most clients and legal services. Most clients know very little about the legal system and legal services, making most of them unsophisticated and uninformed consumers. Unfortunately, many lawyers forget about the invisibility of their services and focus all of their energy on trying to "tell" clients how great their services are . . . despite the fact that the clients simply do not know the difference.

The challenge of selling invisible services to typically unsophisticated clients is a significant challenge, but one that must be effectively addressed in any firm that wants to improve its client relationships and its overall business. Since clients cannot judge the quality of the services, lawyers need to focus on improving the client's experience (because clients most definitely can judge the experience). In the end, success in building great client relationships and delivering what "clients want" in terms of service requires that law firms face up to the reality of their "invisible" services and invest their time, energy, and efforts in creating and delivering a great experience for their clients.

One fact that lawyers cannot deny is that part of their business involves the delivery of legal services. One common theme with all services (and especially professional services) is that services are, by definition, nothing more than a promise to do something in the future, taken primarily on faith, and the delivery of services is almost always more about the relationship among people than it is about the end product. In fact, it is often very difficult to identify the true "end product" of legal services. Some lawyers would argue that it is the final written product that is often delivered to a client, but this perspective seriously misses the boat. Rather, any written work product is just that . . . that tangible product or evidence of the legal services that were provided. Too often lawyers operate under the misconception that the value that they are providing is tangible, when the real value that they deliver is the most invisible of "products"—their advice, counsel, and analysis. When lawyers work with clients and in their business as if their primary "product" is some sort of tangible written product, they tend to undervalue their services and they will almost always fall short when it comes to delivering the types and quality of experiences that clients demand.

Let's consider a simple example of how lawyers fail to see the real value of what they do and deliver. Some time ago I was speaking with a lawyer about the potential to implement some fixed fee engagements in his law firm. Specifically, we were talking about the firm charging a fixed fee for incorporating new companies. After some discussion about how much time is typically involved for a "simple incorporation" (by the way, focusing solely on time is part of the problem), the lawyer shared with me an example of a typical telephone conversation with a prospective client. As he described the situation, a prospective client would call him with questions about what type of entity to use for a new company. After asking the prospective client a number of questions he could usually feel confident in recommending a particular type of entity.

He then shared with me what he described as a fairly typical conversation regarding a prospective client who "needed" (according to his advice) to form a single member LLC:

> You have two choices on how to proceed. You can have our firm prepare the necessary documents and filings for the LLC, and the cost will be approximately $1,000. Alternatively, you can download the forms from the secretary of state's Web site, fill in the blanks, and file the forms yourself, and you will only have to pay the filing fee.

Of course the prospective client will remain merely prospective (and choose to do it himself).

What this lawyer—and many lawyers—fail to realize is that the real value being delivered to clients is the analysis, counsel, and advice. In this case, the real value was in correctly analyzing the client's situation and recommending the LLC entity. It is not the preparation of some standard forms that represents the value to the clients, but the advice that is given. Until lawyers start to recognize this reality and focus on selling and marketing this true value, it will be virtually impossible for them to build their business beyond being simply a group of professionals selling their time to help fix problems. While that may seem acceptable, ultimately it is not the path to success and stability for a law firm.

> Services are intangible—you cannot see, feel, or touch them—but one of the biggest challenges for lawyers is the fact that most clients never know what the services are going to cost up front.

We will talk more about the uncertainty of legal fees later, but services can be difficult to predict in terms of total cost, and lawyers have made the challenge even greater by adopting the view that it is virtually impossible to know the costs in advance (despite the fact that many service providers—including professional service providers—provide more certainty regarding fees and total costs). Another challenge with services is that you usually do not know that they are failing or falling short until it is too late. This is partly because clients do not know whether the services are high-quality or whether the services are fulfilling (or likely to fulfill) their expectations (reasonable or not). This challenge also arises because the services cannot be qualitatively or objectively evaluated by anyone, and especially not by clients.

When all is said and done, services are people oriented (and therefore unpredictable). They are not process oriented. It is about the people. While you most definitely can and should use systems and processes to create a positive experience for the person (i.e., the client), including building a strong framework, tools, and culture focused on the client's experience, ultimately it is the people who are going to make you or break you. What a surprise! Your clients will decide whether you succeed or fail, thrive or struggle, have an okay firm or a robust and self-sustaining law business.

We started this chapter facing (I hope) the reality that clients cannot judge the quality of your services, which is a reality that absolutely must be addressed by lawyers. My purpose here is not to bash clients or to suggest that clients are not intelligent, but it is important to recognize that most clients do not have the background, experience, or training to judge anything relating to your services. The only exceptions are when you are working with in-house counsel, but even these lawyers may not have regular experience with certain types of legal matters and, without this experience, even corporate counsel may be not much better than a lay client at evaluating the quality of your services. On top of a client's inability to make these judgments and assessments (at least accurately), it is virtually impossible for anyone to objectively assess the quality of your services. While judging legal work product might be a little easier to do and have some validity, the invisibility of legal services is further evidenced by the fact that *no one*—especially clients—can reasonably judge the quality of the services.

It Is All About the Experience

As we shared at the outset, clients do not know what they do not know. They do not know whether they are getting quality service or not. They do not know the difference between excellent, good, and poor, whether it is litigation advice, trial work, contracts, briefs, negotiations, legal advice, and so on. Unfortunately, the one thing that they can judge (and which is closely related to the services) is the results, but the reality in the practice of law is that it is virtually impossible to guarantee or even control the results. If clients are judging you on the results, then you and your firm are living on the edge with little or no control over your client's perceptions of you and your firm. This leaves way too much to chance and, in fact, more likely assures that many of your clients will walk away believing that you did not do your job well enough. Not only will you lose a client, but that same client is likely to tell others how you failed to do your job (as opposed to referring you to others), and you will be forced to replace that client with a new client (where the cost of acquiring that new client is six to eight times higher).

Before you start to think that creating winning experiences for clients is a lost cause, we need to focus our attention and effort on what clients can judge (whether they have any background or experience with lawyers or not). Clients can and do judge the quality of your service based on the experience that they have in working with you and your law firm. The experience is where you must focus your time, energy, and dollars in developing, implementing, and supporting an entire system that delivers the type of experience that clients want to have . . . the experience of feeling important, significant, and cared about.

▼▼▼▼▼

Clients cannot judge your expertise or technical skills, but they absolutely can and will evaluate you and your firm based on the overall experience that they have in working with you.

Clients cannot accurately judge the difference between excellent and superior technical skills, but they can and will judge the quality of your relationship and advisory skills. For all of the things that clients do not know and cannot judge, what clients *do know* is whether they feel valued and important, whether they feel that they are treated well, and whether they feel that you care about them. That is three "feels" in one sentence. If you are thinking that this is all too touchy-feely, then you need to step back and reassess. Everyone wants to feel valued, important, and cared about . . . *everyone!* Thus, it is no surprise that your clients are looking for the same things in working with you and your firm. This is one area in particular where you must not try to convince yourself that the practice of law is different from every other business. Clients want to feel that you care about them and their work, and clients are uniquely qualified to judge the quality of the relationship. This is where you must invest your time and energy—on building better relationships with clients, on providing great experiences for your clients, and on making certain that they walk away believing that you cared about them . . . if you fail in this effort, then your clients will really be "walking away"—and for good.

So, what are you to your clients—what impression have you created in your clients' minds in terms of what you are to them?

- Are you a mere technician?
- Are you a mere service provider?
- Are you a necessary evil?
- Are you merely a seller of billable time?
- Are you just a problem solver?

If so, then you are a "dime a dozen" in the legal community. There are dozens and probably hundreds of firms in your own city that are nothing more than technicians, service providers, problem solvers, and necessary evils.

Note that I am not even attempting to comment on or judge the level of your technical skills. Whether you are a lawyer with great technical skills, average technical skills, or even poor technical skills, if you are nothing more than a technician or service provider, then the level of your skills is largely irrelevant when it comes to business development efforts. You may indeed be a highly skilled technician and service provider, but you are still nothing more than a service provider. And as we have said before, your client's perception of you is all that matters, because your clients will judge you based on their perceptions of you, regardless of the factual reality. Certainly, your own opinion of yourself and your services is totally irrelevant when it comes to client service, client relations, and business development.

You Are as Good as Your Clients Think You Are

Let me explain that last statement a little more, because understanding and working with the differences between self-confidence and self-perception is critical. When it comes to client relationships and client development, self-confidence is not everything, but it is close to everything. I assume that we all can agree that unskilled lawyers are still unskilled even if they have an abundance of confidence in their own abilities. However, even the most skilled and experienced lawyers cannot be effective at client relationships and client development if they do not believe in themselves. Now, a lawyer who has the skills and the experience will most likely have the resulting self-confidence that flows from the existence and command of those skills and that experience. Most outstanding lawyers are confident in their own ability; however, one challenge for lawyers is separating confidence and abilities from overall self-confidence.

▼▼▼▼▼

Pure abilities and even experience are not enough to create outstanding client relationships or to drive business development results.

The self-confidence that I am talking about is more akin to self-worth, which is what allows you to take risks and to get outside of your comfort zone. Most of us are comfortable and confident in practicing the law and delivering client services, but most of the skills covered in this book require us to think differently and to act differently. For most people, change (or doing things differently) can be scary, and it is your sense of self-worth that will allow you to do things differently to achieve different and better results. In fact, a strong sense of self-worth and self-confidence can "make you" a better lawyer than your skills and experience would support.

Again, having the requisite skills and experience *usually* results in a strong sense of self-confidence, which is then demonstrated in your actions and behavior. However, that is not always the case, and it is essential that you focus on developing that strong self-worth so that you can achieve your highest potential—for yourself *and for your clients.* A paraphrase of a great Henry Ford quote goes like this: "If you think you can or you think you cannot, you are right." In other words, if you believe you can achieve something then you can. If you do not believe it (or do not believe in yourself) then you most likely cannot achieve it. In fact, if you do not believe that you can achieve something, then your best course of action would be to not even try it. You are probably wasting your time and, if it relates to representing a client, you are also wasting the client's time and money.

Consider our earlier discussion about attorneys' fees and hourly rates. Many skilled and experienced lawyers shy away from the topic of fees and hourly rates in client meetings. This is generally the result of a lack of confidence. If you truly believe in yourself and in the value of your services and advice, you can and will look a client or prospective client right in the eye and confidently tell them what you are worth. If you lack that confidence, or you are uncertain about your value, then you will try to avoid the topic or, when it does come up, you will look down or away from the client and you will stumble around the topic of money. Clients will generally retain you (and keep you) if they believe that you are looking out for their best interests and if they believe that you can help them. While they sometimes ask about qualifications and experience (more often, experience and not qualifications or training), the question that they are really asking (themselves) is whether they believe in you as their advocate or advisor. If you do not believe in yourself, clients and prospective clients probably will not believe in you. Even in the day-to-day practice of law, self-confidence and self-worth can make you a much better and more effective lawyer.

Think about it. Can you imagine a trial lawyer being effective with a judge or a jury (whether in the courtroom or in chambers) if that lawyer lacks self-confidence? If you do not believe in yourself, then how effective can you be in presenting your client's positions, whether it is in litigation or in business negotiations? If you consider yourself to be a highly effective lawyer and advisor, think about the last time that you went up against what you perceived to be an ineffective lawyer on the other side, whether it was in trial work or in a business negotiation. Did you prevail in an argument while your opponent seemed inept? Did you secure a concession on the terms of a deal that you never would have conceded if you were on the opposing side? Have you ever thought that another lawyer was "weak" based on your interaction with him or her? Most often, the fundamental difference is confidence. Whether that confidence comes from within (which it always will in part) or from an abundance of experience, a confident lawyer generally will be an effective lawyer.

Once again, however, do not confuse pure confidence and abilities with a strong sense of self-worth. Many lawyers who are very confident, who have excellent skills and experience, and who are very effective in the practice of law do not have the inner self-confidence to talk honestly about legal fees, to ask their clients and business associates for referrals, to say no to a prospective client who is not right for their firm, or to "fire" a client who has become a disruption and a distraction. It is one thing to believe in your abilities, which will make you a good practicing lawyer. It is quite another thing to believe in yourself enough to do the right things and better things when it comes to the business of law. This second and higher level of confidence will make you effective at building client relationships, will make you effective at business development, and will help you build a great firm or even a great "law business" for yourself within your firm.

Remember, there is also a difference between self-confidence and self-worth versus self-perception. Self-perception is how we see ourselves, but that may not be at all what our clients and prospective clients see. For example, your self-perception may be that you are a very skilled lawyer, but clients cannot judge your skill and, therefore, they have no basis to develop a perception regarding your skills. Similarly, your self-perception may be that you and your firm provide great client service, but some or many of your clients may think differently. Most clients cannot accurately judge the quality of your skills and legal services—they can only judge the "quality" of the relationship, which is nearly always based on the things that you do (sometimes very small) that demonstrate to the client that they are important to you. Remember, clients are uniquely qualified to judge whether you care about them and their business, and this goes way beyond sending a fruit basket or similar gift at the end of the year. In the following chapters we will talk more about relationship-building and client service, but for now it is important to remember that your own perception of yourself and of your services is irrelevant compared to those of your clients and your prospective clients.

▼▼▼▼▼

If your perception of the quality of your client service is based on your skills and your belief in the quality of your legal services, then you are probably misjudging the quality of your client service.

This is one area where the maxim "the customer is always right" rings true. Whatever perceptions your clients and prospective clients (or even the marketplace) have are 100 percent accurate. If your clients think that your service is horrible, then it is horrible. If your clients think that you charge too much, then you charge too much. If your clients think that you are unskilled, then you are unskilled. If your clients think that you do not care about them, then you do not care about them. This is such a vital concept to grasp because it allows us to refocus our attention going forward on those perceptions. Instead of trying to logically or quantitatively "prove" what we think is true, we need to focus our energies, our thought processes, and our actions on changing those perceptions. Until we change those perceptions, they are reality.

For many lawyers and law firms, the reality (i.e., client perception) is that lawyers are technicians, service providers, sometimes problem solvers, and necessary evils who charge a lot of money for services that most laypeople do not understand. This is the perception that you need to change by how you think and, most important, what you do. You have to "show your clients" who you really are to change this perception. What should you be or what should you be doing? We will talk about this in great detail in the following chapters, but every lawyer should be selling solutions for their clients' needs. Every lawyer should be adding real value (typically through their advice, rather than their billable hours). Most important, lawyers need to focus on helping their clients achieve their goals.

Obviously, you cannot help your clients achieve their goals unless you know what those goals are, and we are not talking about just their goals with respect to a particular legal engagement. Those are not their business goals in most cases. Their business goals go far above and beyond their short-term goals relating to a particular matter. As we explore the vital subjects of client relationships, client service, and business development, remember that the true path to being a trusted advisor (and thus the clearest path to business success in the law) is to focus your time and energies on helping your clients (and those with whom you have business relationships) to achieve their goals, whether business or personal. Now, let's take a look at the steps to building a great law firm.

Building a Great Law Firm

Building a great law firm! Certainly, it is easier said than done, but an important first step is to recognize that the most important concept is not greatness, but building. Great law firms do not just happen—they are built! Like any other endeavor, this requires having a vision and a fairly detailed step-by-step plan intended to create and develop your desired result . . . a great law firm. Topics that we have already covered are part of the process of developing a vision for your law firm, as well as key ingredients to building your law firm on a firm business foundation. The final piece of the puzzle is appropriately focused on the heart and soul of any law firm business. It is not the lawyers. It is not legal skills and abilities. It is not day-to-day operational issues. It is clients, client service, and relationships. These are the areas that make or break the business of a law firm.

The balance of this book will cover the five critical steps for building a great law firm:

1. Defining your perfect client. Yes, that is right, you choose the types of clients you want and you have.
2. Defining a plan to pursue that market.
3. Differentiating yourself and your firm. This is one of the most important steps, but also one of the more difficult, especially if you try to differentiate based on skills and experience.
4. Delivering great performance and experiences for your clients. Client perceptions drive client experience, and great client experiences drive your results.
5. Deciding to build relationships. Relationships do not just happen, but flow, develop, and evolve based on how you decide to do business.

I often hear lawyers say, "The practice of law wouldn't be so bad if it weren't for the clients." Well, clients and the practice of law are a package deal: No clients = No business.

The good news is that you have total control (yes, you heard me right, total control) over the clients you have, the clients you choose not to have, and how you work with your clients. If your clients . . .

- Do not see you as a value-added resource
- Treat you like a mere vendor
- Are not building relationships with you
- Do not pay you on time
- Are not the types of clients that you want to have

. . . then the answer can be found by looking in the mirror. You have chosen the clients and types of client relationships that you currently have. If you want better or different clients and better or different relationships, *you* have to change how you think and what you do. The choices are yours, not your clients to make, which takes us right to our next topic . . . defining the perfect client.

PART III

Building a Great Law Firm . . . Step by Step

18 What Does Your Perfect Client "Look Like"?

"I don't know what they look like, but I'll take pretty much anyone." This or something similar is a typical response from lawyers about what kinds of clients they are looking for or would like to have. Another common response is "anyone who will pay." These sound humorous or tongue-in-cheek, but they are very serious responses, and many lawyers are, in fact, looking for anyone, taking anyone, and getting anyone. If you have not already figured it out, this approach is not going to help you improve your law business. In fact, it is so counterproductive that it will often cause your business to stagnate or even regress in terms of revenues, profits, and client service. The reason is simple: If you are looking for anyone and willing to take anyone, then that is exactly whom you will get—anyone—and a law firm based on having "anyone" as a client is not built on a solid foundation.

There are generally two reasons that lawyers adopt this "I will take anyone" approach to client development. First, no one ever told them that they could and should choose the types of clients they want to accept. In fact, many of us are taught that the practice of law means serving clients, which of course it does; however, serving clients does not equate to serving anyone and everyone. Rather than taking whoever comes to you, you should be making a conscious decision about the types of clients you want and will accept. This means deciding

- what types of clients you want to work with;
- what types of clients will help you to build your firm; and
- what types of clients you should "fire."

Remember, whom you have as a client is a choice . . . your choice.

Second, many of us make the erroneous assumption that being willing to take anyone is somehow more productive. It goes like this—if I am willing to take anyone as a client, then my potential market is larger than if I restrict it to certain types of clients. In terms of pure numbers, this is obviously true; however, the error in this logic is that it fails to differentiate between quantity and quality of clients. We often make the same mistake with opportunities, believing that more opportunities will equal better results. There is some truth to this analysis in that you will generally achieve better results if you do more, but this is the type of thinking that has already gotten lawyers into trouble.

The focus on billable hours and equating time with money has resulted in a profession full of lawyers who are focused almost exclusively on their billable time, rather than on the opportunities that exist and that can be created by thinking and acting differently. No wonder clients perceive many lawyers as nothing more than sellers of time, rather than as valuable resources and advisors. But what many of us fail to recognize is that while we are very busy taking on "anyone," the best and right opportunities are either passing us by or being missed because we are so busy with the wrong opportunities and the wrong clients. When it comes to clients and prospective clients, our focus must be on quality, not quantity.

While there will always be a small percentage of firms that are able to create a "law firm machine" that can grow and prosper by accepting anyone and everyone as clients, these exceptions to the rule are not the path to building a great law business. The path is instead paved with clear and conscious decisions about the types of clients who will provide you with the business that you want to have and with strategies designed, developed, and implemented to deliver to you the "perfect" clients who will help you build a great law business.

While there rarely are "perfect" clients, there most definitely are clients who are "perfect fits" with your plans and goals. And, of course, there are also clients who are not only wrong for your business, but will actually drag you and your firm down if you allow them to do so. The business of law is no different than any other business . . . you typically get exactly what you look for (or do not look for) and that which you are willing to accept. If you want to build a great firm, one critical step is deciding which clients you want and will accept, which begins with developing a written client profile.

▼▼▼▼▼

If you strive only to be mediocre, then taking anyone as a client will probably allow you to achieve your goal, and you may even secure an adequate living from your law practice.

Yes, your client profile must be written. Unless and until it is written, it has no practical value. It is as if it did not exist at all. Many lawyers have told me that they have a client profile, but when I ask to see it, they will tell me that it is in their head. When I ask them to describe their "perfect" client, I hear something like, "Well, I have a pretty good idea of what I am looking for." When I ask them to describe the characteristics of their client profile, they generally stumble around with vague generalities and parameters that are so broad they are of little value. Until you write down the characteristics of your "perfect" client, you do not have anything that is going to help you to build your firm.

Writing it down also represents a commitment and creates accountability. Frankly, that is why most of us choose not to write things down—because if we write it down, then we can be held accountable (even to ourselves) if we fail to follow the path that we have written down. Admittedly, writing down your client profile is a double-edged sword. On one hand, it creates accountability, which can be a little bit scary. On the other hand, that same accountability drives results. While your client profile criteria are very important, they are of little value unless you write them down. The other value of a written profile is that it is readily available to review to refocus on what you are looking for and what you desire. Without having it in writing, it is easy to forget. Without having it in writing, it is easy to lose focus, and focus drives better results.

Ultimately, the clients you are looking for and pursuing and the clients you are willing to accept should be the same, but they can be separate decisions. For example, you may decide on the types of clients you want and are going to pursue, but you might also decide to accept other clients (who do not fit your client profile) if they come to you. It is important to recognize, however, that by accepting the wrong clients, you may miss the opportunities to find and secure the right clients. Therefore, there are really two different questions that you must answer regarding clients. The first is deciding on the types of clients you want to pursue. The second is deciding on the types of clients you are willing to accept and keep. But be very careful. While pursuing "perfect" clients and accepting others may seem like a prudent and safe path, do not underestimate the power that accepting and keeping the wrong clients has in terms of limiting or even negating all of your positive decisions and steps with respect to the right clients. One wrong client can drag your business down if you let that happen.

Many of those who develop a client profile confuse the concept of an ideal or perfect client with a target market (see Chapter 19). Target markets are about numbers and mostly quantitative criteria such as revenues, subtitles, numbers of employees, industries, or geographic locations, but client profiles are about the qualitative things that you expect from your clients. What a novel concept—you decide the types of clients you want to have.

Why do so many lawyers say that the practice of law would be great if it weren't for the clients? Because they have clients they do not want to work with, and generally this has nothing to do with dollars. I once had a discussion regarding "unreasonable" clients with a partner who said, "They can treat me however they want as long as they pay." You can certainly choose to take this approach, but make sure that it is a conscious decision—not a result by default. If "no decision" is your approach to your business, you can probably guess the types of clients you will typically have.

With that overview, what should be included in our client profile? Ultimately, it is your decision, but here are a couple of my suggestions. "My ideal clients . . ."

- *Pay on time.* If your clients do not pay on time, then congratulations . . . you have done a terrific job of "training" your clients to pay late. Your clients may choose not to pay on time, but you choose to allow it . . . either by not enforcing your payment terms and/or by allowing them to remain clients. It is your business and you are not an interest-free lender. You have every right to expect and demand to be paid on time. Cash flow is king in any business, including a law firm. If your clients are not paying on time, you are losing money, a form of lost profits. Clients who do not pay on time are hurting the financial foundation of your firm, which also indicates that these clients either do not understand your business or do not respect you as a businessperson.
- *Are pleasant to deal with.* What a unique concept! Working with people whom you like. All of you have had situations where you had clients you did not like and with whom every personal interaction was unpleasant or uncomfortable. Working with clients like this has little upside and big downsides. The only upside is that they might actually pay you. However, we all know that unpleasant clients are usually the most likely to pay late, to ask for (or extract) discounts, or to fail to pay entirely.
- *Are value-driven and focused.* If your clients or prospective clients are concerned only about hourly rates and see you as merely an expense, then you are setting yourself up for trouble. These are the clients who will often question your time and fees because they do not see your value. It is also virtually impossible to deliver a level of service that will satisfy these clients, resulting in unhappy clients, poor relationships, and distractions. Not everyone thinks in terms of value, but if you work only with clients who understand the concept of value and see you as a value-added resource, then your relationships will be enhanced, service will be improved, and you will have a strong foundation for building your business.

- *Respect my time.* We have all experienced clients who demand the impossible, not only in results but in responsiveness. We have all worked with clients who think that they are our only client and act surprised to hear that we have other matters requiring our attention. While it is true that we should endeavor to treat our clients as if they are our only (or at least most important) client, our goal should be to secure and retain clients who respect our time and understand that we are businesspeople running a business. If your clients do not respect you and your time, it will be a significant challenge for you to create and develop the types of relationships that build great law firms.
- *Are willing to offer open and honest feedback regarding me and my services.* We can all guess as to the answer to the question "How are we doing?," but only our clients really know the answer. Our clients' perceptions will determine our success and it is vital that we have the ability to learn and understand those perceptions. While it is difficult to guess whether clients are or will be willing to offer honest feedback, one way to address this issue is to ask up front and to make it clear that this is something we will be asking our clients to do. Clients who are unwilling to help us to be better advisors should not be clients.
- *Are willing to refer me to others.* Quality and consistent referrals are the lifeblood of any great business. Make it a "condition" of doing business with you. Building a referral-based business is one of the easiest, most effective, and most profitable ways to build a successful law business. This requires two things: (1) that you have clients who are willing to refer you to others and, if they are not willing to do so, then they are not the types of clients who will help you to build the business that you desire; and (2) your relationships must be of a type and nature that will allow you to ask your clients for referrals. This is another topic that should be discussed with prospective and existing clients. Make it clear that you will be asking for their help in the future, and also make it clear that you intend to help them with referrals.

Developing a client profile that includes the foregoing is an important step in the process of building a client base that will deliver the results that you seek for your business.

To help you further understand some of the key criteria that you might want to include in your client profile, consider some of the following ideas that were shared with me over the years by various lawyers and law firms:

- Look to their lawyer for legal and business advice
- Are sophisticated on legal matters

- Appreciate the need for and value of good legal advice
- Exhibit community engagement
- Family oriented
- Do not take impossible positions simply to see what they can get
- Want to resolve disputes and litigate only when the economics make sense
- Do not consider their lawyer an opponent (they know their lawyer is on their team and they take advice when given)
- Are responsive when asked for documents, evidence, witnesses, and so on
- Are successful and decisive owners

While your criteria may vary, the most important step is determining the criteria and putting it in writing. We see and find what we are looking for, which is why developing your client profile is so vital in allowing you to have more of the right clients for growing your firm to greater financial success. If you do not know what you are looking for, you will rarely find it. By creating a written client profile, you will know what you are looking for, you will know it when you see it, you will know what to avoid (i.e., you will know when to say no to certain clients who are not "right"), and your client development activities will be focused on securing the types of clients identified in your client profile.

Your client profile is not only critical in securing new clients, but it should be used to help you decide which clients you should no longer represent. (For purposes of this discussion we are not addressing the topic of any ethical or regulatory limits on ceasing your representation of a client. Obviously, you must comply with all applicable rules and regulations when it comes to ending a client relationship, and you must take all appropriate steps to protect and preserve the client's interests.) When asked by other lawyers what my plans were for the next year, the first thing I always said was, "I am going to fire some clients." While they were always shocked and assumed I was kidding, that was always part of my agenda for every new year (and even throughout a given year).

Over time I came to realize how significant the negative impact was on me and our firm when we had clients who did not fit our profile:

- Clients who did not pay on time
- Clients who were difficult to work with
- Clients who were unreasonable and did not respect our time or our efforts
- Clients who saw us solely as an expense
- Clients who simply were not pleasant to work with
- Clients who never referred new business to us and probably would never do so.

Not only were these clients not helping our firm to grow, but they were actually distracting us from our quality clients.

Take just a few moments to think about the clients on whom you spend most of your time. Too often you will discover that you are spending most of your time on the "trouble clients," while your quality clients are being ignored or are being given only the time that is left over after you have dealt with your "trouble clients." This is not the way to build a strong and successful law firm focused on client relationships.

I also encourage you to periodically rank your clients as A, B, C, or D clients. "A" clients are your superstars. These are the clients who fit your client profile. "A" clients pay on time, they are pleasant to work with, and they see you as a valued resource. They respect your time and your business, they offer feedback, and they refer you to others. You want more "A" clients and you should focus your efforts on finding and developing them. Your "B" clients are pretty good clients and are also likely to develop into "A" clients. While not all "B" clients become "A" clients, and every law firm can and should have "B" clients, you always want to focus on improving your client base. If you have a law firm made up of only "A" and "B" clients you are on the path to building a great firm.

"D" clients are easy to identify. These are the clients who do not fit any of your client profile traits. They do not pay on time, they are not pleasant or fun to work with, they see you only as an expense, they do not respect your time or your business, they never refer you business, and they do not help you in any way. They are always looking to take from you, without expending any time or effort to help you and your business. These are the types of clients who are preventing you from securing better clients and building better relationships with your "A" and "B" clients. They are a drain on you and your business . . . and they should be "fired."

The "C" clients need to be carefully reviewed. If they genuinely have the potential to be "A" or "B" clients, then you can and should invest in them and in that relationship. However, do not kid yourself . . . if they are really nothing more than "C" clients or, even worse, are likely to become "D" clients, then they too must be "fired." While it may seem harsh to "fire" clients, remember that every minute you spend with the wrong clients is time that you are not spending with your best clients. Not only is it important for your law firm, but you owe it to your highest quality clients to make sure that you are investing your time with them and in other similar relationships. Imagine what your quality clients would say if they knew that you did not have time for them because you were wasting time on the wrong clients. With this different perspective, the "firing" of clients is not harsh but sound business judgment that is the "right thing to do" for everyone.

If you do not know what your clients look like, then it is next to impossible to find them. Only by developing a written client profile describing an ideal client can you create and implement the type of focus that you need to consistently secure and retain the best and right clients, which are essential to building a great law firm. The right clients can drive the success of your law firm, while the wrong clients can drag you and your firm down.

19 What Pond Are You Fishing In?

Knowing what types of clients you want is very important, but deciding on a target market is equally vital to your firm's financial health. Businesses know that success nearly always comes to experts (rather than generalists), but law firms and lawyers all too often try to be all things to all people. What is perceived as "targeting" more opportunities actually results in your firm missing the right opportunities, pursuing the wrong opportunities, and having a complete lack of focus on what you need to build a great law firm. Why do lawyers often try to be all things to all people? The reason is simple—lawyers think that specializing or having target markets (yes, there can be multiple target markets for the firm and the individual lawyers) risks missing out on opportunities. As we will discuss in this chapter, the opportunities that *appear to exist* for generalists are mostly perceived and the best and most profitable opportunities exist only when your efforts are targeted in some way.

I am sure that most of you have been fishing at least once in your life. When fishing it is critical that you fish in the right pond (for the type and size of fish that you want to catch), that you have the right equipment, and that you have the right bait or lures for the fish you want to catch. For example, if you are taking your young children fishing, your target is quantity. You want and need to catch lots of fish to keep and maintain their attention. Otherwise, you are in for a long afternoon. Therefore, you seek out ponds that are likely to contain many fish, even if they are small fish. You also use equipment and bait designed to catch the small fish that are your target for that outing. In contrast, you would pick a different pond or lake if you were targeting larger fish; you would also change the equipment and bait or lures that you are using. The same is true in the business of law. Most successful law firms target their services and their business development efforts in a few niches. Yes, there is that word that scares many lawyers—niches. Many of us hear the word niches and we immediately begin to formulate all the reasons that we cannot be specialized. In this chapter we will talk about niches and target marketing, their pros and cons, perceptions of them, and their realities.

Clients Want Specialists

I do not remember the exact numbers, but well over 50 percent (and probably closer to 75 percent) of our prospective clients and even existing clients wanted to know if we had experience in the type of matter that they needed help with. A very common question from clients and prospective clients is, "Have you done this before?" We all know that we have an ethical obligation to be competent to represent clients in a particular matter, and we also have an obligation to refer them to another lawyer if we are not competent to handle a particular type of matter. However, most of the matters that we handle do not require prior experience with that type of matter.

For example, if you handle the buying and selling of businesses, it is probably not substantively significant whether you have been involved in buying or selling a particular type of business. Likewise, if you are an estate planning lawyer and have handled complex situations in the past, it is not particularly relevant or important what assets a prospective client has to deal with as part of their estate planning. If you have handled non-compete litigation in the past, then you are likely competent to handle a non-compete matter for any business, no matter what the industry. However, these realities are not necessarily the same as the perceptions of your prospective clients. Many prospective clients have the perception that prior experience with their specific type of matter, situation, and industry is important, and it is that perception that you must address when you look for new clients.

Before going on, let's cover one very important topic in this area. Most clients who are looking for specialized expertise (based on their perceptions) do so out of a concern for competency and the ability to do a good job, and we all know that such specialization or expertise may not have any significant impact on the quality of the work . . . but what about the value of the services and advice? If you are an expert in a particular area, you may see better and different opportunities to assist the client throughout your representation. This provides greater value to those clients. Likewise, if you are an expert and have significant prior experience in a particular type of matter or with a particular industry, there is a strong probability that you will be able to handle this matter in a more cost-effective way, resulting in a lower overall cost (and thus higher value) for your clients. While many clients may not be thinking this way when they ask the questions, this is something that you need to be thinking about in terms of establishing a target or niche market.

> ▼▼▼▼▼
>
> It is very likely that you can add more value and be a more valuable resource if you are specialized. Therefore, specialization, developing niches, and target marketing are all focused on adding value to your clients.

So, clients typically are looking for experts or specialists and that perception should be the foundation for your decision to develop and market niches and specialties. Whenever I suggest the value of niches or target markets to lawyers, I will invariably hear many objections. Lawyers perceive that by being a generalist they have more opportunities. That is certainly true in terms of the quantity of opportunities. If you are a business lawyer and you will represent any business, then you have more potential clients than if you were niched or specialized, but there are two shortcomings to this perspective. First, the quality of the opportunities is obviously minimal. Unless you are looking to build a law firm on pure quantity and develop some "commodity" type of legal service, you cannot succeed by "focusing" on everyone. In fact, you cannot really call that focusing at all—it is actually a complete lack of focus. Only by targeting and focusing on quality opportunities can you build a strong foundation for your firm.

Second, it is virtually impossible to focus and have any significant success when you are trying to be all things to all people. Let me give you a typical example. I will often hear business lawyers say that their "target" market is closely-held businesses. I then ask a couple of questions to show them that this is not a target market at all. "Are you interested in working with home-based businesses doing less than $50,000 a year in revenue?" Usually, the answer is no, but these are closely-held businesses. "So, are you interested in representing closely-held businesses with revenues in excess of $1 billion?" Usually, the answer is no. Thus, we have already established that they are not really interested in working with all closely-held businesses, but we have "narrowed" it down to companies with revenues between $50,000 and $1 billion. Can you see the problem here? That is still not a target market or any type of niche, and it is impossible to effectively market to such a diverse group of clients. While lawyers have the perception that this is a target market, it is not, and their results (or lack thereof) will demonstrate that it is not a true target market.

Business development results require focus, both in terms of thinking and activities. It is impossible to focus on a prospective client base that is too large. It also makes it very difficult (if not impossible) to develop a marketing and business development plan and know what to do as part of your business development activities. Lawyers have a limited amount of time to engage in business development activities, which means that those activities must be well thought out, well planned, targeted, and focused on quality.

> ▼▼▼▼▼
>
> If your supposed target market is too broad then your business development activities will necessarily be sporadic, unfocused, and unproductive. Only with a clear picture of who you are and who you want to represent can you be effective at business development.

You may get clients without being focused or targeted, but your results will be based more on luck than on strategy and tactics. It will also be impossible for you to develop a business development process or system that will consistently deliver the results that you need to achieve your business and financial goals. Most lawyers do not have a process or a system to consistently deliver the results that they need to achieve success. Without that process or system, lawyers and law firms are at risk and they are more likely to go to their comfort zone, which is being the lawyer practitioner, and then hoping that the business will come. As we have said before, hope is not a business strategy.

The book *Good to Great* by James Collins (HarperCollins 2001), discusses the "hedgehog concept" as a vital part of any great business. The hedgehog concept is this: Figure out the things that you do or can do very well (even better, things that you can do better than anyone else). Then figure out from this group the things that you can do profitably or most profitably. Finally, evaluate the things that you or your firm really enjoys doing in terms of the type of work or types of client. Then figure out what meets all three of these criteria—you can do it very well or the best, you can be financially successful doing it, and you enjoy doing it—and this should be your niche or specialty. By focusing on these one or two areas, you can differentiate yourself with clients and prospective clients, which is a difficult challenge when it comes to all professional services, including legal services.

Differentiation is not easy, but niching or specialization is one of the most effective means of differentiation for lawyers. The key to seeing the value of niching in target marketing is to, once again, consider the prospective clients' perceptions. When they talk to you, they are thinking expert and specialist. If your answer to them is, "No, I am not an expert or specialist," you have an immediate and difficult challenge to overcome. Yes, there will be times when you can overcome that perception with information, logic, and persuasion, but wouldn't it be great if your answer to that question was, "Yes, I am a specialist in this area."

You Are Already Niched—Spread the Word

By the way, most of you already have niches, but you have not yet used them to your advantage and turned them into target markets. Many lawyers tell me that they do not have any real niches or specialties, not even within any particular industries. However, when I ask them a few questions, I discover (along with them) that they are already representing specific industries more than others. Thus, they already have a niche, but they are not using it to their advantage in terms of their business development efforts. It is very important to remember that a niche market is not necessarily based on legal specialty areas. For example, patent and trademark work are legal specialty areas, but one of the most effective ways to specialize is by particular industries. You may be a business lawyer, but if you decide to focus your representation on business issues relating to residential construction companies, landscapers, medical practices, plumbers, accountants, insurance agencies, hospitals, or food distributors, you now have a niche. You can even decide to focus on a particular industry before you become an expert in that industry. This allows you to differentiate yourself in the market.

You need to make sure that the market you are targeting is big enough to provide the clients and revenues that you desire, but other than that, you can pick any industry for your niche. Being niched also allows you to build better relationships because you are knowledgeable about a particular industry, which means that you can talk more intelligently with clients and prospective clients in that industry. You can and should read their publications. You can and should attend their trade shows and even join their associations (typically as an "associate member"). You can become an expert on their industry, which means that you are more valuable to clients in that industry. If you know and understand their industry, these clients will perceive that you care about them and their business. This is the foundation of relationship building, which means better clients and hopefully, more referrals. In the end, niching and target marketing deliver better clients, better relationships, and more referrals . . . a sound foundation for any business.

One common question from lawyers is whether they can have more than one niche. The answer is a qualified yes, but you have to be very careful that you do not lose your differentiation with too many niches. Let's look at one obvious situation where multiple niches can be effective within a law firm. The firm itself may have a broader target market, but recognize that having that broad target market makes it more difficult for the firm itself to develop a clear and effective message. At the same time, the lawyers can have their own niches or specialties. For example, if a law firm represents businesses, that is a pretty muddled message that will not have much impact on anyone. However, an individual lawyer within that firm, when meeting people and building relationships, can and should communicate that the firm represents businesses and that he or she specializes in working with real estate development companies. Thus, the law firm can retain a broad scope of services, but the individual lawyer can use the niche and the specialization to advantage in his or her business development efforts.

▼▼▼▼▼

This is the great thing about a law firm with more than one professional—it can have many specialists with "niche markets," and the firm can and should market those specialties rather than a broad law firm message, which is confusing and generally ineffective.

Many lawyers are concerned that, if they mention only one or two niches or specialties when talking to someone, they are losing opportunities if that person does not have a need for that niche or specialty. There are several flaws in this argument. You must remember that nine out of ten people that you meet or speak with do not have a need for your services at that particular point in time. Thus, these conversations are not sales opportunities, but merely opportunities for you to differentiate yourself and to potentially begin the process of building a relationship. It is important to realize that your first meeting with anyone (especially if it is not an introduction with respect to a specific need) is unlikely to result in any new business today, yet this is the type of example cited by many lawyers. While what you say and do when you are out networking and meeting people is important, this is just the first small step toward building relationships and developing new clients, and the most important thing that you can do is to differentiate yourself.

Having a niche or specialty is an effective way to differentiate yourself, and it is memorable. Most people whom you meet will not remember a broad, vague, or general overview of what you do, but they will remember something that is unique or special. That is just how people's minds work. Many people believe that lawyers are boring, especially in conversations. Why? Because lawyers tend to be vague and general in describing what they do, and because lawyers tend to talk too much. This leads me to another topic relating to the perceived opportunities versus reality when meeting and talking with people. If you ask a lot of questions up front, you can do a more effective job of communicating to the person what you do. We will talk about asking questions in the next chapter, but asking questions is also the best and quickest way to differentiate yourself and to begin to build a relationship.

People like to talk about themselves and their business, but only if they are asked. One of the most important business development skills that you can learn is asking questions of people you meet, of prospective clients, and of existing clients and then listening to what they say. By asking questions, you demonstrate an interest in them, which is the foundation of building relationships, and relationships will be your best source of business.

Why Be a Generalist When You Can Specialize?

Before getting back to the question of multiple niches, let's refocus on the perceptions that we communicate when we are a specialist versus a generalist. Please read out loud the following statements and listen to how they sound. Think about what perceptions they create in your mind as the listener.

- My name is Jeff Nischwitz. I am a partner with Smith & Smith, a firm that specializes in helping family-owned businesses transition the business from one generation to another.
- My name is Jeff Nischwitz. I am a partner with Smith & Smith, a business law firm, but I specialize in working with entrepreneurial companies that are looking to rapidly grow their business.
- My name is Jeff Nischwitz. I am a partner with Smith & Smith, a general business firm.
- My name is Jeff Nischwitz. I am a partner with Smith & Smith, and we work with small businesses and their owners.
- My name is Jeff Nischwitz. I am a partner with Smith & Smith, a general business firm, and I do corporate work.

Which of these will you remember? Which made an impact on you? Which left a positive impression and which left a negative or neutral impression? It does make a difference.

Not only must you have a target market, but that market must define your message, individually and for the firm. Your individual and firm "message" flows from and is consistent with your target market. By the way, your "message" is not just words but also actions. You can say whatever you want about yourself or your firm, but you will be judged by what you do and how you think (as evidenced by your actions). You may talk a good game, but you must walk that talk at all times. Anyone can claim to be something, but you will ultimately be judged by what you demonstrate through your actions. For example, if you talk about "partnering" with your clients, but your actions demonstrate that you are merely billing hours, then you will not be seen as a "partnering" type of business. If you claim to be a specialist and niched in a particular industry, but you know nothing about the industry, you do not get involved in the industry, and you do not invest in becoming an expert in that industry, you will quickly be found out. Therefore, you not only must have a message that fits with your desired niche or area of specialty, but everything you do must support that message.

In addition, your client profile and your target market must be the foundation of any marketing or business development plan. Anyone can keep busy with "activities," but the successful lawyer will invest his or her time in activities designed to advance the firm's message to the right clients in the right market. This requires not only careful planning, but also assessing everything that you do (or consider doing) to make sure that everything fits with your client profile and target market. This means that everything you do must have a purpose and that purpose must be consistent with your profile and your target market.

▼▼▼▼▼

Everything that you say and do (internally and externally) should fit with and be designed to further your search for the ideal client within your target market.

For every business development effort, the following question should be asked: "Will this activity help me/the firm identify and develop prospective clients who fit our client profile and are within our target market?" If the answer is no, then you should not engage in that activity, no matter how great or small the investment. Lawyers have often told me that they paid for certain advertising that was "low cost" only to have to admit to me that the advertising was not really targeted to their market. Every dollar you spend or hour that you invest toward activities that are not focused on your client profile and your target market are wasted dollars and wasted hours. Only by investing your time and money strategically and tactically and focusing on your target market can you achieve the kind of results that you need to grow your law business.

Let's return to the topic of multiple niches. You and your law firm can have multiple niches, but you have to be very careful not to confuse them (and thereby lose their effectiveness) by having too many niches. For example, I recently had a lawyer share with me his brochure, which had a list that started out "focused in these areas" and then proceeded to list 27 bullet points. No way! People simply will not believe that you can be an expert in that many areas. While they may be objectively provable, your assertions are not likely to be believed and, therefore, people will view you as a generalist at best.

The same concern for confusion applies to the question of whether you can take on work that is outside of your niche or specialty. The short answer is yes, you can. Niching and target marketing are about what you are pursuing, which is a separate question and decision from what you are willing to accept. However, if you accept work (too much work) that is outside of your niches and specialties, you can lose focus and thereby your effectiveness with respect to those niches and specialties. In summary, you can and should have multiple niches and specialties, but do not have too many and be careful when taking on work outside those specialties or else you will lose the value that you sought to achieve.

We have said it before but it bears repeating: When it comes to clients and prospective clients, perception is reality. People and businesses are attracted to experts and specialists, especially when it comes to products or services that are high value and/or high investment. Even if we know that we do not have to be experts or specialists to deliver high-quality services, prospective clients do not know that. Instead of trying to convince prospective clients that you can do the job just as well as an expert, why not be that expert? Instead of trying to change a prospective client's perception, be the expert and avoid the objection altogether. Likewise, in the world of lawyers where everyone "looks the same," differentiation is vital (but difficult) and niching and specialization are among the most effective strategies for being different. Almost by definition, you cannot "target" everyone or any market that is overly broad. Doing so is akin to throwing darts blindfolded—you will occasionally hit the board and even occasionally hit a bull's eye, but most of the time you will hit the wall.

Since prospective clients are attracted to experts, take advantage of this business opportunity by developing niches, market yourself as a specialist, and target your business development efforts on your niche areas of specialization. See Appendix A for a worksheet to help you identify existing target markets and desired target markets for you and your firm. If you consider all of the other businesses around you, you will see that most are specialists or niched in some significant way. Even businesses that now offer a wide range of services typically began as niched companies and only expanded their products or services once they had built a firm foundation. While opportunities for generalists may be more numerous, it is the quality of the opportunities that will determine the success of your business.

To enhance your law business success, decide who you want to represent, become the expert and specialist for those target clients, develop a message, and plan to demonstrate your differentiation to your target market and the results will follow. Throwing a line into any pond will not deliver the types of clients who will grow your law business, but fishing in the right pond, for the right fish, with the right equipment and "bait" is the path to building a great law firm.

Appendix A

Target Markets Worksheet

What Are Your Current Target Markets?

What clients, businesses, or industry markets are you currently targeting?

- Be specific.
- List only markets that you are proactively targeting.

What Should Be Your Target Markets?

What clients, businesses, or industry markets would you like to be targeting?

- Be specific.
- List markets you are not targeting, but should be.

20 What's So Special About You?

What is unique or different about you or your law firm? Success in the business of law requires that there be something special, unique, or different, but most lawyers and law firms are doing a poor job of differentiating themselves with clients and prospective clients. While many lawyers believe that they are differentiating themselves, many of their claimed differences are illusory, are not visible to prospective clients, or cannot be proven (and thus, do not really "exist"). Differentiation is one area where most lawyers are struggling as they try to build their business in a market growing more competitive every day. In this chapter, we will explore how important differentiation is, how we are generally failing at our differentiation attempts, and we will identify some potential avenues for differentiation with prospective clients.

With respect to differentiation, we need to get one thing clear at the beginning: better is *not* different. Very few clients and prospective clients know what "better" looks like, they cannot judge the quality of what you do, and they certainly cannot differentiate between the quality of various lawyers. We were all trained to be logical and think logically. We were trained in critical thinking and critical analysis, which did not leave much room for the "soft" areas of people and relationships, but that is the world we live in when it comes to the business of law. Do you remember the discussion about perception and reality? Perception is a key to differentiation, since differentiation is usually achieved by creating a certain perception in the eyes and minds of our clients and prospective clients. This perception is almost never about quality of service or legal skills because clients "do not know what they do not know."

Despite this fact, most lawyers and law firms attempt (unsuccessfully) to differentiate themselves based on the quality of their skills and services. We are talking about attempts to differentiate based on quality of legal services, not the quality of the "service." Certainly, the quality of the experience a client has with you or your firm can and should be a major source of your differentiation. However, whatever you may think of the quality of your legal services is not going to be an effective means for you to differentiate with clients and certainly not with prospective clients. Simply put, perception is reality and that perception is the key to differentiation. As we further explore the concept of differentiation, please keep this basic principle in mind: Better is not better. Different is better!

As a trained professional, you may not like the foregoing principle, but it is a business reality for lawyers. For nearly every business, it is very difficult to differentiate based on quality of the product or the service, but that is what everyone attempts to do. Just as in the business of law, most buyers or potential buyers cannot accurately judge the quality of the products or services and claimed "better quality" is rarely provable. If you cannot prove it, it is not a point of differentiation. You may believe it to be true in your mind, but what your clients and prospects "see" (what is in their minds) is what matters when it comes to your law business.

When I ask lawyers what makes them so special or different or why someone should hire them instead of another lawyer, I rarely get an answer that makes sense or that would have much of an impact on a prospective client. In fact, most lawyers admit that they do not really know the answer or that they have a very difficult time putting it into words. Many will even admit that there probably is not much of a difference between themselves and another lawyer. There are differences (even clear differences) in the eyes of clients and prospective clients, but we tend to focus our energy and our thoughts on our legal skills. When it comes to differentiation for lawyers, focusing on legal skills is a waste of your time. It will almost never differentiate you. The interesting thing is that most lawyers know this, but we continue to fall back on skills and quality differentiation attempts because that is our comfort zone.

> ▼▼▼▼▼
>
> The mindset of most lawyers is that being a good lawyer is good enough. Unfortunately, no one told the clients and prospective clients that this is true and no one has yet to come up with a way to allow clients and prospective clients to figure out who is the best lawyer.

We were trained to be good lawyers. Our law firms told us that we needed to learn to become good lawyers. We continue to try to differentiate based on quality of work and skills because that is where we are most comfortable and, frankly, finding true differentiation is hard—not impossible, but hard. Being different requires us to think and act differently because, ultimately, thinking and acting differently is the key to creating differentiation in the minds of our clients and prospective clients.

Take a few minutes and think about (and actually write down answers to) these questions:

- Who are you?
- Who is your firm? Not what is your firm, but who is it? Law firms are nothing more than a group of people.
- What is your personal culture and what is your firm culture?
- How do you see clients?
- How do you perceive your role as a lawyer and the role of your law firm with clients and in the community?
- What do you deliver? What does your law firm deliver? What do clients get from working with you and your law firm? What is your deliverable? What is your law firm's deliverable?

If you are not sure about the answers, then imagine how confused your clients and prospective clients are!

Every client and prospective client wants to know the answer to this question: Why you? Whether they ask that question out loud or not, they will ask it at some point in the decision-making process. If it is a prospective client, they are asking before they hire you. If it is an existing client, they are asking that question as they decide whether to continue to use you as their lawyer. Many times lawyers have told me that a client left them and they do not know why. Part of the surprise is that they mistakenly assumed that once a client, always a client. Not true. Clients are continually asking that question—why you?—and you need to make sure that you are answering that question for them throughout the relationship.

If you think that the questions above are "touchy-feely," you are right. They are not logical and often are not quantifiable, but these are the questions you need to be asking yourself and these are the questions that your clients are asking themselves. Remember, if you do not know the answers to these questions, your clients and prospective clients certainly do not know them either.

What Is Not Different

If you want to see pretty clear evidence of how ineffective most law firms are at differentiating themselves, take a look at and compare law firm brochures and Web sites. While the exact words vary and the "look and feel" is sometimes different, most brochures and Web sites share similar themes and messages, most of which are ineffective in terms of creating desired differentiation. Here are some of the most common attempts at differentiation from law firm brochures and Web site content:

- Highly skilled or experienced
- Quality service
- Reasonable fees or value
- Trusted advisor

For most lawyers and law firms, (without more to support them), these are ineffective in differentiating you or your law firm.

Claiming to be highly skilled or offering quality service does not work. Clients and prospective clients do not know if it is true, they cannot judge it, and they cannot compare it between lawyers and law firms. In fact, clients and prospective clients expect this as the minimum standard so that "telling them" that you are a good lawyer or that you provide quality service is almost insulting to them. My guess is that most of you have never had a client or prospective client tell you that they are looking for mediocre or average skills or service. Admittedly, there may have been times when they told you that on a particular matter they do not believe that it requires the highest level of skill or experience, but this is really a cost minimization concept. In fact, it probably tells you that this client or prospective client has concerns about your overall fees or hourly rates and they want to make sure that you staff the project appropriately. Rather than this being an area to potentially differentiate, it is really a client or prospective client expressing a concern as to whether you will staff a matter with the right person who has the right skill level for the particular matter and the dollars involved. In other words, clients want and expect you to be highly skilled, expert, and to deliver quality service. Therefore, skills, quality service, and general expertise or experience are not effective means for differentiating yourself or your firm.

> ▼▼▼▼▼
>
> We are not covering law firm web sites in detail in this book, but the "look and feel" of a Web site or a brochure can be effective in differentiating a law firm (positively or negatively). For example, using the scales of justice on your Web site or brochure will communicate to many people the perception of traditional, old school, or "just plain lawyer." In contrast, if your Web site or brochure looks different than that of any other law firm, then it can be an effective differentiator.

One key exception is that specialized or niche experience can be an effective differentiator. For example, if you have extensive experience in employment law, that can be a differentiator, but only if you use it as such. If you market yourself or describe yourself as a business lawyer, that is not a differentiator. But if you market yourself and describe yourself as an expert in employment law, then that certainly can serve to differentiate you from other general business lawyers.

For many of the same reasons, the concept of reasonable fees, value added, fees appropriate for the matter, and similar themes are ineffective in attempting to create differentiation or even to create a positive message. Nearly everyone says the same thing whether in print, on a Web site, or verbally. It is rare indeed to see or hear a law firm or lawyer describe themselves as expensive, although a few lawyers have taken this approach and it has proven to be very effective. With these few exceptions, lawyers and law firms are all saying that their fees are reasonable, that their fees are appropriate, that they focus on delivering overall value, and that their fees are appropriate for the particular type of matter. Everyone is saying it, which means that it cannot be a differentiator.

▼▼▼▼▼

The other problem with trying to differentiate based on skills, quality of service, or experience is that, since it is generally not quantifiable, it is so subjective as to be ineffective. You may have a belief in your mind as to why it differentiates you, but if listeners (clients and prospective clients) cannot or do not reach that conclusion, then it is not an effective differentiator.

Like skills, experience, and service, this focus on reasonable fees or value is also something that is difficult if not impossible for a prospective client to accurately assess. Reasonable compared to what? Reasonable to whom? Clients and prospective clients are generally unable to effectively and accurately compare and determine reasonableness of fees. You may think that your fees are reasonable, and you may even think (and know) that you can objectively prove them to be reasonable, but you probably cannot do so with a client or prospective client—either you do not have the opportunity or they are not familiar with the information that would allow them to reach the same conclusions that you want them to.

For example, I used to say that my hourly rate was reasonable, but the rate was $200 an hour. I firmly believed that it was reasonable based on comparison to other lawyers with my years and level of experience and expertise, but clients and prospective clients do not have that information and it is difficult for them to verify it. While I firmly believed that my $200-an-hour rate was reasonable, some clients did not think it was reasonable, and their perception was the only reality that mattered. Not only is it difficult for clients to accurately assess and judge reasonableness or appropriateness of fees, it certainly is not a differentiator when most other lawyers are saying the same thing. Clients and prospects cannot make a distinction. Like so many other attempts at differentiation, reasonableness or value of fees is almost totally subjective, which means that different people will reach different conclusions based on their own personal perspectives. Such a subjective standard is almost impossible to successfully use as a differentiator.

Very few lawyers market themselves as being very expensive, although the few that do have been effective at creating differentiation based on the high rate of their fees or hourly rate. Many clients believe that you get what you pay for; they are willing to pay more for the best and, in their mind, only the best would insist on higher than normal fees. So, while reasonableness or appropriateness of fees is not an effective means of differentiation, charging higher-than-standard or market fees can be an effective differentiation strategy. Remember this—clients are like all other consumers of any product or service . . . they will ultimately make their buying decision based on two things: the perception that the value they will receive exceeds the cost to be paid and the perception that you can help them with their problem. If they do not believe that you can help them, they will not hire you no matter how cheap you are (and if they do, those types of clients are not going to do anything to grow your law firm business). No matter what your rates or fees are (high or low), clients and prospective clients will not pay unless they see a perceived value coming to them from your services. For all of these reasons, reasonableness of fees, appropriateness of fees, or value added are not going to be effective methods for you to differentiate yourself or your law firm.

The other common differentiation tactic for lawyers certainly has the potential to be an effective differentiator, but for most lawyers, it has proven to be just words. Most lawyers want to be viewed as something more than a mere vendor service provider. In fact, the holy grail for lawyers is achieving the status of trusted advisor, business advisor, or "counselor." Certainly, taking the steps to attain this status with your clients is not only desirable but necessary in this new business market. However, the mistake that lawyers have made is in trying to differentiate by merely using the *label* "trusted advisor" or "advisor."

When reviewing Web site content and printed brochures for law firms, it is very common to see self-proclaimed designations such as "trusted advisor," "advisor," "valued resource," or similar descriptions. There are several problems with attempting to differentiate in this way. First, many lawyers and law firms are saying the same thing about themselves, which means that it loses impact. Second, clients have no way of judging whether you actually are what you claim to be unless and until they have an opportunity to either work with you in some way, they receive a strong referral from another client, or you do such an effective job in your initial meetings that they at least get a sense that you function more as an advisor than as a mere lawyer. However, the "trusted advisor" differentiation effort suffers from the same challenge—clients really cannot quantify or determine whether you are what you claim to be, which makes it a subjective assessment and, thus, a differentiation challenge. A third impediment to effectively using the "trusted advisor" role as a differentiator is that there is no common understanding of what it is, and if people are not sure what it is or what it means, then they cannot evaluate it or use it to differentiate you.

> Another challenge is that many lawyers rely on the self-described role of trusted advisor as a differentiator when trusted advisor status is something that you obtain or achieve based on what you do and how you work with clients. It is not something that you can self-proclaim.

Differentiators need to be provable, but this means that if you claim to be a trusted advisor, you must be able to clearly and effectively answer this question: If you are a trusted advisor, what exactly does that mean? Many lawyers are not prepared to answer that question. First, because they have not thought about it and they hope that merely proclaiming themselves trusted advisors will be enough. Second, lawyers have not thought about what it really means to be a trusted advisor and are not actually functioning in that role. If you do not know what the role is, you certainly cannot be a trusted advisor to your clients and you cannot effectively communicate a differentiation message.

In addition to all of this, there is another significant challenge in attempting to differentiate yourself based on being a so-called trusted advisor. Because trusted advisor status is so integrally related to what you do, how you think, and how you function with a client (as well as the client's perception of the value that you bring to them), it is nearly impossible to go to market and effectively differentiate yourself as a trusted advisor. You simply cannot prove it to the market. You can prove it to clients only over some period of time, which certainly allows you to differentiate yourself with each individual client, but it requires a great deal of time, coordination, and strategic and tactical effort to coordinate a process and system of referrals and strong recommendations based on your trusted advisor role.

For example, let's assume that you are doing all of the right things with some of your clients to demonstrate to them that you really are a trusted advisor and that they can look to you for advice and counsel that will help them in meaningful and valuable ways. Certainly, with these clients you have differentiated yourself but how do you then take that and differentiate yourself with prospective clients? That is the difficult challenge. The only way to effectively accomplish this task (transferring your proven differentiation into a message to prospective clients) is through referrals and, for the most part, referrals are not effective unless there is a process and a system behind them.

In other words, most of our clients will not refer business to us unless we ask, consistently and systematically, for those referrals. As much as they may believe in us, most clients are not thinking about us and our business as they go about their day and their business. We will be talking more about referral systems and processes in Chapters 33 and 34, but without a process or a system, it will be very difficult to effectively market and differentiate yourself to prospective clients as a trusted advisor. For all of these reasons, proclaiming yourself to be a trusted advisor or some similar term will likely be ineffective in helping you to differentiate yourself and it will be difficult as a method for growing your law business.

What Is Different

Now that we have explored differentiation attempts that are generally ineffective, let's talk about some key concepts that will take you on the path toward effective and marketable differentiation. There are really two different parts to differentiation. The first is understanding or developing your personal or law firm points of differentiation. The second involves figuring out *how* you are going to effectively communicate those points of differentiation. As you have already seen, the much more difficult task is to find a way or the means to effectively communicate your points of differentiation, but many lawyers and law firms are stumbling on even the first part—figuring out what makes them different.

In order to figure out what does make you different, you obviously have to answer this question: What makes you or your law firm different from most other lawyers or law firms? Ideally, you can come up with a list of things that make you different from every other lawyer, but let's assume that being different from "most others" is sufficient. Once we eliminate the nondifferentiators (which we discussed above), many lawyers have a difficult time being able to tell anyone what makes them unique. In fact, many lawyers have told me that they do not know what makes them different. My response is always the same: If you do not know already, you need to figure it out very quickly and start sharing those differences with your clients and prospective clients. If you really do not see yourself as different from any other lawyer, then it will be very difficult to build your firm in any significant way. As the old saying goes, "viva la difference," and this is very much the way that clients and prospective clients look at you and make the all-important buying decisions regarding legal services.

When assessing or determining how you are different, here are some areas that you should consider:

- How you think—particularly how it relates to clients, client service, and what you are seeking to deliver for (not to) your clients.
- How you *do* things. As we have already discussed, clients will ultimately judge you based on what you do, not what you say. *Do* you do things differently than most other lawyers or law firms?
- Do you have a client-focused service culture? And, if so, can you prove it?
- Do you have a specialty or a niche practice area that you can market and communicate to clients and prospective clients?

Ultimately, you must be able to answer the question of why your clients should keep using you and why your prospective clients should choose to use you. If you do not know the answer, then your clients will either be unable to answer it or they will reach the wrong conclusion.

For example, if you claim to deliver great client service, that is not a differentiator (for all of the reasons listed above) and it is impossible to prove it. Therefore, it is ineffective. However, if you commit to returning phone calls within 24 hours, that is objective, measurable, and provable. Now, you better have a system in place that allows you to follow through and honor that commitment, but clients can clearly measure you against that service commitment. That has the potential to be a differentiation point. Similarly, it is ineffective to merely claim to be different because you focus your efforts on the client's goals. However, if you demonstrate that focus by examples, case studies, or even in the types of questions that you ask your clients, then you may be able to objectively *demonstrate to them* that you are client-goal focused and that this may differentiate you. This sounds subjective, and it is, but when I say that you must be able to prove a claimed point of differentiation, what I mean is that you must have a means (typically by actions) by which a client can conclude that it is true or not. That is what makes it provable.

> ▼▼▼▼▼
>
> Your claimed differences must be objectively provable. If you cannot prove it in some demonstrable way, then you cannot prove it to clients and prospective clients and thus, you cannot effectively use it as a point of differentiation.

As we said at the outset, first you must decide what differentiates you. Then, you must find a way to *show* your clients the difference. If they cannot "see" it, then they cannot judge it and, by definition, it is not an effective or even real differentiator. In case you have not already realized it, many or most lawyers and law firms look and sound the same. For that reason, differentiation is so important, but simultaneously is a challenge and an opportunity. Differentiation is critical, but if everyone is looking and acting the same then that makes differentiation easier. You just need to be more creative, get outside of the box and outside of your comfort zone, and be willing to invest time, creativity, and energy in the process of finding the differentiators and then in developing an effective means to "show" your clients that you are different.

One of the most overlooked aspects of differentiation is the development of a clear, accurate, and easily communicated value proposition or *unique selling proposition* (USP). If you are not sure what a USP is, you should not feel left out. Many business professionals, whether in professional services or otherwise, have not given much thought to their unique selling proposition. The value proposition and the USP are simply sales and marketing terminology for what makes you so special, so valuable, or so unique. While these concepts are certainly a function of differentiation, they actually involve the creation for yourself and separately for your law firm of a clear, succinct, and value- or benefit-driven description of the thing or things (do not make it too broad) that make you and/or your law firm unique or special. Developing a USP or value proposition takes time and thought. It is not at all unusual for an individual or small group of lawyers to spend hours and even days working through the process of developing and creating an effective, accurate, and provable USP or value proposition.

One of the most effective means of developing a really effective USP or value proposition requires that you continually ask yourself (with respect to each believed differentiation point) this question: So what? Only when you continue to push yourself and to dig deeper into what really makes you unique or special can you develop a truly differentiating USP or value proposition. For example, if you said to me that your value proposition is that you have 20 years of securities litigation experience, I would ask you, "So what?" Why is that important? Why is that special? Why does that make you valuable? Ultimately, prospective clients want to know why they should do business with you and what they will get out of it.

▼▼▼▼▼

Clients (even legal clients) want to know whether you can make them money, save them money, or somehow simplify their life or business. Your USP or value proposition must address these bottom-line fundamentals.

Certainly, there is a value to the fact that you have 20 years of securities litigation experience, but the experience alone is not enough to communicate that value with very many prospective clients. Certainly, there are other lawyers in your area who have the same degree of experience. With some clients it may be enough to simply tell them how much experience you have and they will become your client, but most clients will talk to other lawyers, or will talk to other people about other lawyers. You cannot assume that they are talking only to you, which means that you need to consistently differentiate yourself. If you have peeled off all the layers of the onion and you are down to the core of what makes you special or unique and why it is valuable to the clients you work with, then you will have an effective USP or value proposition. It is not easy and it may take a good deal of time, effort, and creativity, but it is worth the investment.

Your Commercial

A topic very closely related to the USP or value proposition is your "commercial." Whether it is for you personally or for your law firm, you need to have a "commercial" (actually several commercials) that you can use when you have an opportunity to talk about what you do or what your law firm does. This is sometimes called your "8-second commercial," your "30-second commercial," or your "elevator speech." You will note that the time increments on all of these are very short, the emphasis being on quickly and effectively communicating something different, unique, or memorable about you to the listener. You have only a short period of time to make an impact on someone, and you most certainly will make an impact on them, but it will be negative unless you do something affirmatively and differently to make a positive impression.

Many lawyers have told me that they do not believe that they need to have any sort of "commercial," but they are dead wrong. Many people do not like talking to lawyers, especially in a social setting or informal business setting. Why? Typically, people tell me that lawyers are not interesting or, frankly, are boring. Why? Because lawyers have not put any effort into being different or unique.

Let's face it. Lawyers often evoke negative feelings in people. You may not like it, but it is a reality. Think back to our discussion about some of the different (and negative) perceptions that people have about lawyers. Now pretend that you have some of these perceptions and that you have just met someone at a business function or even in a social setting. You ask them what do they do and this is what you hear: "I am a lawyer" or "I am an attorney." What happens? All of your biases and perceptions regarding lawyers immediately jump into your head and you judge that person (and others are judging you the same way) based on those biases and perceptions, and nothing about what you said or how you said it has done anything to change those perceptions.

You may be thinking that you have time to make up for a bad initial impression, but that is not the case. People judge each other very quickly and you have only a few seconds to make a positive or at least different impression. A common perception of lawyers is that they are dull, uninteresting, or knowledgeable only on the law (which is a subject that most people do not understand). Therefore, people are immediately hesitant to even want to talk to a lawyer, and if your opening line is a dull, generic, or unimaginative statement about what you do, they are already thinking about how they can get away from you.

You do not need to wear a funny hat or sing and dance to make an impression on the people you meet, but you must take a little bit of time to develop a "commercial" that quickly gets people's attention, makes them at least interested in talking to you a little more and, at a minimum, creates some level of differentiation. Let's look at a couple of simple examples. When I was a practicing lawyer, my primary focus was business litigation. For the longest time that is what I told people that I did—business litigation—but eventually I realized that most people do not know what "litigation" is. As a result, I made sure to use the term trial lawyer instead of an unknown word ("litigation"). Do not assume that the people to whom you are talking know anything about what you do or even that they care, which means that you need to think about their listening perspective in carefully choosing the words and phrases that you use.

Think about what other people say to you when they introduce themselves and answer the question about what they do. Most of the time, they will tell you something descriptive about their business such as "I am the CFO with ABC Company and we manufacture widgets." Granted, this is not an incredibly dynamic introduction, but it has told you a little bit about what they do and it may get your attention or create a desire to ask some more questions. I am certainly not suggesting that this is an effective "commercial," but it is better than simply saying that you are a lawyer, an attorney, or that you practice law.

One suggestion that I would make is that you consider not even referencing the word lawyer or attorney or anything relating to the law. For example, if you are an estate planning lawyer you might introduce yourself by saying that you "help people plan for their future." Some people might assume that you are a financial planner or do a variety of other things, but that is okay. Most people will ask you more questions to find out exactly what you do, so your introduction has opened the door to allow you to tell them more about who you are and what you do. That is what you want to achieve. You want them to be asking you questions, which takes the pressure off you in terms of feeling under the gun to describe or talk about yourself. We are very uncomfortable talking about ourselves *unless* we are asked about ourselves. Then we are more than willing to start sharing our story with others.

Let me share a couple of other examples with you. These are not intended to be things that you will necessarily copy, but they will give you an idea or maybe help you to start thinking differently about how you can describe yourself and what you do to others. There is a law firm in Cleveland—Cowden, Humphrey, Nagorney & Lovett—that has the following tag line: "Entrepreneurs Advising Entrepreneurs." Their lawyers will often use the same tag line as their "commercial" when they meet someone new. This is a powerful "commercial" for two reasons. First, it is memorable and thus has branding impact. Second, it tells you a great deal about the lawyers, the law firm, and their clients.

Always remember that people really do not care about what you do, but they do care about who you are. Your "commercial" gives them a first glimpse of who you are, much more than what you do.

Who do they represent? Entrepreneurs. How do they think? Like entrepreneurs. This law firm has less than 15 lawyers, which in some minds represents a small law firm. Consider the difference between these two introductions: "Entrepreneurs Advising Entrepreneurs" versus "I work with a small law firm that works with businesses." Which is memorable? Which differentiates? Which tells you something about the lawyers and the law firm? Obviously, it is the first one, and this is the type of impact that you want to make on people and prospective clients. Remember, better is not better. Different is better.

The other example that I would like to share with you is one that I used in the last four or five years when I was practicing law. I'll share the "commercial" with you (although it always varied a little bit) and then discuss it in more detail:

> I am a partner with Nischwitz, Pembridge & Chriszt in the warehouse district. We typically work with business owners and executives and we practice law differently.

This proved to be a very effective "commercial" for me. Let's look at what it accomplished.

First, it told people that I was an owner in the law firm. This might not make an impression, but it might, so I wanted to make sure it was included in my "commercial." Second, mentioning that we were in the "warehouse district" would typically make an impression or stimulate additional conversation. The warehouse district in Cleveland is an area of renovated warehouses converted into office space, and people often wanted to talk more about our offices and what it was like to work in the warehouse district. In addition, there was a general sense that working in the warehouse district connotated being new, creative, cutting edge, progressive, forward-looking, and so on. Thus, I had potentially communicated a great deal about myself, our law firm, and how we think and work. Frankly, for many people, the warehouse district is "cool," and that made us "cool" in some people's eyes.

Third, notice that I never said that I was a lawyer. I certainly made that clear in what I said, but I did not go with what I consider to be a stiff and unimaginative statement of what I am or what I do. Fourth, I never talked about what we do (remember, no one cares what you do), but instead used the words "work with" to communicate a sense of partnership or a team approach with our clients. Admittedly, not everyone will come away with this impression, but my "commercial" was intended to have the most positive impact possible on as many people as possible. Fifth, by mentioning "business owners and executives" I communicated some sense of the level of our law practice and, as was usually the case, it generally caused the listener to ask some more specific questions about exactly what type of law we practice.

Rather than me spewing it out to them, I set it up so that they would ask me about it and I would provide the additional information only when I had been granted an "invitation" from them with their questions. Finally, by stating that "we practice law differently," I almost always got a question back as to what that meant. Absolutely, I had to have differentiation points to share with the listener, but I did not want to start rattling off what I believed to be our differentiators. Instead, I wanted them to ask me what they were, and my introduction usually set the stage for the question and my presentation of the differentiators.

Why was this "commercial" so effective? It was memorable and made me memorable. It was different and differentiated me. It encouraged and almost forced the listener to ask questions, which gave me an invitation to provide more information. It told them a great deal about me, our firm, and our clients. It also gave them some insight as to how I think and how our firm thinks and works. There was a lot packed into this 8- or 10-second introduction. I cannot overemphasize the significance of how this "commercial" encouraged further discussions (on various topics) and induced most listeners to ask me more questions. Your commercial is not about dumping on someone a long list of what you do,

> ▼▼▼▼▼
>
> If you can get people to ask you questions (with genuine interest because they really are curious), you have achieved a significant goal by differentiating yourself and your law firm and by making a memorable and positive first impression. That is what your "commercial" is all about.

because no one cares what you do, and for the most part, everyone else does things that way. You want to do things differently, which means that you need to be different, be creative, be unique, and be memorable.

What's in It for Them

Before moving on, there is one more differentiation topic that we need to cover—one of the most critical topics for anyone in business to understand and, ultimately, implement into their sales efforts. The topic is features versus benefits. We are going to talk about the difference between features and benefits, but note this key point at the beginning: People (which means your clients and prospective clients) care only about benefits. Benefits are what they get from you or from doing business with you. Features are things like what you do, experience, background, or other information that is more factual in nature, but people do not buy for features. They buy based on the benefits that they expect to receive or achieve. Admittedly, some people can identify the benefits from the features, but why would you want to leave that to chance? Instead of focusing on features, you need to focus your attention and messages on benefits, which means figuring out what the benefits really are and then figuring out an effective method to communicate them.

This is not a challenge just for lawyers, but for every industry and every business. Once you start to understand and see the differences between features and benefits, you will start to see how other people in business are relying too heavily on features and ignoring the benefits. Whether or not you lead with features or benefits is not the most important question. What is most important is that at some point in time you dig deep enough with clients and prospective clients to figure out what benefits they want and make sure that you communicate to them how those benefits will be achieved by working with you. That is a fundamental and critical ingredient of your business development results.

To make this easier, we will first look at some features versus benefits examples outside of the law. One of the easiest examples is with automobiles. Why do most people buy Volvos? Alternatively, what is it that Volvo focuses most of its marketing and branding on? Safety, of course. Whether it is demonstrably true or not, Volvo has worked hard to promote itself as the manufacturer of the safest (or one of the safest) automobiles. So, if you buy a Volvo, the benefit you are buying is safety, right? Wrong. Safety is a feature. Yes, the long list of "safety features" (steering system, braking system, airbag system, ability to handle impact, and so on) are features, but even the description of "safety" is still just a feature of a Volvo. If you really dig down to the core decision-making, most people buy a Volvo because they want to protect their family. The benefit is keeping their family safe. Therefore, a truly effective Volvo salesperson will mention the various "safety features," but will make sure to talk about the potential buyer's family and the safety of their family. It is possible that a potential buyer is interested in another potential benefit, which is what someone would want to try to discover by talking to the person and asking lots of questions, but most Volvo buyers are interested in the benefit of keeping their family safe.

Let's consider another automobile example. Why do most people buy a Porsche? Pretty simple: speed or status; right? Wrong. Speed is a feature. Status is a feature. You have to dig deeper to find the benefits. What are some of the reasons that people like to drive fast? It is fun, it makes them feel good, it gives them a sense of adventure, it makes them feel special. The same types of *feelings* apply to the feature of status. Ultimately, people will buy a Porsche because of the benefits relating to how it will make them feel by owning or driving that Porsche. Those are the benefits. A Porsche salesperson who talks only about how fast the car will go is taking a chance that the potential buyer will not get a true understanding of the benefits to them from owning that Porsche. The successful Porsche salesperson will talk to that prospective buyer about those underlining benefits or feelings to move the prospective buyer to make the buying decision. The prospective buyer has an interest in the Porsche because of how they think it will make them feel. The salesperson helps show them how it will make them feel and thereby helps the customer get what they really want.

I was talking about this topic (features versus benefits) with a group of financial professionals. I asked them who had recently purchased an automobile and one of them told me that he had recently purchased a very high-end Infinity. I asked him why he bought this particular car, and he started to give me a long list of features. I kept pushing him and saying, "But why did you really buy the car?" I kept digging deeper until he finally said, "To be honest, there is a certain degree of status with owning an automobile like this and I liked how it made me feel driving that car." That is the benefit that he bought and that is the type of focus you need to have when talking to clients and prospective clients. You need to focus on the benefits that they will receive and hopefully want, rather than throwing out a long list of features that really do not mean much.

Now let's take a look at features versus benefits specifically with respect to the practice of law. Following is a list of typically listed features relating to lawyers or law firms, each of which is followed by other deeper level features (but still not benefits), which end in a description of some type of benefit.

- Twenty years of industry specialization/niche specialist—expert—more efficient—lower cost—higher likelihood of favorable transaction—lower risk of mistakes or unfavorable transaction—fewer worries—*make or save more money in the transaction*

- Small law firm—more attentive—better service—lower fees—better value—individual attention—*feel valued*
- High-quality client service—better value—lower risk—fewer worries—*feel valued*
- Understand your business—invested in relationship—better advice—*better result for client*

As you can see, all of the features that we typically tout really boil down to a couple of basic benefits: lower costs, lower risk, enhanced likelihood of success, security, comfort, feeling valued, or peace of mind. These are the benefits that clients are looking for and frankly expect.

How many times have you experienced a disconnection between your client's expectations and reality? For example, you "sell" a prospective client or an existing client on a new matter based on your years of experience and expertise, but that certainly does not guarantee a favorable or desired result. However, your client or prospective client perceives the benefit as being guaranteed success. When the results are not as desired or expected, the blame naturally falls on you. You know that it is not your "fault," but in a way the disconnect between the features you were selling and the benefits that the client perceived is your responsibility.

▼▼▼▼▼

The mistake we often make is that we talk only about the features, without ever thinking about what the underlying benefits are or whether the clients can even figure out (correctly) what those benefits are.

Thus, there are two reasons to focus on benefits. First and foremost, people buy products and services (including legal services) based on the perceived benefits or perceived value, not based on features. Therefore, it is critical that you stop focusing on features, start understanding benefits and value, and start educating clients and prospective clients on the benefits and values that they will receive from working with you. Second, having a clear understanding of the benefits and value will minimize (you can never avoid) miscommunications or disconnects between expectations with your clients. Making it clear what benefits and values to expect will ultimately improve your overall client satisfaction level, since client satisfaction is nearly always a function of how well the results meet or equate to expectations. Client satisfaction usually is not based on the actual results but on how those results measure up against expected results, benefits, and value received.

Differentiation for lawyers is a challenge, but it is vital to dramatically improving business development results. You need to focus your message on what clients and prospective clients want to hear. You need to develop a message (including a "commercial") that clearly, quickly, and effectively communicates true differentiation points. Those points must be provable and you must build a system and process around delivering them. And always focus on the benefits and the value, not the features. Keep asking yourself why or what is so special about that and you will eventually dig down to the core of the benefits and the value. It is up to you to invest time and energy on deciding who you are, who you want to be, and then effectively and consistently communicating these differentiation points to the people you meet, the clients you work with, and particularly with your referral sources. Everyone wants to know why they should do business with you. It is your obligation and responsibility to make sure that you clearly and fairly communicate to them the "why" that will allow them to make a secure and comfortable decision in favor of working with you.

What Clients Want

21

While most lawyers think that they provide great service and value, and that their clients love them, we all must face the fact that many of our clients are dissatisfied. Rather than putting our heads in the sand and "hoping" that our clients are happy, we need to recognize what we do well and what we do not do well when it comes to client service. Even more important, we need to understand what clients do not like and how we can do a better job of addressing these client dislikes and delivering what clients want. The crucial first step is to stop talking about service (even great service) and to instead focus on delivering a great experience for your clients. Remember, most clients cannot judge what we do, but they are perfectly qualified to judge (and they do judge) the experience and whether or not you communicate to them (through your actions) that they are important and that you care about them.

Some time ago, a business owner shared with me a great example of how we as lawyers are missing the mark with clients. This owner had recently seen a television commercial for a local law firm. He could not even remember the nature of the practice, but he definitely remembered what he did not like about the commercial. Here is what he said:

> At the end of the commercial the lawyer [presumably a member of the firm] looked into the camera with a very serious look and said, "We are serious about the law." My immediate response was that I could care less whether you are "serious about the law." I want to know if you are serious about me and my business.

This is a perfect example of thinking that the firm is more important than the clients. What this business owner is telling us all is that we need to be more serious about him and his needs—more specifically, that we need to focus our valuable time and energies on the client, instead of on ourselves.

This gets back to a point we made earlier about how many lawyers tend to take an internal focus on what they do and the messages they communicate. One of the most important rules of sales and marketing is to focus the message on the listener, which is the client or prospective client. Instead, we too often focus on ourselves and try to push forward messages about us, rather than focusing on *them*. Ultimately, clients and prospective clients do not care how good you think you are—they want to know what you can do for them, what value you bring, and whether you can help them.

We have already talked a lot about what clients are really interested in and about delivering great experiences for them, but we also need to focus on several key client dislikes. In nearly every client survey that I have seen, the complaints or shortcomings fall into the following categories:

- Poor communication
- Unexpected delays
- Reactive instead of proactive lawyering
- Fees

We will talk more about fees later, but all of these encapsulate what clients see as the shortcomings of lawyers and law firms. You will also notice that there is a lot of overlap between these various client dislikes.

▼▼▼▼▼

Although we generally should not focus on negatives, sometimes it can be valuable to do so. Identifying what clients dislike provides a clear road map for delivering what they do want, which in turn allows us to more effectively deliver great experiences for our clients.

Poor Communication

Poor communication usually means that clients do not know what is going on (because they have not heard from their lawyer in a timely and consistent manner) and/or communication is unclear or confusing. Most clients did not go to law school and very few ever practiced law. Therefore, our communication must assume that their knowledge and understanding is at the most basic level. If they understand more than the average person, they will let us know. Therefore, our communication should be not only timely, but delivered in a manner that is easily understood by a layperson. Legalese does not cut it when communicating with clients.

Litigation is an area that requires particular attention to tailoring the communication to the client's level of understanding. For example, clients may not know the differences between a pretrial, a pretrial conference, a settlement conference, a final pretrial, and a pretrial hearing. Most clients also do not know the difference between a motion to dismiss and a motion for summary judgment, yet those are the words that we tend to use in telling clients what we are going to do. We assume (often without even giving it a thought) that clients know what we are talking about, and that if they do not understand, they will ask. That is a mistake. More often they will not ask either because they do not know what they do not know or they do not want to sound ignorant or unsophisticated. It is our obligation to make sure that our clients know what is going on, what is being done, why it is being done, and what everything means.

It is often suggested that lawyers should make it a habit to copy their clients on everything—every letter, every draft document, every memorandum, every set of telephone notes, and so on. I do not believe this is the answer. While this practice may be appropriate (although my guess is that most clients do not want to receive copies of everything and they should at least be asked), this is really the easy way out and does not address the underlying issue—communication. Communication is about understanding, and we help our clients to understand by being thoughtful in our communication, by making sure that our communication is consistent, and by making sure that our communication can be understood. Simply papering a client to death does not deliver the type or level of communication that clients want and deserve.

Unexpected Delays

Unexpected delays are another common frustration expressed by clients, but this is also mostly about communication. Note that the problem here is not "delays," but *"unexpected delays."* With nearly everything in life our greatest frustrations come not from delays, but from the unexpected. If we are prepared for delays (or have more reasonable assessments), many delays actually cease to be delays. Things now proceed in due course and as planned. As lawyers with any level of experience, we have a pretty good idea of how long things take. Unfortunately, we make two mistakes with respect to time and potential delays. First, we almost always underestimate the time it takes for anything. We underestimate how much time it will take us to complete a project, and we underestimate delays in communicating with other lawyers or other parties.

How many times do you reach your client by telephone on the first call? How many times do you reach opposing counsel on the first call?

How many times do you reach a lawyer in your office on the first call? How often do you play phone tag, voicemail tag, or e-mail tag? How often do things go exactly as planned? How often are you able to accomplish tasks or projects without any interruptions? The reality is that almost everything that we do in the practice of law is fraught with delays, interruptions, and obstacles, and yet we often fail to compensate for this in our planning and in our client communications. Typically, we underestimate the entire process of anything we are doing, despite the fact that the entire process depends on people.

Our underestimating of time (particularly in communicating with clients) ultimately arises from a certain level of fear. We want happy clients, and delays make clients unhappy. To avoid an unhappy client (at least at the beginning), we underestimate the time involved so that they get the sense (a false sense) that things will move along quickly. Of course the inevitable result is that things do not move along as predicted (or as assumed by the clients if we do not give them any information), and they become unhappy later when the real timetables (which we knew all along) become clear. Clients want to know how long it will take. While it is very difficult to be absolutely specific on this topic, we need to be more realistic about our time estimates on everything and we need to make sure that we are communicating something about timing to our clients. Remember, it is not the delays that upset clients, but the unexpected delays.

> ▼▼▼▼▼
>
> We are trained and experienced lawyers, and we know very well that most things we do are measured in weeks, months, or even years. They are not measured in days, yet our communications with clients tend to be in terms of days and hours.

Reactive Lawyering

When I mention the subject of reactive versus proactive lawyering, many lawyers tell me that their clients are not in the position to judge this aspect of how they deliver their legal services. While this may be "technically" correct, once again, clients are uniquely positioned to make this determination based on their perceptions. Remember, perceptions are absolute reality when it comes to client service. If clients think that you are reactive (versus proactive), then you are, in fact, reactive in their minds, which is the only place that client service matters—in the minds of the clients. There are several ways that clients perceive their lawyers as reactive. One primary area is in communication. Many lawyers believe that answering client's questions when those questions are raised or updating clients when updates are requested equals quality communication. That is generally not the case. Quality communication generally means that the clients do not have to call and ask questions or to request updates because the questions were answered without being asked or the updates were given in advance. I personally had this experience as a client several years ago when I was pursuing a business investment.

For a variety of reasons, including several very compelling business reasons, it was important that we move forward quickly with the venture. This meant that we had to make a decision as to whether we were going to go forward even sooner. All of this was clearly explained to my lawyers, but the process did not move quickly and, in fact, was dragging along at a very slow pace. Looking at it objectively, the primary reason for the delays was the opposing counsel's unavailability and/or unresponsiveness. While this was not within my lawyer's control, I took issue with the fact that I received no updates whatsoever about the status of the discussions (or even the efforts to make contact) except when I asked for an update. When I sent an email or called to find out the status of the discussions, I did receive a relatively prompt reply or voicemail message back (often in the evening). However, at no time did I receive a proactive email or telephone call updating me on the discussions or the efforts to contact the opposing counsel. My lawyers probably felt that their communication was adequate. In fact, most lawyers would view this communication (answering my questions) as effective and appropriate, but not all clients see it that way.

Think about your own experiences as a client or customer in any setting. If you have a question or a problem, you certainly want it to be answered, but isn't it true that often you are thinking that you should have been given the information without asking? If you buy a product, but have to call the manufacturer with a question, then that is an inconvenience. You should have been given all the information at the outset. This is the way many clients think with respect to their lawyers, and I was one of those clients. I appreciated getting updates and answers when I asked, but given the fact that my lawyers knew that I was on a tight time frame, my expectation was that I would be kept updated without asking. This is not an unreasonable expectation, and unfulfilled expectations are often at the heart of client dissatisfaction. Proactive lawyering means proactive communication to make sure that your clients are kept updated at all times and on all matters.

Another reactive versus proactive perception that clients have relates to the legal work itself. On several occasions clients would tell me that they "felt" as though the other side was in control. They "felt" as though they were always reacting to a position taken or a strategy implemented by the other side. Whether this was true or not was irrelevant. I may have anticipated the positions or anticipated a move by the other side, but my clients perceived that we were reacting to what the other side did, rather than proactively implementing our own strategy. As we have talked about many times, this may be an inaccurate perception, but an inaccurate perception is still reality to clients. Ultimately, this is mostly about communication, but the effect of poor or inadequate communication can be the perception that you are a reactive rather than a proactive lawyer and in many clients' eyes, that means that your service is less than it should be.

▼▼▼▼▼

Clients want and expect their lawyers to be in charge and in control, just as the clients themselves want to have a feeling of control.

We have now seen that perceptions are often at the heart of client dissatisfaction. Before moving on to the topic of attorneys' fees and client dissatisfaction, let's talk a moment about the term "client dissatisfaction." Many of you may be reading this and thinking that you do not have any or many "dissatisfied" clients. First of all, it is almost a certain bet that you have more dissatisfied clients than you know about. Many times you do not hear about the dissatisfactions from a "dissatisfied" client, but for any number of reasons (real or claimed), they end up no longer being clients. We may try to convince ourselves that we did everything "right," and that may be objectively true, but a dissatisfied client is still a dissatisfied client and the ultimate responsibility is ours.

A second and more important issue relates to my definition of a "dissatisfied client." What I have discovered in the business of law is that aspiring to have "satisfied clients" is setting the bar much too low. Merely satisfied clients do not help build your business. Merely satisfied clients are not stable, and thus you and your law business are at risk with these clients. Merely satisfied clients do not refer other clients to you. Merely satisfied clients are usually not "A" or "B" clients. Seeking to have merely satisfied clients usually results in a dissatisfied client if you fall short of your minimal goal of satisfaction.

Your business needs excited clients, enthusiastic clients, raving fans, and clients who feel that working with you has been a great experience. Your goal needs to be delivering great performance and great experiences, not mere satisfaction. Therefore, when I talk about the risk of having dissatisfied clients as a result of poor communication, unfulfilled expectations, delays, and so on I am talking about the critical risk of ending up with clients who are, at best, merely satisfied. Merely satisfying clients should not be your goal, and it is vital that you and your firm build cultures, systems, processes, and habits focused on delivering great performance and great experiences for your clients.

Uncertain Attorneys' Fees

Now, let's talk about what clients really do not like, and the topic is fees. Contrary to what many lawyers believe, hourly rates are not the problem with most clients. Certainly, there is often a disconnect between the size or complexity of the client or matter relative to the hourly rates, but that is more of a problem as it relates to whether a client or matter is "right" for a lawyer or law firm. It also relates to how matters are staffed, which are all ultimately client service issues. In the end, however, hourly rates and even total invoice amounts are not at the heart of the problem. The heart of the problem with attorneys' fees is their uncertainty.

Whenever the topic of attorneys' fees comes up—especially the topic of the billable hour—many attorneys get very defensive, and immediately want to tell everyone that billing by the hour is the only way to do it, especially in a business setting. We are going to talk a little bit about alternative fee arrangements in Chapter 23, but for now you can assume that the billable hour is not dead and is not likely to die soon. However, that does not change the reality (aka the problems) of the billable hour.

One of the first and foremost realities to keep in mind is that with rare exceptions, lawyers are the only people with whom individuals and businesses work without knowing the cost in advance. Certainly, our experience as consumers in buying products (whether personally or in business) is that things have a specific price. The price may be negotiable, but we are quoted a price, we pay it, and we receive the product and any related support and services. The cost for what we receive is very clear, fully explained, and not subject to variation. Even with personal and business services, really hard estimates and pretty narrow ranges are the standard, not the exception. Even in the information technology industry, which is fraught with perceived unknowns in terms of total costs, there is a great deal more certainty with fees than in most legal matters.

Let's face one fact at the outset—we as lawyers are very hesitant to commit ourselves on fee estimates, unless we are forced to do so by the clients (e.g., insurance companies and in-house counsel) and larger companies have "forced" this accountability on many lawyers. We know that there are a lot of variables and uncertainties with respect to many legal matters and representations, particularly as the matters become larger and more complex. The same fear or risk aversion is a factor in the still minimal use of fixed fee arrangements among lawyers. No matter how strong the arguments or how clear the logic, it is important that we understand the perceptions of clients and prospective clients (and even the markets) in dealing with lawyers. Legal matters are one of the very few areas where clients do not have a clear understanding of the cost going into the matter. At a bare minimum, this certainly causes many clients to be concerned, frustrated, uncertain, confused, nervous, and even fearful going into any legal engagement. These realities and perceptions must be considered and accounted for in how you deal with and work with clients, especially in the area of communication.

Two of the biggest problems with the billable hour are that it is not client focused and it is not service focused. The reality is that the billable hour is almost entirely geared for and intended to benefit lawyers. In fact, Ronald Martin of Holland & Hart in Colorado Springs has described the billable hour as one of the "profession killers," and he identified these "billable hour rules":

▼▼▼▼▼

The billable hour minimizes the law firm's risk; assures that the firm is fully compensated for its services; and puts nearly all of the risk on the clients. Whether we want to admit it or not, the fact is that the billable hour is all about the lawyer, and not about the client.

- The longer it takes to do the work, the more the firm is paid.
- The more bodies that are thrown at a matter, the more the firm is paid.
- The more inefficient the firm is, the more the firm is paid.

Profession killers indeed!

You may be reading this and saying, "But we do not spend more time on a matter unless it is necessary. We do not involve more lawyers unless they are necessary. We assign staff appropriate to the needed expertise and the complexity and significance of the matter. We always work to be as efficient as possible." You are probably correct, but every one of the above-listed "billable hour rules" is still an absolute truth. The longer it takes, the more people who get involved, and the more inefficient the work, the more the firm will be paid (unless the firm voluntarily or involuntarily reduces the bill or unless the client refuses to pay). These are the facts relating to the billable hour, and we must consider them in determining how we are going to work with clients and how we are going to communicate with them.

▼▼▼▼▼

Clients are not used to being told that cost is uncertain, that it will depend on many facts and circumstances, and that there is no cap or limit on the total amount of fees on a particular matter. That is not part of their prior experience and it is certainly outside of their comfort zone.

Imagine that you have a problem with your employees. They are not working together or there are a number of conflicts or challenges among them. You contact a human resources consultant who comes to you and discusses several potential solutions. You believe that you need outside help and that this particular consultant can help you, and therefore you are ready to retain the consultant to help you. Imagine further that when you ask how much it will cost, the response is "I charge $200 an hour. I really have no idea how long it will take, nor can I give you any assurances or guarantees regarding the results. I may be able to offer a solution that works in a relatively short period of time, in which case the total cost could be $10,000. However, it may take much longer (I cannot tell you how much longer), I do not know whether it will work, and in the end the cost could be $50,000, $100,000, or even higher. When would you like to get started?" How do you feel after that conversation? What are you thinking? How confident are you in the consultant's ability to solve your problem? How concerned are you about what the total cost will be? How concerned are you that you may spend lots of money and not get the result you want or need? This is precisely how most of your clients think and feel after having a fee discussion.

Even if we do nothing to change how we charge for our services or bill for our time, or in any way alter the billable hour concept, we have to at least recognize that uncertainty of fees is a concern for clients and is a challenge to be overcome, typically through more consistent, more effective, and more client-focused communication. When it comes to attorneys' fees we must put our "client hats" on and consider what the client is hearing, thinking, and feeling when it comes to our fees. The billable hour may not be dead, but the days of actually doing the work without any consideration of the client's perspective on our fees is dead or at least it should be.

22 Forget Great Service . . . Deliver Great Experiences!

I rarely find lawyers who say that they are not already providing good service to their clients. In fact, most lawyers tell me that they do provide good service to their clients. Some even believe that they are providing great service to their clients, although I rarely have anyone who can tell me exactly how they are providing such good (or even great) service or what good or great service looks like. Nor can they point to any evidence or information from their clients that confirms that their level of service is great or even good. Rather, it seems that most lawyers assume they are providing at least good service based on nothing more than their gut reaction or the fact that they are not getting an excessive number of complaints. In the prior chapter we talked about what clients want and some ways to deliver in those areas, but the real problem is that lawyers (like many businesspeople) have set the service bar too low by focusing on "service" (whether good or great) as the goal.

The problem with focusing on service at all is that it is too focused on the "stuff" of the working relationship between clients and lawyers. As we have talked about repeatedly, lawyers tend to focus on the quality of their legal services, rather than the quality of the service provided. This happens for a couple of reasons. First, lawyers are most familiar with and can best judge the quality of their services. Therefore, this is the standard that they apply. Second, we have mistakenly gotten it into our heads that the only standard to which we should be held by clients is the quality of our services. However, clients generally cannot judge (at least not accurately) the quality of our services and, therefore, for us to judge the quality of our service by the quality of our *legal services* is a mistake. We may provide the highest quality of legal services, but clients will ultimately judge us based on the quality of the experience.

Instead of focusing on services, lawyers need to focus on delivering a great experience to their clients by understanding the client's true interests and goals, by educating them, by preparing them, and by managing their expectations. It is also important that we totally shift our focus from our own services to our clients so that we can develop a truly client-centric mindset. This means that we need to develop processes and systems around the delivery of a great experience to our clients. It also means that we need to make every decision with a "client hat" on. By delivering a great experience to our clients, they can and will become our raving fans and they will then help us to grow our business by staying with us, by doing more business with us, and by bringing us new business through referrals.

> ▼▼▼▼▼
>
> A critical first step in delivering great performance and great experiences is to always keep your focus first and foremost on the experience, and not on the results.

Nearly every client we work with or prospective client that we talk to is focused on results. They want to win, prevail, get their way, get the best deal, and so on, and there are two reasons for this focus with clients and prospects. First, like most people, it is all about them and they are very focused on getting what is best for them. This is not unusual and we need to anticipate it in how we work and talk with clients and prospects. Second, results are the easiest thing for them to understand. They may not understand our industry, our services, or the law, but they can certainly understand and develop in their own mind what it is they want and then expect to achieve with our help.

As we all know, however, we rarely (if ever) have control (and certainly never have total control) over the results of our efforts. We can do our very best and provide the best and highest quality legal services, but there are always many factors that are beyond our control that will ultimately impact the results. No matter what the nature of your legal services, the "other side" and the opposing lawyers are always factors in the results that are achieved—not only the results, but also the timeliness of the results. If the matter involves litigation or a trial, other factors such as the system, the judge and/or the jury, and time itself can influence the results. By the way, we also forget about the facts and their impact on the results. If it is a business matter, other factors may include economic conditions and the overall business environment.

With all of these things that are out of our control, we also often forget about the other key factor that is usually out of our control—our client. Wouldn't it be great if our clients were always rational, reasonable, and never changed their minds? Unfortunately, the reality is that our clients are unpredictable and this lack of predictability is another piece of the puzzle that is outside of our control. For all of these reasons, and as much as we would love to control them, we do not control the results in most matters. If we do not address this early in the relationship, we are at serious risk of a bad experience with our clients if they are looking solely to the results to judge the quality of our services and even the quality of our "service."

Given our lack of control over the results, we need to instead spend our time and efforts focused on the "client experience," because the experience is something that we have much more control over. Ultimately, we cannot control our clients' perceptions, but we need to direct our efforts toward their perceptions by focusing on delivering a great experience and, therefore, creating a great performance in our clients' eyes. After all, clients' perceptions are always right and we need to invest our time toward changing their perceptions rather than ever trying to convince them that we are right. If a client has a bad experience (and thereby perceives bad service), it is next to impossible for us to prove to that client that we provided good service. Rather, we need to direct our efforts toward changing their perceptions (preferably from the beginning) so that they have a great experience and therefore see our performance as great.

While we do not control results, we do have a great deal of control over communication, whether it is from us to our clients or from our clients to us. In addition to communication, most of the ingredients of delivering a great experience and, thus, great performance are uniquely within our control, and these are the key areas when it comes to consistently delivering great experiences for our clients. Just as questioning and listening are keys to building better relationships, questions are also the key to delivering great experiences for our clients. These are not questions specifically related to their legal matter, but questions directed to our clients' wants, values, and interests. We need to know and fully understand our clients' true interests, values, goals, and expectations. We not only need to know these at a superficial level, but we need to know what supports each of these interests, values, and goals. We need to know what our clients hope or expect to achieve from working with us, whether it is in terms of tangible results, indirect results, or intangible results. We need to dig deep and explore what their real motivations are.

Are they really focused on the result in this matter or are they more focused on what the result in this matter will do for them in other business or personal matters? Many times our clients' decisions, actions, and behaviors are driven by things that we do not understand because we never asked or we did not dig deep enough. If we take things at face value and accept our clients' superficial input on what they are hoping to achieve, we will never understand the real issues and, therefore, we are in danger of failing to provide the type of experience that they want. While many of their interests and goals may at first sound like results (and they may be), we need this information as the starting point for the process of understanding their needs and then beginning our own process toward creating a great experience for them. In other words, understanding our clients' true interests, values, goals, and expectations is the first step in the process of providing a great experience.

Educate, Prepare, and Manage

Okay. Now we know what they want, what is important to them, and what they hope to achieve. So what do we do with this information? Simple—we educate them, we prepare them, and we manage their expectations. Let's start with educating them. What do we educate them on? Everything. We educate them on the process. We educate them on the law and how it impacts their matter and issues. We educate them on the system. We educate them on their situation and on what we do not control. Clients and prospects come to us with preconceived notions about everything covered in the above list. They may know nothing about any of these areas, but they have perceptions that have already been formed before they even speak to us. Obviously, most clients come to us believing that all of the facts and circumstances are in their favor and that the law *must* support them. "It is only right," they tell us, so they come to us totally believing that they are right and that they will prevail or achieve their goals.

Naturally, they also come to us believing that their situation is unique or that it has occurred so often that the answers must be obvious and, of course, are obvious in their favor. All of our clients come to us with a wide range of biases, and it is up to us to educate them in all of these areas, but we must educate them only after we understand their true goals, interests, values, and expectations.

> ▼▼▼▼▼
>
> Educating our clients on timing issues (how slowly most processes move) is a great example of how to manage their expectations.

Litigation is a great example of where we often fail to properly educate our clients up front about how long things actually take. In our courts, for example, a matter filed in the county courts would rarely come to trial earlier than 18 months after it is filed. It is also common to have two or three continuances, and it was the rule (rather than the exception) that you would appear for trial with witnesses and be told that you had to be rescheduled due to some pressing criminal matter or double or triple booking of civil matters. As trial lawyers we were very familiar with this reality, but we did not always do the best job of telling our clients up front that this is what they could expect. Over time, I learned that it was vital to tell my clients up front that this would be the reality—that things would take much longer than expected and cost much more than expected—so that they knew what they were getting into from the beginning. This accomplished two objectives. First, it prepared them so that they were not surprised. This is important since surprises are rarely good when it comes to client relationships and client experience levels. Second, it helped them to make better decisions along the way. Fully informed clients make better decisions relative to their entire matter, and that should be our goal—to help our clients make better decisions.

Next, we need to prepare them. We need to prepare them for what will happen, for what might happen, for the opposition, for the opposing party, and for the people on the other side of a transaction. In short, we need to prepare them for everything. Most of our clients do not have any experience with lawyers or their experience is very limited. They do not know what to expect, and it is our foremost obligation to prepare them for what will happen or what might happen. We have all had the experience of clients being surprised or even shocked about something that happened or did not happen, but it was not shocking to us at all. Why? Because we have the experience and we knew to be prepared for it, but we often forget to prepare our clients for what we already expect. We get so caught up in rushing in to represent our clients and to do our work that we often forget how little they know—we simply do not take the time to prepare them for what is coming.

How many times have we had clients express frustration or even anger at delays in some aspect of our representation? In most of those cases, we are not surprised with the delays because we have seen them before and we knew they were coming, but for our clients they are unexpected. It is our responsibility to make sure that our clients are not surprised. If we prepare them for everything, then we take back control over the experience and we lay the groundwork for them having a great experience because things will happen as we predicted and as we prepared them. If things go better than expected, then we are really heroes to our clients, but if we can at least prepare them, then we minimize the risk of them being surprised, and surprises are never good when it comes to our clients.

The final area is managing our clients' expectations. First of all, this is *not* about the old saying of "underpromise and overdeliver." I have never liked that saying, although it is very prevalent in the business community, because it is all about us and rarely if ever about the clients. It also sounds very manipulative and deceptive. When we talk about managing expectations we are not talking about deception, but about using the things that we have talked about (education and preparation) to manage our clients' expectations. The process of educating and preparing our clients is really the heart and soul of managing expectations. If we tell clients what to expect, then most of what happens will be expected. If we expect delays and this is communicated, then delays will be expected. If we establish reasonable timetables, then clients will not be surprised.

By the way, we need to establish reasonable timetables not only within the process of the overall matter, but also for our work. We are infamous for making promises that we cannot or do not keep. This can be the kiss of death when it comes to client service and certainly client experiences. Most clients will be happy with whatever timetables we create as long as we honor them. By asking questions and understanding their needs we can reach a mutually agreeable timetable for most services, but we need to then meet those timetables. The worst thing we can do is to make promises and fail to honor them. As much as we do not want to admit it, that makes us unreliable and it will often cause clients to lose confidence and, in some cases, not to trust us in other ways.

▼▼▼▼▼

We often make promises to our clients without evaluating our ability to honor them. We "think" that we are doing the right thing by promising a quick response or a quick turnaround, but we are really doing a disservice to ourselves and to our clients if we cannot keep that promise.

Many of you have probably heard this definition of integrity—"doing what we say we will do"—and this is very true with our clients. We need to make promises that we know we can keep, and then keep them. This is one of the best ways to not only provide great experiences, but to build great relationships. By managing our clients' expectations, we can take back control over the experience and assume significant control over their perception of our performance.

Building a Client-Centric Law Firm

As we have already mentioned, our goal is and should be to deliver great performance to our clients, not merely good service or even great service. Great performance and great experiences are ways that we can very effectively differentiate ourselves and our law firm, but they require that everything we do be focused on our clients. We need to put ourselves in our clients' shoes with respect to everything we do, everything we say, and every decision we make. This requires that we implement delivery systems within our firm that are focused more on the experience than on the technicalities.

As we discussed earlier in terms of making better use of our support staff in communicating with clients, this is an example of having a delivery system that is focused on the experience. If we fail to timely return telephone calls, then our clients may not have a good experience. However, if we implement a system that assures that they get prompt responses and communications (even if not directly from us), then we enhance the experience. It is very challenging to deliver a consistent quality of experience to our clients without implementing systems to support the entire process. Systems create consistency, and consistency will help us to drive great experiences. By exceeding expectations (which we have managed), we create an environment where our clients can have great experiences and thereby perceive great performance by us and by our law firm.

Before moving on to how delivering great performance can help us create and receive more and better opportunities in the future, we need to spend a little bit more time exploring this concept of building a client-centric firm. Frankly, very few law firms actually talk about or use the term client-centric, yet most law firms would say that clients are their "number one priority." But are we acting according to that belief? Is everything that we do and say focused on our clients? Do we make all of our decisions in terms of what our clients want or think? Do we build our business operation around the client experience? My guess is that our words and actions are falling short of creating a law business that is truly client-centric.

If we want to be totally focused on clients, then we need to find out from our clients what we need to do better and then do it.

If we are truly client focused, then all of our decisions will be made with our "client hats" on, which means that for every decision and even every discussion we should ask ourselves, "What would our clients think?" If we are carrying on discussions or making decisions that we would not want our clients to hear, then we need to rethink those discussions and those decisions. Our discussions, deliberations, and decisions should be an open book (or at least we should be willing to have them open) for our clients. Do we write our time entries and bill our clients with a client hat on or are we solely focused on meeting billable hour requirements and satisfying some standard that has nothing to do with client service or client experiences? We have opportunities every day to put our clients first, but do we?

Do you remember the discussions about features versus benefits? We can also examine client service using these same concepts. Delivering great experiences for our clients is a feature of what we do, and all of the methods, practices, systems, and processes that are part of delivering that great performance are also features. The ultimate benefit for clients is that they are working with a lawyer or a law firm that truly cares about them and their legal or business needs, as well as the benefits that flow from working with a person or firm that is interested in enhancing the client's success, having access to a true trusted advisor, and being able to make better decisions for themselves, their business, and/or their family. Likewise, there are benefits to you and your law firm of delivering great performance and great experiences.

Developing Raving Fans

We have already talked about how delivering great experiences for clients is the means by which you can achieve the goal of securing and retaining more clients, better clients, and more consistent clients. These will all help to enhance your business success, as well as to provide a firmer foundation for the future of your law firm, not only in terms of profits, but in terms of lowering your business risks. One specific benefit of delivering great experiences is that these higher quality clients—clients who have had a great experience—will often become raving fans. In the end, that is your goal . . . to develop, nurture, and retain clients who are raving fans, clients who see the great value that you can deliver, clients who appreciate the value that you add and want to be around you and to work with you, and clients who respect you and value your services and advice.

Most important, we all want and need clients who will enthusiastically and regularly refer new clients to us. Referrals are the future of your law firm business. For nearly every law firm, this is the business truth. It is not advertising, it is not cold-calling, and it is not networking. While all of these may bring business to your law firm, referrals are critical to your business success because they come with little proactive selling effort, the cost of acquiring these new clients is much lower (which enhances profitability), and your success in converting prospects into clients is significantly higher with a referral. There is no

> ▼▼▼▼▼
>
> For any business, including a law firm, your goal is to have "lifetime clients" who refer more high-quality "lifetime" clients to you.

magic to the formula, but the magic is in developing processes, systems, methodologies, and ways of thinking that will allow you to deliver the essential great experiences.

Excited clients are your best sales agents. Yes, that is right, even in the business of law, you want and need sales agents. These are not outside representatives, but clients or others in key relationships who will enthusiastically and consistently refer new business to you. It is well-known in the business world that the cost to acquire a new client is six to nine times higher than to retain an existing client or to secure new business from an existing client. The same cost analysis applies to referrals, since referrals are essentially an extension of your existing clients. If you can consistently deliver great performance, show your clients that you care by giving them a great experience, and make them feel valued, then they will sell for you.

One note: even if you deliver great performance and great experiences, do not assume that your clients will refer people to you without being asked to do so. Remember the numbers that we talked about earlier: For every five people who are willing to make referrals to you, only one (only 20 percent) will do so without being asked. Why? Often it is because they do not think you need referrals. Even more often, they are not sure who to refer to you or they are just too busy to think about it. You need to stay "top of mind" with your clients and key relationships, and you need to consistently ask them for referrals, follow up on referrals, and make it clear that you would like them to "sell" for you. You do not have to use the word sell, but you do have to make it very clear that you want and would appreciate their help in building your business.

One very important caution—under no circumstances should you ever give any indication that you are asking for referrals or asking for help because of challenges in your business or because business is down or slow. People (even your best clients and relationships) will generally refer business only to lawyers and law firms (or any other businesses) that are successful. Making a referral is risky, and we all want to be confident that the work is done right, on time, and that the relationship will not be damaged or harmed in any way as a result of the referral. That means that they must be confident in you and your firm, and confidence flows from success, not challenges.

Some time ago, I was meeting with a partner in a law firm, and he wanted to talk to me about referral strategies. He shared with me a script he had created that he was going to use as the model in contacting clients and others to ask them for referrals. It went something like this:

> As you know, the economy has not been good the last several years. As a result, our business is down. Until this downturn in the economy, we had been growing pretty consistently, but the last couple of years our business has slowed down and we are looking for ways to increase our

> business. Because of this, I want to talk to you about how you might be able to help us to increase our business and to get more clients by referring others to us.

No, no, no! As I told this partner, under no circumstances should he ever say anything to anyone about business being slow or ask for referrals because he "needs" them.

He seemed troubled by this, and he indicated that it was true—that the reason he was asking for referrals was because business was down. We then talked about how referrals are important no matter whether your business is up or down—that referrals are simply good business all of the time. We then came up with a new script that went something like this:

> Like you, we are always looking for ways to grow and improve our business. The best way for us to grow our business is through referrals from our clients, which I am sure is true for your business. I want to talk with you for two reasons: (1) to find out more about what you are working on in your business and to see how I can help you in growing your business; and (2) to make sure you understand all of the ways that we can help clients, to share with you the types of clients and opportunities we are looking for, and to ask for your assistance in introducing us to others who might benefit from our services and how we do business.

The end result is the same in both approaches—asking for referrals—but the message is very different. The difference is in how those messages are perceived by clients, which can prove to be the difference between whether you receive referrals or not.

Remember, referrals are the best and most profitable way for you to grow your law business. Referrals are not just something you pursue when business is down, but something that you develop a system around so that you are creating raving fans and asking for referrals all the time. And always remember that clients will refer others to you because they trust you, they respect you, they value your services and advice, and they are confident and comfortable that you will not damage their relationship with the person or business they refer to you. This means that they need to also be confident in you and your law firm, and they will not be confident if you approach them from the perspective of your business being down and needing help versus wanting to grow and improve your business.

We have already talked several times about the concept of leverage—doing and achieving more with less—and referrals are a perfect example of leverage. Referrals deliver new business to you with little expenditure of time or money on your part. Thus, the investment is low, but the returns are great—a perfect example of leverage. Raving fans sell for you so you do not have to. Raving fans also expand your sphere of influence without you having to invest (and sometimes waste) time and money expanding that sphere of influence on your own time or nickel. Every person in business understands the concept of returns on investment, but we often forget about the returns that we are getting (or not getting) or that we are capable of getting from our relationships, whether with clients or others within our sphere of influence.

Remember, clients do not know what good service looks like, but they do know what a great experience feels like and they know when you have delivered great performance for them and with them (as opposed to them). They do know very well how they feel after they receive the benefit of your great performance and the great experience that you delivered for them and with them. They can understand the benefits once they have experienced them, and these benefits will build your law business on the firmest foundation possible. A foundation of quality clients, lifetime clients, and raving fans will build your law business through the magic of referrals.

The returns that we receive from our relationships are going to be at the heart of our success in the business of law, and it all starts with clients.

For many law firms, the delivery of legal services has become the primary focus of the firm and the lawyers, and the delivery of legal services is often considered the lifeblood of the firm. In reality, it is clients who always have been and always will be the lifeblood of any law firm, and given that truth, we need to build our law firm, our lawyers, and all of our people around the idea that clients come first and that everything we do and say should be focused on our clients' best interests. This is the foundation for a truly client-centric law business, and this is the real path to consistently delivering great experiences and great performance for our clients.

In the final analysis, great performance means showing our clients that we care about them. We can do that in many different ways but it all starts with our clients clearly understanding that we are focused on them, we are committed to them, we are invested in and with them, we are supporting them, and we are truly their "partner" in going forward with whatever representation or assistance we are providing. If we show our clients that we really care about them, we will have clients for life and we will have raving fans who will help us achieve our goals in the future.

23 The Billable Hour Is Not Dead . . . But Should It Be?

This book is not about the "death of the billable hour," and we are not about to undertake an exhaustive examination of billing alternatives. However, it is important to spend a few minutes digging a little deeper into the billable hour (what it is and what it is not) and taking a "different look" at the billable hour going forward. In recent years, many lawyers have stated that the billable hour is "here to stay," but there is really no way to tell its future. Some more senior lawyers can state with confidence that the billable hour is here to stay during their professional career, but we all know that the billable hour is of relatively recent vintage (circa late 1950s), and, frankly, it would be naïve to think that the billable hour's reign is permanent and unchanging. Ultimately, our clients will decide whether the billable hour is here to stay—a decision that will be determined in part by what other lawyers begin to offer clients as alternatives. While the legal marketplace certainly has some unique aspects, it is still a marketplace that will ultimately be driven by the same basic business factors that drive all markets for every product and every service; different, yes, but still essentially a supply-and-demand marketplace.

Whenever a discussion with lawyers turns to the billable hour, I invariably hear comments like, "There are no other viable alternatives," "the other alternatives just won't work," "the billable hour is the only billing method that makes sense for our business," and "legal fees are too unpredictable for anything other than billable hours to work." The reality, however, is that there are alternatives, there are other avenues, and alternative billing arrangements can work and have been proven to work in various practice areas and law firms. They are not necessarily easy or perfect answers, but they are options worth considering, especially if you truly want to be client focused. In examining the law business market, one of the main factors behind the continued strength and viability of the billable hour as the "industry standard" is the current lack of alternatives with other law firms. While certainly the law firms have not banded together to try to create some type of "billable hour monopoly," the fact is that law firms benefit from the fact that most of their competitors continue to rely on the billable hour as the industry standard. Without clear alternatives and options, clients are not yet in the position to push for change as they have in other industries, but the time may come when the alternatives exist, and then every firm is going to have to make a business decision about its course of action.

As we noted earlier, the biggest flaw in the billable hour system is that it is not client focused. Some of you are probably ready to argue that it is client focused—because it allows clients to pay only for the services they need—but the billable hour system really exists for the benefit of the firm. When a client works with a firm under a billable hour system, who bears all of the risks related to the costs of those services? Of course, it is the client. No matter what, the firm continues billing and the client continues paying until the client either runs out of money or runs out of patience, changes lawyers, or there is a resulting fee dispute. Most lawyers argue that the billable hour is necessary to protect the firm from not being able to recover fees for the work that it performs. They cite the unpredictability of lawyers, the law system, and legal matters as reasons that the billable hour is necessary. But think about it. All of those uncertainties and lack of predictability are risks for the client as well, yet the billable hour puts all of that risk on the client. This is another challenge for lawyers in that clients see their lawyers as service providers who are on the clock, rather than as trusted advisors who are there to help them.

You may question this view by clients, but it is very rare indeed that I meet anyone who has dealt with lawyers who does not at some point indicate a concern or frustration with the fact that they are "always on the clock." Clients do not call their lawyers because they do not want to be put "on the clock" for everything, which results in clients making bad or at least uninformed decisions. Lawyers are always frustrated with clients who do not call them first, but the main reason the clients do not call first is because of their fear of that "clock." People are hesitant to call their lawyers in advance because they are not certain of the need (or the value added), and they do not want to be charged until they know they need to be charged. This is the reality in the legal marketplace, and it is a reality that we cannot ignore as we evaluate how we do business and how we serve our clients.

Let's be very clear on one thing when it comes to billing arrangements, and that is that there most certainly are alternatives. The following is one list of alternative billing arrangements that either my law firm used or which I know other law firms are using:

- Flat or Fixed Fees—whether for an entire engagement or for certain parts or aspects of an engagement, a fixed or a flat fee is charged to cover the designated scope of services.
- Contingent Fees—we are most familiar with contingent fees in the personal injury arena, but they can be used in any type of legal matter where the fee is based in whole or in part upon the "success" achieved based on agreed parameters.
- Value Billing—this is where the amount of fees is somehow based on the value received or realized by the client without regard to the amount of hours expended (whether high or low).
- Results Billing—this is similar to value billing, but it really amounts to having the fees determined in whole or in part based on specific and objective results sought and achieved by the client. For example, a certain fee is agreed on if the law firm is able to achieve the result of terminating a client's lease obligations (perhaps within some parameters of the cost to achieve that termination).
- Periodic Retainer Fees—the client pays an agreed amount monthly for either a certain designated range of services (i.e., the lawyer or law firm is available for regular consultations and certain designated services without any time billed on an hourly basis) or the client agrees to pay a certain amount on a periodic basis to cover all work for a client or all work related to a particular matter.
- Fee Caps—these are essentially "not to exceed" amounts either for an entire matter or for particular parts of a matter.

Of course, there are also hybrid fee arrangements that integrate various alternative billing methods as agreed on by the client and the law firm. I will not even begin to try to analyze every conceivable alternative billing arrangement under the applicable codes of professional responsibility; however, there is no code of professional responsibility that I am aware of that in any way per se prohibits alternative billing arrangements. Instead, viability and permissibility are based on facts and circumstances and the applicable standards under each particular code or set of regulations. While lawyers have often told me that one or another alternative billing method is unethical, I have yet to have any lawyer show me that this is true per se for every instance of that proposed alternative billing arrangement.

The purpose of outlining these alternative billing arrangements is to get everyone to understand that there are options and that how we bill for our services is a choice—a business decision—and we need to spend more time evaluating and understanding that as a decision, rather than simply concluding that the billable hour is the only way to do business.

One of the most often-cited objections to alternative billing arrangements is the uncertainty for the law firm in terms of whether or not fees are collected or the amount of fees collected, but every time that I have heard this objection, it is based on looking at each individual matter or representation on an isolated basis. We all know that personal injury lawyers have been using contingent fees for years. While the personal injury lawyers would love to be profitable on every single case, we know that is not the reality and they know that is not realistic. Their goal is to achieve profitability (in fact, to reap great profits) based on their overall success with their caseload. Viewed in isolation, certainly there is a significant risk of not being profitable on a matter if it is handled on some sort of alternative billing arrangement, but the goal is to achieve overall profitability.

One interesting phenomenon is that many of us are already working under either alternative billing arrangements or at least significant limitations that are demanded by our clients. For example, the insurance industry and many general counsel have done an effective job of insisting on greater control over legal fees and related legal costs. One way that they have achieved this control is by insisting on budgets and estimates. They have also been able to use their bargaining power to achieve lower hourly rates and caps, fixed fees, or similar alternatives because they have enough buying power to insist on those concessions. If that is the case, then what is the message to the rest of our clients—we cannot work with you on alternative fee arrangements unless you are a large insurance company or a large client? That is not a client-centered practice.

> ▼▼▼▼▼
>
> What would our clients think, say, and do if they knew that we were giving favorable billing arrangements to certain clients, but not to them because they were too small or, frankly, because they had not asked?

Many trial lawyers tell me that it is "impossible" to use alternative fee arrangements such as fixed fees or retainer fees because of the inherent unpredictability of litigation. While it is unpredictable, we are certainly capable of doing a better and ultimately an effective job of estimating if we break down the representation into smaller pieces. There are always more and different ways to look at the services and the opportunities to implement alternative billing arrangements, but we have to be open to those new ideas and we have to be willing to get outside of our comfort zone to offer them. The bottom line is that fear is the biggest obstacle to implementing alternative fee arrangements. Our fear of not being paid in full for our services again gets back to the dilemma: Are we focused on getting paid for what we do or are we focused on delivering to our clients an outstanding value—a return on their investment? You may not like to look at it that way, but that is ultimately how clients look at it . . . now and in the future.

Another common objection is that clients do not want alternative fee arrangements. I must confess that I find this objection the most difficult to understand. Certainly, clients who are used to the billable hour might be hesitant to undertake an engagement whereby their fees could potentially exceed rate times billable hours, and these are the types of clients who are interested only in having a one-sided arrangement. In other words, they are very happy to have the fees be lower than the standard hourly rate, but they are not (without being better educated) willing to have the fees be potentially higher than standard rates times hours. This is obviously not acceptable, since these alternative fee arrangements are intended to spread the risk between the law firm and the clients, not to put all of the risks on one side or the other. The reality is that straight hourly billing puts all of the risk on the client and very little risk on the law firm. That is also one-sided, which is a reality we need to consider as we evaluate our fee arrangements and interact and communicate with clients.

Once clients are educated, the quality clients (the types of clients you want and need for your business) will come to understand the benefit of an alternative fee arrangement that balances the risk between client and law firm. If you really believe that clients do not want alternative fee arrangements, I challenge you to find a client who is excited about being charged by the hour, no matter what the work is, no matter how much time it takes, no matter how much time is wasted, and no matter how much value (or lack thereof) is delivered with those services.

The billable hour may not be dead, but at least it is or should be under the microscope. We need to understand and see how the billable hour is not client focused, and we need to at least analyze our billing arrangements in order to make good and well-informed decisions about how we are going to proceed. This is not a black-and-white issue, but like much of the law, it is certainly a gray issue, and the time may come when we do not have a choice but to pursue alternative fee arrangements. Ultimately, it is up to you and your law firm to decide whether you are going to "stand pat" because that is the way you have always done it, or whether you are at least open to looking carefully at billing alternative fee arrangements in order to not only make what you believe to be good business decisions for your firm and your clients, but to be in a position to coherently and persuasively educate your clients as to why your fee arrangements are what they are. As we said at the outset, the biggest objection that clients have to legal fees is the uncertainty, and it is our obligation as professionals, as advisors, and as a profession to make every effort to inform, educate, and communicate with our clients on this often difficult topic.

PART IV

Building Relationships to Success

24 Stop Selling and Start Building!

Let's get one thing straight from the beginning: With the exception of practices driven by traditional advertising *the key to sales and marketing for lawyers and law firms is building relationships.* Lawyers may have different opinions about the business of law, but I have yet to find a lawyer who will challenge this fundamental concept. In fact, most lawyers will not only acknowledge this truism, but will use it to justify their failure or refusal to make or implement various business decisions relating to their law business. Lawyers everywhere are saying (either to the world or to themselves) that their business is "all about relationships." With all of this agreement that relationships are the heart and soul of a lawyer's practice, you would think that every lawyer would be thriving and flourishing with relationships as the foundation. Unfortunately, this is not the case because too many of us fail to understand that relationships do not just happen, but must be developed, built, nurtured, and supported in many ways.

Not only do we sit back and wait for relationships to happen and/or act as if their existence and quality is outside of our control, but many of us do not even know what to do or how to do it when it comes to relationship building. Too often, we fall into the trap of thinking that relationship building is akin to "country club marketing"—we play golf, they like us, and they hire us. In today's business and legal marketplace, "country club marketing" does not work anymore (or at least, it does not work as easily or as often as it may have worked in the past). Clients (i.e., buyers and consumers of legal services) may not be more sophisticated in legal matters, but they are more sophisticated in how they buy these services, what they are looking for, and what their expectations are—not only in the beginning but throughout the representation. Unfortunately, the idea of *hoping* to build relationships by meeting a lot of people and *hoping* that at least a couple of them will like us and pick up the phone and call us when they need us is neither a consistent nor reliable way of building a business, legal or otherwise. Instead, we need to better understand what relationship building is all about, what the steps and processes are, what clients and prospective clients are looking for, and all of the other details relating to the "science" of relationship building.

Yes, relationship building is and will always be an art in many ways, but there are scientific and systematic aspects of relationship building we can learn, understand, and implement that will expand our relationship-building opportunities, accelerate the relationship-building process, and ultimately deliver more and better-quality relationships. Remember, we are selling the invisible (professional services), and any business selling invisible services must become an expert at relationship building, must be effective at relationship building, and must be productive at nurturing those relationships and turning those relationships into new business, ongoing business, and referral business. For all of these reasons, relationship building is truly the path to success in building a great law business.

Nearly every lawyer knows (or at least says) that relationships are the key to acquiring clients, keeping clients, and growing their law business, but in practice few lawyers are focused on building relationships and doing the things they must in order to build them. In part, this is because we are not always sure what we need to do to build relationships, and we mistakenly believe that they will just happen if we are nice guys, nice women, or good professionals. In reality, building relationships has nothing whatsoever to do (at least not directly) with legal services or the quality of our legal skills. Relationship building requires committing to the success of other people, as well as developing systems to help us to achieve the desired relationships. In the end, relationship selling has nothing to do with selling, but everything to do with delivering results for other people. The key ingredient is obvious—it is about giving, being selfless, looking for opportunities to help others in whatever way we can help them, and focusing on others throughout our business day. Ultimately, that is the path to great relationships that will in turn build your law practice into a great law business.

When we talk about looking out for others' success, it comes down to the fundamental principle that we need to be passionate (yes, there is such a thing as passion in business) about our clients' success. Notice, I did not say our own success or the success of our law firm, but passionate about the success and results achieved by our clients. I am not suggesting that we need to sacrifice ourselves personally and professionally for our clients, but that we need to put our clients' true interests, needs, and goals at the top of our priority list. We all have a "to-do" list, but how many of us include on that list efforts to help our clients beyond just doing the "legal stuff" that they need to have done. How many of us are asking our clients about what is going on in their lives or businesses, what challenges and opportunities they have, what they are looking to accomplish, what they need help with, and how we can be an integral part of their path to success? This is what separates mere lawyers from trusted advisors.

> We need to be passionate about our clients' success, our clients' opportunities, and our clients' legal matters. It is not always about winning or losing, but it is about making sure that our clients' interests come first.

The importance of relationships is never lost on us as lawyers, and we all "talk the talk" about how vital relationships are to our business. Unfortunately, many of us are not "walking the talk" when it comes to relationships. Instead of developing and nurturing them, we have been waiting for them to happen, and that will not work. This should not be a surprise to any of us, since it is about *building* relationships—it is not about *finding* relationships. Relationships do not just happen. In fact, developing relationships is much like farming. We must plant seeds, nurture them, "water" them, and ultimately harvest them. But many of us do not "plant the seeds" for building relationships because it is just a little bit scary.

It is scary because the relationship building sometimes requires us to get outside our comfort zone. It is also scary because relationships require us to focus on things outside of our legal skills and experience. They require us to focus on people rather than services, and that can be scary. We also know that you cannot simply throw seeds into the ground and expect a bountiful harvest. You need to spend time making sure that the soil is ready for the seeds. Once planted, you need to water and nurture the crop, keeping it free from weeds (i.e., "D" clients) to allow the crop to flourish. In short, a successful crop requires constant attention and nurturing.

The exact same thing is required in relationship building. You must always remember that relationships do not happen overnight, which means that we are always investing for the long haul. We also need to remember that we must always give before we can expect to receive. That giving may take various forms, and certainly is not limited to giving referrals (although referrals are a great way to build and enhance relationships and generate return referrals), but we certainly must come to the relationship table with a giving attitude, a selfless approach, and a genuine interest in helping others achieve their goals. Quite simply, that is the heart and soul of relationship building in any business or profession. Most of the rest of this book will focus on skills, strategies, tactics, systems, and processes (as well as ways of thinking) that will allow you and your firm to become not just legal experts, but relationship-building experts. And remember this—great legal skills might pay the bills, but great relationship-building skills will grow and build your law business.

No Time Like the Present 25

When it comes to training associates in business development and marketing skills, there is *no time like the present!* In fact, yesterday would have been even better, but yesterday is gone, today is here, and it is time to get all of your associates thinking and acting like rainmakers. Instead of waiting until associates become (or are on the eve of becoming) partners to begin working with them on business development, we should begin training associates pretty much on day one of their employment. The results will be monumental for everyone. Great companies realize that every single employee will have a positive or negative impact on the company's sales efforts (which includes client service), and they build a sales culture throughout the organization. Not only do they talk about sales, but they train every person in sales, from the top executive to the sales manager, to the top sales producer, to the newest sales producer, to the worker on the shop floor, to the secretary, to the receptionist, and, yes, even to the janitor. Why? Because every person impacts sales by how they think, how they act, and how they interact with each other. It is vital to understand that creating a sales culture—where everyone is a part of the sales effort—is what separates great businesses from good, mediocre, and lousy businesses. The same applies to law firms, especially with respect to associates and business development training.

Great businesses recognize that every employee is a part of the sales effort.

Unfortunately, the standard associate model for law firms usually goes something like this:

- Work hard
- Learn to be a good lawyer

- Work harder
- Worry about clients and business development later

If you ask the management of most firms, they will tell you that this is their philosophy on associates and business development. They will not deny it. In fact, they will give you a list of reasons why this is a good approach with associates. They will tell you that associates have enough to worry about learning to be lawyers and that they do not have time to learn about how to get clients. They will tell you that most new associates have so much to learn about the practice of law, dealing with clients, dealing with partners, dealing with long work hours, learning the substantive law, learning the legal system, and so on, that it would be too much to expect associates to learn about business development at the same time. That is a recipe for mediocrity.

Many years ago I was teaching a business development workshop for a firm of about forty lawyers. Partners and associates were present, but at the end of the workshop the managing partner at the firm stood up and said something to this effect:

> For the associates who are here, I don't want you to worry too much about this presentation or business development. We hesitated to include you, but we decided to do so just so that you could start to hear a little bit about the topic. However, we do not expect you to do much in the area of business development. For now, we want you to focus on becoming good lawyers.

This is not an unusual approach—in fact, this is a fairly standard philosophy in many firms, but it has many shortcomings.

First, most associates *want* to learn about business development. Yes, there are associates who are not interested in business development, especially in their early years, however, my experience has shown that the associates who do not have an interest in it at all are the same lawyers who are not interested in it as senior associates or even as partners. Many associates want to start working on business development early in their careers, and would love to receive the training and support to begin that process. They know that, ultimately, the firm will expect them to play some role in business development and that success will depend (to some degree) on their ability to bring in new business. These associates can see their future and want help now with the skills, training, and mentoring that will allow them to achieve business development success as early as possible.

When your firm intentionally excludes associates from business development training, you are telling those associates that you do not expect them to be marketers. You may think that the message is that you do not need them to be marketers *now,* but the message to the associates is much broader. Associates can logically conclude that if the firm really wanted them to become rainmakers, it would be training them as soon as possible, rather than waiting. Even if there is no misunderstanding about the firm's long-term expectations for its associates, associates can naturally feel ignored or left behind. If the firm is not providing the training and support that associates want, then the firm has created a breeding ground for dissatisfied and disappointed associates. As you can guess, unhappy associates (especially those who feel a disconnect between their interests and the firm's interests) will likely leave the firm, costing the firm hundreds of thousands of dollars.

Second, this approach most often assures that the associates will be significantly delayed on their path to becoming rainmakers and that the firm's business development results will be seriously delayed and diminished. Let's start by considering a basic business question. You know that certain activities are designed to deliver (and are likely to deliver) sales for your business. You also know that these activities often require some period of time before they deliver the hoped for results. You also know that the desired activities (for most people) take or require some training and "practice" in order to deliver the desired results. Knowing all of this, do you (A) immediately implement appropriate training and support for your people as they begin engaging in these desired activities, or (B) withhold training, instruct your people to do nothing, and wait for a number of years before taking any action regarding these desired activities? Ding, ding, ding! The correct answer of course is A—immediately begin training and implementation. But most firms choose to wait, to delay training, to delay implementation, and, ultimately, to delay results, usually in the name of waiting until the associates have learned to be "good" lawyers.

It does not take an advanced degree to recognize that delaying the training and implementation necessarily will delay the results. In fact, there is a compelling argument that the results not only will be delayed, but will be exponentially reduced over time. Let's consider a hypothetical (but perhaps real world) example. Assume that the partnership track is ten years for an associate. We will also assume that associates spend their first three to four years learning to become "good" lawyers. So, in year five they finally receive some business development training, and we will even assume that they immediately start practicing their business development skills. However, we all know that business development

▼▼▼▼▼

The reality in today's legal market is that highly valued lawyers are those who are also good business developers. While there is still a place for the pure producer/technician, economic realities make business development a vital ingredient in the mix of a lawyer's professional skills.

results are often not immediate, especially for newer lawyers. While there are those rare occasions when the results flow quickly, rainmaking and business development skills take time to develop and relationship building takes time, especially if you are starting from scratch.

Therefore, even the best associate (one who started his or her business development activities in the fourth year) will typically see some progress in the first three years of working at business development (years four, five, and six), which should accelerate in the next three years (years seven, eight, and nine). However, even a normally progressing associate will typically take six to nine years to really become a productive rainmaker and then, hopefully, the results will continue to grow and expand over time. With this "traditional" training and business development model, associates typically will not start to become productive business developers until they are in years ten through twelve of their practice. Assuming that they are effective at business development, and further assuming that they practice for an average of thirty years, they will have fifteen to twenty years of productive business development time. That certainly seems like a good number of years, but let's consider the alternative training model.

Instead of waiting three or four years to even begin the training process, assume that associates begin some form of business development training and practice in their first year. Assuming the same timelines, this would mean that associates would begin to become productive business developers in years seven to nine (before they are considered for partnership—a critical timing issue). It will also add three to five years to their productive business development years overall. This may seem like a small difference, but since the expectation is that business development will improve over time, the inevitable conclusion is that business development opportunities and results will be lost forever for every year (or even month) that the training, support, and activities are delayed.

Putting it simply, the "traditional" model, which delays business development training for associates for several years no longer fits the realities of the legal marketplace. Today, consumers of legal services are more sophisticated and competition is greater, and these realities place even greater importance on business development training and support. In today's competitive legal environment, there is no good reason to intentionally delay associates from beginning to work on business development and there are many great reasons for them to begin immediately.

▼▼▼▼▼

While law firms are certainly well intentioned and do intend to get associates involved in business development after they have become "good" lawyers, the reality is often that the training never comes.

Finally, many firms that delay business development training never get around to providing that promised training and support, which leaves the associates unprepared and untrained for the responsibilities that will later be expected of them. In many firms there is no associate business development training program for any level of associate, which means that associates will tend to pass unnoticed from their third to their fourth to their fifth to their sixth to their seventh year without any training program or mentoring system and without any guidance to help them get started. The result is that you end up with senior associates with little or no business development training or results, yet the firm is disappointed that the associates are not bringing in more business. Why? Because the associates were never shown what to do, how to do it, when to do it, or even why to do it. Partners are busy with their own legal work and business development efforts, and they rarely will invest the time to teach the associates what they know about business development.

Another shortcoming of delaying the process is that it is unfair. In nearly every firm, some value will be given to business development roles when it comes to consideration for partnership. While there will certainly be some lawyers who achieve partnership without any clients or business development skills, those numbers are dwindling every year. Law firms are looking for lawyers who contribute to the success of the firm in many different ways, and no one can dispute that a lawyer who is not only good, but also brings in clients, has greater value. To create a structure that assures that most associates will not have achieved significant business development success before they are up for election to the partnership is not fair to the associates and, ultimately, hurts the business of the firm.

I have spoken to many partners responsible for business development who express frustration that their associates are not bringing in more business. Typically, when I ask about their associate business development training, I will be told "We don't really have a formalized program." The world of law firms and business development has changed, and most associates do not know what to do. Associates often tell me that they want to work on business development, but they do not know what to do and no one is showing them.

The reality is that business development for lawyers must be learned. There are various activities (which we will talk about in later chapters) that are designed to create business development results for lawyers, but most lawyers do not know what they are. The result is that associates (and even partners who never received training or mentoring) are engaging in what they believe to be business development efforts, but they are really just wasting their time. Taking your friends to ball games or to dinner is not business development. Having lunch with the same three people four or five times each year is not business development. Business development for most lawyers is a learned skill, which includes learning the right activities, developing a system of business development activities, learning how to conduct those activities, and preferably, being supported and mentored in those efforts. There are very few born rainmakers in any profession, and this is particularly true in the business of law.

If you want to grow and improve your law business, you need to grow and build rainmakers. This requires a formalized training program, a formalized mentoring program, and a system to support the firm's business development activities, including associates. These are essential ingredients for creating a law firm that runs and grows like a business and that has and maintains long-term stability for everyone.

What Should I Do Today? 26

Deciding what to do each day to develop business seems like a simple matter, but most law firms are ignoring it or overlooking it as they go about the business of law. Even lawyers who want to be rainmakers often have a hard time following through and actually doing what they would like to do . . . and what they need to do. One of the biggest reasons for falling short (or not even beginning) is the absence of a personal business development plan. Too many lawyers rely on hope as their business development strategy, but it rarely produces significant results. Lawyers were not trained in how to build relationships, and, unfortunately, the lawyers in the firm who have had success in building relationships and generating new business did it the "old-fashioned way" (which no longer applies). They do it without knowing why it works or are too busy to pass along their success secrets to others. The client profiles and target markets discussed in Chapters 18 and 19 must be an integral part of your marketing plan, including the what, when, and why of each lawyer's business development activities. This chapter takes a close look at the "how tos" for lawyers looking to begin (or expand) the journey to becoming rainmakers.

▼▼▼▼▼

To succeed in business development, most lawyers need a plan—a plan for what they are going to do and why they are going to do it.

Before we talk about some of the "how-tos," we need to talk about relationship-building tools. Many of these tools are about your mindset, and it starts with understanding that nothing we do is about "closing a sale"—it is all about beginning a relationship. The key word is "beginning," which means that we need to focus on beginning and building relationships, rather than hoping for, pursuing, or expecting immediate sales. Statistics show that over 90 percent of the people who we talk to do not have (in their mind) a perceived need for our services when we are speaking to them. Therefore, it is unreasonable and unrealistic to expect an immediate sale (i.e., a new client) upon meeting a new person or shortly after meeting a new person. I am not suggesting that we need to wait forever—that is another problem that we suffer from as lawyers in that we always say that these things "take time"—but we need to be more realistic in our expectations.

Many people already have a lawyer, but they may not have the right lawyer and they may not have a particular need for our particular niche. But we need to make sure that they know who we are, that they remember us, and that they remember what we do (or what differentiates us) when and if the need arises. In fact, if we do a really terrific job of relationship building, that process will serve to differentiate us, and people will actively seek us out to be their legal counsel because we are different . . . a difference that comes from demonstrating a commitment to their success.

Another key point in relationship building is that you must monitor your own efforts in a formalized manner. Not only must you have a plan, but you need to be accountable to yourself (and to others) by developing a system to continually monitor your relationship-building efforts. Contrary to popular belief (that relationships are based on just getting to know people and finding people who like you—although finding people who like you is an important element), building relationships is much more science than it is art. It is about having a system and a process to help you do what you know you need to do, to communicate your interest in your clients, and to show your clients in tangible ways that you are committed to them. In the famous book series titled *Don't Sweat the Small Stuff* (Hyperion 1997) the overall theme is that the "small stuff" (that we are sweating over) often distracts us from what is important in life, but in building relationships it absolutely is the "small stuff" that makes the difference, that gets people's attention, and that demonstrates a tangible difference between us and everyone else.

We will be exploring how building credibility and trust occurs when we embark on a formal and accelerated process of relationship building. However, the foundation of all of those efforts, of all of our plans and of all of our activities, is a sincere desire to help others succeed, not a focus on helping ourselves. It has been said that there are six reasons to build relationships:

1. To make friends;
2. To help friends achieve their goals;
3. To help friends save or make money;
4. To help friends create new clients;
5. To help friends add value to their customers and clients; and
6. To be perceived as a valued resource.

These cover a pretty wide range of thinking and activities, but *none of them* mention you or your business. They are all about the other person, the client, or the prospect. They are all about being unselfish and totally committed to and passionate about helping others to be more successful.

As we mentioned earlier, an individual and firm business development plan is vital to being effective and successful. You must have a plan for what you are going to do, and most important, why you are going to do it. Your plan not only needs to be specific, but it needs to answer these fundamental questions:

- What are you going to do?
- When are you going to do it?
- *Why* are you going to do it?

Contrary to popular belief, you cannot market by accident. In fact, marketing by accident is essentially an oxymoron.

Marketing suggests a plan, a goal, and a strategy, while accidents are just that—luck—and things that might keep you afloat, but will not build your business. Like Justice Potter Stewart in the Supreme Court decision regarding pornography, many lawyers think that they will know a client or a prospect "when they see it," but by then it is too late. Instead, we need to decide what types of clients we want, know where they are likely to come from, and target our activities in a way that is most likely to achieve success in building relationships, referral sources, and new client prospects from our targeted pond.

We talked earlier about making decisions and doing research on the question of target markets, niches, and specialty areas, but it is also vital that our personal and firm marketing plans track the results of that research. There are many lawyers who feel that creating a personal marketing plan is a waste of time and, frankly, that is a cop out. Lawyers do not like to create personal marketing plans because they are outside of their comfort zone. Lawyers are not used to being thought of (or thinking of themselves) as salespeople, and creating a personal marketing plan means that they are now salespeople. These are dirty words to many lawyers. The fact is that creating your own personal marketing plan (even if driven by the firm) is in your best interest. The only true path to success, stability, and security is to be a rainmaker and to have your own "book of business." This does not mean that lawyers should build their own "books" in order to be able to leave the firm, but only that security no longer exists by simply being a good lawyer. Instead, security comes from being a good lawyer who has clients. That is the business reality for lawyers today and in the future.

One of the main reasons for having a firm and a personal business development plan is, as we discussed earlier, to create accountability—accountability to yourself and, ideally, to others in the firm—because that is what will drive you to follow through on your plan. Without a plan that holds you accountable, you are likely to do what most of us do—invest in new business development efforts only when you have free time, and most of those efforts will be misdirected because, when you find a "free moment," you will do what is easiest, rather than what is most important. We will always have pressure to deliver legal services, whether that pressure is imposed by our firm or our clients. A written plan means that we can pull it out and quickly and easily determine what we need to do next, what is most important, and how to go about those next steps.

▼▼▼▼▼

The reality is that we will almost always have only a small percentage of our time available for business development efforts, which means we need to make business development easy. Having a plan makes it easy.

Without a written business development plan, we will most likely look at that stack of legal work on our desk and do it first. First, it is our comfort zone. Second, we know exactly what to do. Third, if we have to think about business development, we are less likely to do it. That is why it is so vital to have a process and a system, including a written business development plan.

How detailed should your business development plan be? The more detailed the better. Not only should it include activities and targets, but it should include goals. I have worked with many lawyers, all of whom seem to have a different driver or "hot button" when it comes to what motivates them to actually undertake business development activities. The key is to find a plan, a system, or a process that works for you—one that you will actually use because you are most comfortable with it. In Appendix B you will find an example of some worksheets that I have used with lawyers to help to determine their level of interest in certain business development activities, assess past business development activities, target future activities, and track business development activities. As you will see, these worksheets will help you to figure out what you like to do or want to do, what you are most comfortable doing, and what you see as most valuable. You can then use that information to develop goals and a plan for achieving those goals. Appendix C contains worksheets that you can use to develop plans and goals for your business development activities.

We cannot overestimate the value and importance of having a written business development plan. It does not have to be lengthy or complicated, but it must be in writing. We have all been sitting at our desks knowing that we need to work on business development, but without a written plan we will not know what to do or when to do it. All of those piles of legal work (our comfort zone) will be staring us in the face and nearly all of us will reach for the "billable hours" before we pick up the phone and call a client, a referral source, or a key contact. In so many ways, business development is like the Nike slogan—"Just Do It." If we would just pick up the phone or walk out the door and start doing the things that we know we need to do to build relationships and our client base, we would achieve the success we seek. But we are busy. We are afraid. It is outside our comfort zone. In short, we do not know (or have not planned) what we need to do right now, at this moment, to help grow our law business. A business development plan is precisely the map that we all need to achieve greater success in building our law businesses.

One critical element of our business development plan is the ability to understand who our clients are (or who we want them to be) by asking these questions:

- Where do they go?
- Whom do they spend time with?
- What organizations do they belong to?
- What do they read?
- Whom do they do business with?

The answers to these key questions will guide and frame our business development activities.

Many of us in the practice of law fall into two categories when it comes to business development:

1. "I hope" that new clients will come to me; or
2. "Here I am"—we spend (or waste) our time being out in front of people, meeting lots of people, talking to lots of people, but never with a plan, a focus, a mission, a goal, or even any idea of what we really need to do to build relationships and to get more and better clients.

Make no mistake—some activity is better than no activity, but strategic activity is going to be the path to generating more and better clients. This means that you need to have some niches and you need to engage in activities that are most likely to work in the ponds that are stocked with the right prospects.

This demonstrates one of the great values of niches or specialties. With a niche or a specialty (or even a target industry), you can take your limited time and focus it on understanding the needs, interests, and goals of clients within your niche, specialty, or target market. By definition, it is almost impossible to have that type of knowledge with respect to all companies, all prospective clients, or any overly broad category of clients or prospects. For example, if your target market is small business owners, you could join

▼▼▼▼▼

The narrower your focus, the greater your ability will be to get involved with those clients, to understand their industries, to become part of their organizations, to support their goals and issues, and to become knowledgeable about their businesses so that you will become a value-added advisor who can help them in their business.

the local chamber of commerce. There could be hundreds of small business owners in that chamber, but how many dozens of lawyers? It is simply too broad.

One topic noted above—whom prospective clients do business with—is one of the most overlooked opportunities for new clients. Rather than starting from scratch, figure out whom your target clients already do business with and invest your limited time and resources in sales efforts directed to those people, companies, or industries that already do business with your targeted prospects. This allows you to achieve the ultimate goal of leverage (achieving more with less) in your business development efforts. This is, again, fishing in the stocked pond, where you know the fish that are likely to be there and you are ready with the right message (or bait) that will help you catch more and bigger fish today, rather than hoping for something that may never come by fishing in some undetermined, unspecified, and untargeted pond.

Not only must we have a plan, but we must also have goals. Goal setting is critical for not only the firm, but for the individual lawyers, and this is particularly true for business development efforts. It is very important for the firm and every single lawyer to set business development goals. Without goals, we generally fail to achieve. That is a fact of business life that applies to lawyers and law firms, just as it applies to other businesses. Part of this process also involves determining what goals you are going to set and thus what you are going to measure. For me, the most important measurement in business development terms is dollars collected. This may seem obvious, but most firms tend to measure dollars billed, rather than dollars collected. Some lawyers believe that collection is not their problem, but the goal of the firm is new revenue, and it does not become revenue until it is billed *and* collected. You want to create an environment where everyone (including the lawyer) feels responsible and accountable for collections—not only collections, but timely collections.

With that said, each lawyer should be setting goals for dollars collected, and they should be split between new clients and existing clients. It is not evil or unethical to aspire and seek to enhance your business from existing clients. In fact, for every business existing clients are the best and most profitable source of new business, either with those existing clients or with referrals from them. We all know that existing clients are the best source of new business, but are we asking our existing clients for referrals on a regular and consistent basis? In the final analysis, new clients and new business from existing clients are both important, and both should be measured against reasonable goals.

▼▼▼▼▼

The cost to secure more business from an existing client is significantly less than the cost to acquire a new client, yet very few lawyers set goals for and measure new client business versus existing client business.

Perhaps even more important than goal setting and measuring with respect to revenues is goal setting and measuring business development activities. The biggest (and most often missed) reality for professionals is that activities drive results. Results do not just happen, but they occur *from* the activities pursued. Let me explain that further. While goal setting is important, lawyers and other professionals often set goals but never invest a minute of time in figuring out what they are going to do in order to achieve them. As you might guess, typically these goals are not achieved. In fact, activities are so critical that law firms should measure their lawyers' business development efforts as much from their success in implementing the efforts (in quantity, quality, and nature) as from the results.

If a lawyer sets out a plan of activities that *should* deliver the desired results, and the lawyer achieves the desired objectives for the activities, then it is reasonable to assume that the results should follow. If the results do not follow, then certainly some time and attention should be spent in figuring out whether the activities should be changed or whether perhaps the lawyer's skills in implementing the activities need to be improved. But, the activities need to be measured much more than the results. We do not control the results, but we do control the activities. Without a plan for the activities, most of us are unlikely to achieve the desired results when it comes to dollars.

Let us consider an example. Assume that a lawyer in 2005 generated $200,000 in collected fees. We then assume that this lawyer set a goal for 2006 of $250,000 in collected fees. If the lawyer does not develop some plan and system for the activities he or she is going to engage in to achieve the dollar goal, then the lawyer's success in achieving the dollar goal will mostly be based on pure luck. If the dollar goal is achieved, then the lawyer was lucky. If the dollar goal is not achieved, then the lawyer did a bad job. But without knowing which activities will support the achievement of the dollar goal, there is no way to really judge the lawyer's efforts.

Yes, the results are objective and measurable, but they tell us nothing about what the lawyer did or did not do, what the lawyer did well or did not do well, or what the lawyer can or should do better or different in the future. There is no opportunity whatsoever to learn if everyone is measured based on just the end result, rather than the activities. This is such a vital piece in achieving consistent and desired business development results, yet very few firms or lawyers are doing it. They set goals, but they never figure out what they need to do to achieve them. As a result, they often fail.

Now, let us consider an example of activity goals, rather than goals involving end results or fees collected. My goal may be to increase fees collected by $50,000, but my activity goals may be the following:

- Talking to my existing clients at least once every 90 days
- Meeting with existing referral sources at least once a quarter
- Having at least two meetings with referral sources every week
- Writing at least three articles during the year
- Giving at least three speeches during the year
- Attending at least two business networking events every month.

These are activity goals that can be measured (you either did them or you did not) and then you can compare your activities with your results, and make the necessary adjustments *in your activities,* because it is the activities that you control, not the end results. While we are talking about activities, we also need to talk about what are real and what are not real business development efforts.

On this topic, we need to make one thing perfectly clear at the outset—business development is *not* about meeting people. It *is* about building credibility, trust, and *relationships!* All too often professionals of all types confuse activity (simply meeting lots of people) with productivity (building relationships that will drive new business). Not only are the results different, but the skills and tactics are totally different . . . and these differences are dramatic in terms of the results that you can expect to achieve.

Appendix B: Business Development Activities Worksheets

Business Development Activities

Below is a list of business development activities for you to consider and rank in order of importance (your perceived value) and interest. Please make sure to rank importance and interest without regard to each other.

Business Development Activity	Importance Ranking	Interest Ranking
Networking Group		
Existing Client "Touch" Calls		
Quarterly Meetings w/ Existing Clients		
Firm Newsletter		
Writing		
Speaking		
Referral Source Meetings		
Referral Source Calls		
Networking Events		
Attending Non-Law Seminars		
Joining Civic Groups (e.g., chambers, Rotary, Kiwanis)		
Joining Nonprofit Associations		
Joining Business Associations (e.g., trade associations)		

Personal Business Development Activities

What personal business development activities have you engaged in during the past six months? What worked and what did not work?

- Be specific.
- For each personal business development activity, briefly list your view of the results.

Firm Business Development Activities

What business activities has your firm engaged in during the past six months? What worked and what did not work?

- Be specific.
- For each firm business development activity, briefly list your view of the results.

New Personal Business Development Activities

What personal business development activities would you like to engage in over the next six months? Why?

- Be specific.
- For each business development activity, briefly list why you want to do it.

New Firm Business Development Activities

What business development activities would you like to see the firm engage in over the next six months? Why?

- Be specific.
- For each firm business development activity, briefly list why you want the firm to do it.

Appendix C: Business Development Planning and Goals Worksheets

Personal Business Development Goals

During the next six months I *intend* to engage in the following personal business development and marketing activities.

Activity (be specific)	**Goal** (objective & measurable)	**Timetable** (specific date for achieving goal)

Firm Business Development Activities

During the next six months the firm should *commit* to engage in the following firm business development and marketing activities.

Activity (be specific)	Goal (objective & measurable)	Timetable (specific date for achieving goal)

Business Development Planning Sheet

(Use one planning sheet for each business development activity.)

ACTIVITY:	
STEPS	**DEADLINE**

GOAL: ____

____

DEADLINE: ____

____

Stop Wasting Your Money 27

For most law firms, traditional advertising exists solely (and admittedly) as a means of branding or "keeping their name out there" (or at least they think so). Unfortunately, few firms have the financial resources to truly brand themselves and, therefore, I encourage you to stop wasting your money on advertising that is not likely to bring you new business or effectively brand you. At a minimum, we need to at least recognize what our advertising and traditional marketing efforts are *and what they are not,* rather than placing false hope in advertising as a means to grow and enhance our law business. Not only is most law firm advertising ineffective, but it can actually serve as a distraction from the types of business development activities that are most likely to deliver your desired results. You need to face the fact that so-called branding advertising and marketing will not bring you new clients, and it is new clients that will help you build your business.

Whenever a law firm tells me that they are "beefing up" or "stepping up" their marketing efforts, I am usually pretty confident that that is all it is—marketing—and that they are probably not doing the things that are likely to secure them more clients, better clients, or more business from existing clients. When I inquire further, I usually hear stories about new or additional advertising campaigns, increased sponsorships of events or causes, or new written marketing materials (we will talk more about marketing materials later in this chapter). None of these are about business development (and new clients)—they are only about keeping your name "out there." While branding does have its place, the financial and business reality is that few law firms can effectively brand themselves.

The main reason is that law firms (and even most businesses) do not have the dollars needed to brand themselves. Coca-Cola brands itself. Pepsi brands itself. Walt Disney brands itself. Wal-Mart brands itself. These and many other large companies do invest in branding, and it is effective, but the dollars required for effective branding are beyond the capabilities of most law firms and even most businesses. In fact, traditional branding for larger companies is much more than just "getting your name out there," since they expect to achieve increased business as a result of these marketing and advertising campaigns. When Pepsi invests hundreds of millions of dollars in a new advertising campaign, it absolutely expects that its sales will increase, especially relative to its competitors.

There are really two essential elements of branding: (1) a clear, compelling, and attention-getting message; and (2) repetition. Repetition costs money—big money. And, most law firms do not have the resources to undertake an effective branding campaign. Running an occasional (or even monthly) quarter-page or even full-page ad in a local business magazine is not going to brand your firm. It is certainly not going to have enough of an effect to cause people and prospective clients to seek you out because they recognize your name. With all due respect to these publications, they are "selling" the concept of branding, but law firms are not likely to reap the desired results from their investment. There are just not enough dollars available for the firm to achieve client or prospective client recognition.

Another "investment" by law firms is in sponsoring events. While this certainly demonstrates a commitment to various community or charitable causes, these decisions should be based on the decision to be involved, to help, and to support, not on the theory that putting your name on a charitable cause or event will bring you new clients. For most law firms, new clients come from one-on-one relationships. They are based on people, not advertising campaigns. Certainly, there are some law businesses that develop new clients from traditional advertising, but most of these have a unique practice and their advertising is focused on getting more clients, not on branding.

This distinction is critical in evaluating the value and effectiveness of advertising or marketing. Does it produce results in the form of more clients or additional business? Actually, the question is better stated as, "Is it *intended* to produce more clients or additional business?" If it is, then it can legitimately be considered a business development effort, and it can be pursued in an effort to test and measure whether it is effective at achieving the intended results. As

▼▼▼▼▼

If advertising is not intended to garner more clients or more business, then it is essentially branding and it should be recognized as such.

you can gather from the foregoing, I am not a big fan of law firm advertising, unless it is intended to secure more clients. If a law firm really wants to invest its limited time and dollars in traditional advertising in the "hope" of achieving branding or name recognition, then obviously it can do so, but it should do so with its eyes wide open.

For most law firms, advertising will not produce new, better, or different results. It is not intended to produce those new, different, or better results, and it should be limited or even eliminated. For most firms, new clients will come because they heard about you from someone else, whether it is another lawyer, another client, or someone who has heard about you from a lawyer or another client. That is the fact of business life for law firms, and our business development efforts should be directed to those areas that offer the best opportunities for new client development.

I also want to discuss marketing materials. First and foremost, written marketing materials are *not* a part of business development. While they may be a necessary "evil" in that most of us need to have some sort of written marketing materials (and they may require some level of investment to achieve a desired perception on those who receive them), they probably will not bring in new clients, probably will not bring in new business, and probably will not increase business from existing clients. Whether it is a new firm brochure, professional bios, pamphlets, a Web site, or anything else that is passive in nature and not one-on-one, in most cases marketing materials are a distraction. They may be necessary, but they are a distraction because lawyers start believing that marketing materials will bring in new clients, better clients, or more business from existing clients, and they do not engage in the personal relationship activities that are necessary to achieve more business for their firm. At best, written marketing materials and a Web presence are tools and resources to *support* individual business development efforts. They are nothing more. They are tools to help develop and grow business through other means.

For example, when I stated earlier that a brochure will not attract new business from an existing client, I am sure that some of you immediately thought I was totally wrong. I have heard the argument before. If an existing client reads in a brochure about another practice area, the firm may get business in that other practice area because the client now knows that the firm does that type of work. Yes, that is an outside possibility, but do not kid yourself—most clients do not read the brochures at any length. If they have a need in a particular area at that particular moment, and they happen to read about that practice area in a new brochure (assuming they read the brochure in the first place, which is unlikely because most brochures are too long and too boring), then they *might* think of calling the lawyer and asking for help in this new area. If all of those circumstances do not exist, then the odds are that they will not remember that practice area three months, six months, or a year from now when they have that new need. It is not about the written materials, but about the system and the people who are using those materials to support their business development efforts.

> ▼▼▼▼▼
>
> Only through repetition, systematic contact, systematic education, re-education, and the personal touch you as a lawyer provide, can you be confident that your clients will be kept up to date on your range of services.

Several years ago, I became aware of a law firm that was going through some key personnel changes when several lawyers left the firm. Obviously, it was important for the firm to not only retain the existing clients, but also to make sure that the right things were done to create new business for the firm. Instead of focusing on individual business development efforts, the firm immediately invested dollars in a new logo and in new marketing materials not because some of the names had changed but to actually change the firm's look and feel. Unfortunately, a few years later, the firm ceased to exist, and while there may have been many reasons for this downturn in business, you have to wonder whether a significant factor was too great a reliance on logos, branding, and written marketing materials, rather than stepping up and improving the business development and relationship skills and efforts of the lawyers.

We need to stop looking to the marketing department to bring in new business. Professional services are relationship-driven businesses, and they always have been. Professionals must build relationships to grow their business. The marketing department (and written marketing materials and even a Web site) are merely tools to support the professionals, nothing more. Once we recognize this, we can start investing our time and money where it really needs to be invested—on relationship building and systematic approaches to business development.

28 What You Do Is What You Get

It is a harsh reality for any professional that business development results are generally in direct proportion to the quantity and quality of business development activities. It is that simple. Yes, there are a select and lucky few lawyers who attract clients with little or no effort. Perhaps the lawyer has a parent or other relative who is a key decision-maker with a client or prospective client or is a community leader. And there are times when business more or less "falls into a lawyer's lap," but this is clearly the exception and these "lucky" rainmakers are rarely a solid foundation for a law firm. Most lawyers are afraid or uncertain with respect to clients and business development. Why? Because neither they nor their law firm knows where the clients or business are going to come from. They do not have a consistent, reliable, predictable, or successful process or system for bringing in new clients or new business from existing clients. It is this lack of a predictable and reliable business development system that makes law firms nervous about the future.

Despite this uncertainty, and the general understanding that having a reliable business development system is not only important but vital to the financial success and stability of a law firm, too many firms continue to rely on the "I hope" business development model—"I hope" that we have enough clients and enough business to pay the bills and to be profitable. For many firms, business development and revenues are treated as if they are beyond the firm's control. In reality, however, both are well within the reasonable control of every lawyer and every firm because they both flow from what the lawyer and the firm do.

Before we get into some specific business development activities, let's explore the starting point for many lawyers. I want you to take a quick survey. List all of the people whom you know. If you are not willing to take the time to do it right now, just quickly imagine the universe of all the people you know and then ask yourself these questions:

- Do all of these people know what my firm does?
- Are they all clients?
- Why aren't they clients?

Most lawyers will acknowledge that they have fallen far short in terms of turning the people they know into clients and referral sources. Generally, it is because they have not been proactive and consistent in letting people know what they do and what makes them different, they have not asked existing clients for referrals, and they have not asked the people they know to become clients.

Lawyers are hesitant to admit that they are salespeople and they do not like to talk about the concept of asking for the sale. But, legal rainmakers are very clear and unanimous that, at some point in the process, you have to ask for the business. You have to make it very clear to the people you are talking with that you want to do business with them and that you want the opportunity to show them what type of value you can bring to them and/or their business. If you do not ask, they will rarely pick up the phone and ask you to be their lawyer. That will happen occasionally, but it will not happen often enough to build your firm into a business that will deliver the results you want.

Another key factor in improving your business development efforts and results is to make sure that you and your firm recognize and act on the fact that everything you do is business development. It is not just when you go to networking events or take clients or referral sources out to lunch or dinner, but absolutely everything you do is business development. The "product" you deliver in terms of the services and experience are part of business development. Your billing practices and follow-ups, as well as collections, are all part of business development. Everything that your firm does has a potential connection with clients and prospective clients and is part of business development, and your entire organization must realize that. At a law firm (like any other business) everyone is part of the business development effort. Everyone needs to know and

▼▼▼▼▼

The quality of your service is a part of business development, but how you deliver the service is a bigger part of business development.

believe this to be effective as a law business in marketing and selling your services. You must develop a plan, you must work the plan, and you must measure the results.

For many lawyers, the "do" of business development is one of their biggest, if not the biggest, challenges. Obviously, the first challenge is the desire to "do" business development. You will notice that I did not use the word willingness, but an intentional and, optimally, passionate desire to do business development and to do the things that it takes to bring in more clients, better clients, and more business from existing clients. Given a choice of a lawyer who does nothing with respect to business development and a lawyer who is merely willing to "try it," willingness to "try it" certainly is better than no activity, but I encourage you to recognize that the gap between "nothing" and "willingness" is not as great as we often want to believe.

A lawyer who is merely *willing* to work at business development will:

- Be easily distracted from his or her path;
- Be less likely to follow through on his or her plan (if he or she even has one);
- Be less likely to invest the time and energy necessary to learn and practice business development skills and habits;
- Be much more likely to revert to his or her comfort zone (the practice of law);
- Be easily frustrated when his or her activities fail to generate immediate or significant results; and
- Be ineffective at business development.

Having said all this, you should not ignore the lawyers who are (for now) merely *willing* to work at business development. In fact, the willing lawyers may be the ones who you need to devote most of your time and attention to. Give them the support and training that will help them to see business development as not only something that they must do or should do, but as something that is in their best interest, that is fun and inspiring, and that will ultimately provide them with the greatest level of satisfaction from being a lawyer.

> ▼▼▼▼▼
>
> Business development can be fun. A lawyer who is passionate and driven about business development (i.e., passionate about people) will not only be a great asset to the firm, but will also get the most out of being a lawyer, will make the biggest difference with clients, and can be part of the critical foundation of a successful law firm.

Certainly, there will always be a place for the pure "technician lawyer"—the lawyer who is outstanding at what he or she does (i.e., the pure legal services that he or she delivers to the firm's clients). However, the smaller the firm, the less room there is for pure technician lawyers. Today, even in larger firms, it is more and more important for pure technician lawyers to find other ways to deliver greater value to the firm's clients. Clients (not legal services) are the lifeblood of a law firm. This is a critical financial reality that firms must recognize with respect to every aspect of their operations, and especially with respect to business development efforts.

Whether we have a willing or an energetic lawyer for business development efforts, the bigger obstacles usually lie in not knowing what to do or not knowing how to do it. Many lawyers want to be business developers, but they do not know what to do or how to do it. Given the choice between doing nothing and doing something, there is greater value in doing something, but not a significantly greater value. Often a lawyer who is simply "doing stuff" under the guise of business development—and not necessarily doing the right things, the best things, or using the best tactics—will get tired and frustrated and will eventually quit, and then everyone loses. We already talked about the importance of beginning business development training early on for associates, but that training, support, and development is just as important for partners.

For some reason we tend to assume that partners (simply by virtue of being partners) know how to develop business, but many partners are asking the same questions about what to do and how to do it. They may have some of their own clients, but it is amazing to see how many partners have such small "books of business" despite their years of experience. When judging business development for lawyers, the question is not about whether they have clients, but about the quality of the clients and whether typical annual revenues from those clients are at or near optimal levels. There is no objective number that applies to every lawyer based on years of experience (although some firms try to look at it this way)—it is an individualized question that must be addressed by both the lawyer and the firm in determining appropriate goals and examining where business originated.

In a particular law firm, a lawyer with a $500,000 "book of business" may be considered a "rainmaker," but if $400,000 of the $500,000 "fell into the lap" of the lawyer more through luck and happenstance than through any particular business development efforts, then that lawyer is underperforming. This also forces us to take a closer look at what a "book of business" really means. The key word is "book," defined as consistent, sustainable, and, in most cases, traceable to some form of consistent, intentional, and systematic effort. One of the biggest shortcomings of law firms is the lack of any sort of formalized business development system and a coinciding lack of disciplined use of such a system. Like most businesses, a law firm's ideas and plans are implemented when a system of reinforcement, support, and accountability exists, and this concept is particularly applicable with respect to business development.

PART

V

The Seven "BEs" of Business Development

The Seven "BEs" of Business Development

While there are many different aspects of the "dos" of business development, it is important to try to simplify some of the skills, tactics, and approaches, since simplicity and ease of implementation are essential to an effective plan. For that reason, I have developed the seven "BEs" of business development. These are seven key areas to focus on in business development, but they actually have very little to do with what you do in business development. They are all about what you must BE when you engage in business development activities, and they are:

1. BE interested, instead of trying to be interesting.
2. BE there, engaged and active.
3. BE knowledgeable and informed.
4. BE an investor in people and relationships.
5. BE specific, especially with referral sources.
6. BE systematic in your business development efforts.
7. BE purposeful in everything that you do.

We talked about the concept of Be-Do-Have in Chapter 4, and this concept is vital to being effective in business development, which is why in the next several chapters we will focus on what you will need to *be* in order to achieve your desired business development results.

Be Interested 29

While all of the “BEs” of business development are important, one—be interested—is probably the most important, since it gets at the very heart of what business development is all about. It is first, last, and always about people, and the skill and mindset of being interested in people, in their business, in their needs, and in the solutions that they need that will drive your business development results. Unfortunately, too many people believe that business development, marketing, and networking are all about “being interesting.” Trying to be interesting usually results in talking a lot and listening very little. Being interesting is all about you and not about the person you are talking with. Being interesting is about being egotistical, while being interested is selfless. Recently, a business friend shared this quote with me: “People will respect you for what you know. They will love you for what you don’t know.” Initially, I did not totally understand, but I have come to see its clarity and wisdom in that too often we work hard at being experts and “knowing it all,” which may gain us some level of respect. However, it is when we seek to understand and to learn more about people and their businesses that they will come to love us. This is where relationships (long-lasting relationships) are built and extended.

The simplest way to differentiate being interested from being interesting is the difference between talking and listening—the difference between telling and asking questions. We probably have all heard that asking questions is a critical skill in sales, but too often our question-asking skills are focused on manipulating the listener and somehow leading them to say “yes” to our products or services. Yes, being interested does involve asking questions, but this is about asking questions with a sincere and genuine interest in learning more about people, their businesses, their interests, and their needs.

> ▼▼▼▼▼
>
> While identifying needs or pains with a client or prospective client is important, in business development it is all about the skill of learning about the person.

Most of us are uncomfortable talking about ourselves. We feel uncomfortable or on the spot in a social or business environment when we have to start telling someone about ourselves. I am not sure of the reasons behind this, but it is very real for professionals and even for many sales professionals. However, we become much more comfortable when another person asks us (with a sincere interest in the answers) about ourselves. This is much more than simply asking someone, "What do you do?" (the most common opening line at any business or networking event)—it is about going to a deeper level of asking people about themselves and/or their businesses with a demonstrated interest in the answers. You must be truly interested in them and the answers to your questions.

You can start throwing out questions, but people can judge whether you are really interested in the answers. Sometimes (rarely) your level of interest can be judged based on what you say, but it is usually revealed through other observations or even feelings that people get about you and your level of interest. For example, how you shake their hand tells them something about you. Are you engaging them with your handshake or eye contact, or are you giving them the obligatory shake before you move on to someone else? Do you maintain interested eye contact or are you scanning the room looking for someone else or some "better" opportunity? Are you fully engaged—mentally, physically, and even emotionally—in your discussion with them? Do you demonstrate some level of energy from being part of the conversation? Are you excited about what they are saying and do you show that excitement? Are you sharing in some significant way with them to demonstrate your genuine interest in them and their situation? These are all very demonstrable things that you can do to prove to someone that you are genuinely interested in them, and that you are not just playing along or being a mere participant in the business development dance.

We already touched on the topic of asking questions, but it is important to spend a little more time on this very important skill, which requires that you go beyond the superficial or the traditional questions. For example, nearly everyone in a business or even social environment asks the question "What do you do?" However, most people do not ask another question after hearing that answer unless (and this is big mistake) they follow up by trying to drill down for an opportunity to sell them something. We have all been victimized by this very obvious tactic and many of us have probably been guilty of doing the same thing. If you are interested in them, you will follow up with more questions to learn something more about them and their business.

When I meet someone new, my number one goal is to learn something beyond the superficial regarding their business and them personally. On the personal side it may relate to some interest of theirs, to their family or children, or to some common or mutual acquaintances. A great (and different) opening question is "What do you do when you are not working?" Discovering mutual acquaintances is a powerful accelerator to relationship building. How much the relationship bridge is built depends a great deal on who the mutual acquaintance is and the level of connection that each of us has with that person, but you should always explore that topic in any conversation.

You should also ask a new acquaintance deeper questions about their business such as who they work with, who their referral sources are, who their best customers are, how they get their business, how their business is doing, and so on. It is simply amazing the amount of personal and private information that people will share with you if you ask and do so in a way that demonstrates that you are sincerely interested in them and the information. Numerous owners of closely held businesses have told me revenue figures, profit figures, profit margins, and similar information about their business, information that is definitely not public knowledge. They do this because I have demonstrated to them in some tangible or even intangible way that I can be trusted and also that it may be worthwhile for them to share that information. You cannot get that information by trying to sell anything, except for selling yourself as someone who is interested in them.

Too many people go to events with the express purpose of meeting as many people as they can and collecting lots of business cards, and they leave thinking that they have had a successful night of networking. Why? Because they met lots of people, but meeting people is not what it is about. It is about building relationships. While it is difficult (and perhaps impossible) to actually build a relationship in a single meeting (more on that later), the first meeting is about beginning to construct the relationship bridge—not only beginning to build it, but making some assessments yourself as to whether it is worth building. We all make judgments about people, and it is important that you start making some determinations about whether the people you meet are the right type of people (note, I did not say in the right business) so that it makes

> ▼▼▼▼▼
>
> One key point concerning business-related events is that you should focus more on quality rather than on quantity.

sense for you to invest more of your valuable time getting to know them and hopefully building a mutually beneficial relationship. These are judgments that we must all make as part of our business development efforts, but it is always best to focus on a few quality conversations at a business or even social event, rather than playing the numbers game where quantity prevails over quality.

While it is very unusual to actually build a relationship in a single meeting, it can be done, especially if you are open, honest, and totally focused on being interested in other people. Several years ago I attended a chamber of commerce event (a wine tasting) with about 100 other people in attendance. I spoke to six or seven people during the hour or so before dinner, and, frankly, most of the people did not really interest me except for a husband and wife I met near the end of the "networking" part of the event. They seemed like a very fun couple and they owned a nearby business. We agreed to sit together for the wine tasting and the result was that the three of us had an incredible conversation about business, personal topics, philosophies, and so on. which lasted for over three hours. To this day, we talk about that evening as one of the most memorable for each of us.

What is most significant about that encounter and our conversation is that they invited me to an event at their place of business approximately one month later. I attended and, again, there were many people in attendance, but as the event was winding down they asked me to stay and just a handful of us sat around a table chatting. At some point in the conversation, the owner introduced one of the guests to the entire table as one of his most trusted vendors. He described him as a person whom he had complete trust and faith in and as someone whom he could recommend to anyone with complete and total confidence, a list he described as being a very short. He then proceeded to tell the entire group that, for him, I was also a person in that category.

In one evening (albeit a three-hour conversation), this business owner (and his wife) and I had developed a very deep and strong relationship, a relationship that had put me in a very select group with this couple. I felt privileged and honored to have so quickly become part of this couple's "inner circle," and this came about because of my commitment to being genuinely interested in people, my commitment to quality people and quality relationships (rather than quantity), and my willingness to be open and honest even at a business event. These types of relationships may not always be built so quickly, but if you make it your mindset to be genuinely interested in people, they can and will happen, whether it is in one evening or over time.

The final point on being interested relates to a system or process you can use when it comes to your networking activities. It is always my goal when I meet someone new to learn something interesting and personal about them. I make a note of that information (usually on their business card), and I then record it in my contact management program. I not only enter their name, address, and telephone number, but I make a note about when I met them, where I met them, perhaps some of the topics that we discussed, and some of the personal and private information they shared with me. Then, when I inevitably follow up with them, I have that information in front of me and I can ask about some of those topics.

For example, how are your kids doing in soccer or swimming? How did they enjoy camp? How was your ski trip to Colorado? In fact, I rely not only on technology to help me remember this information but, as in the way many of us learn, by listening, writing it down, and then recording it in my contact management program, I often remember this information when I next run into them, even many months after our meeting. Some of you may be thinking that this is a mere tactic I use, but it is not. What it demonstrates to that person is that I was interested in asking them, I was interested enough to really listen, I was interested enough to write it down, I was interested enough to put it in my contact management program, and I was interested enough to remember it and bring it up in the future. That makes me different from almost everyone else, and the same technique can work for you.

This is not about manipulative tactics, but about being genuinely interested in people and differentiating yourself. Being interested in people will make you interesting, so focus your business development efforts on asking questions, listening, and being interested, and stop trying to be interesting. It will improve your business development results.

Be There 30

Of the seven "BEs," "be there" is probably the easiest (in many ways) to achieve. While quality is always important, the "be there" piece of business development is about taking action, about doing something, about making the effort, and being there in terms of opportunities to meet new people, to review existing relationships, or to spend time with clients. Part of this involves having a plan (more on that later), but another part is making the commitment and following through on it to spend time with people outside the firm. Too many lawyers spend (or waste) most of their lunch time either working at their desk or eating lunch with their colleagues. This is not the best way to spend your valuable time. Yes, there is always the argument that spending time with your fellow lawyers builds teamwork, helps you work together better, and helps you better understand opportunities to work together, but in most cases these intra-firm lunches are either about discussing existing matters or they are social. In these cases, they are just lunch, and "just lunches" will not help you in your business development efforts and certainly will not create better business opportunities or enhance your business results.

> You need to get involved and you need to create or take advantage of opportunities to be around people.

I have talked to lawyers who said that they would like to get involved, yet they spend years simply talking about it. I have met lawyers who have told me that they want to do something, but because they do not know what to do, they have chosen to do nothing. Typically, they do not use the word "chosen," but it is a choice. You have the choice whether to get involved, get out there, and do something, or you can sit and wait for something to happen. Results of some kind are more likely to flow to the person who does something than to the person who sits in their office and waits. Generally, the so-called reasons for not getting involved or getting out there are really excuses for either a lack of or insufficient motivation to participate in business development efforts. Lawyers tell me that they do not attend after-hours events because they want to get home to their families, but they think nothing of working through the night to fulfill billable hour requirements. They tell me that they do not have time to meet with clients first thing in the morning (perhaps because of family commitments), but they make time to work out. Lawyers tell me that they are too busy during the day to have lunch, yet I find it hard to believe that a lawyer does not have time for even one business development-related lunch each month or even each week.

Am I suggesting that you have to trade off family versus workouts versus billable hours versus business development? The answer is yes and no. Yes, it is important to recognize the importance and value of business development and to invest time in it. No, because you can have it all if you are committed to it and if you plan for it. I was at a seminar for lawyers several years ago and the topic was, generally speaking, time management. The speaker asked a lawyer what his biggest concern was about being a lawyer, and the lawyer said that he worked too many hours. The speaker asked him what time he usually left work and, after a struggle, got an answer. The speaker then told the lawyer that for the next 30 days, he should commit to leaving the office precisely 30 minutes sooner every day. He also asked this rhetorical question to the attendees: "If you knew that you had to leave the office at a designated time every day for 30 days, would you do things differently during the course of your day?" The answer of course is yes. If we are committed to it we will make adjustments during our day to make sure that we honor that commitment. The same is true of business development. If we are truly committed to it, we can find the time to invest in it. And it is an investment of your valuable time. Business development is important for you and for your firm and you will make time for it if you believe in it, if you are committed to it, and if your firm supports you in recognizing the value of your business development time.

Community Involvement

Another important way to be there relates to getting involved with a non-profit or some other community initiative. This can be an important business development tool but only if you go into it with the right approach. First and foremost you must get involved because it is important to you. If you want to make a difference, then you should get involved, and it will provide you with opportunities to meet new people who can ultimately help you in your business.

You must be passionate about the cause that you are getting involved with; otherwise you immediately will be seen as just another person trying to generate new business by getting involved.

It is also important that you be very cautious about trying to directly sell to others involved with a noprofit (e.g., other board members). Yes, you must make it very clear who you are, what you do, and whom you do business with. However, you must be careful not to start trying to sell to other board members, especially too early in your involvement. Every nonprofit board has people who get involved solely to expand their business network, and most experienced boards can see these people coming a mile away. Often, they will try to keep them off the board or, once on the board, their relationship-building opportunities will be doomed because they have gotten involved as a "salesperson" rather than as someone who is genuinely interested in supporting the cause and building relationships. As we have touched on several times, the selling of legal services is almost always about a relationship, whether it is with a client, prospective client, or referral source. When it comes to getting involved with nonprofits or community projects, there are two critical things to remember: (1) first and foremost, it must be about the cause; and (2) focus on building relationships, not on selling your services. By the way, in my experience I have found that many nonprofit boards are desperate to get lawyers involved. Frankly, they are looking for "free" legal help with some of their legal needs, and this is a great way to immediately get involved and to bring value to the nonprofit.

While it is almost always a mistake to come in and start selling board members on your services, there is one strategy that can be effective without being offensive. First of all, it is vital that you get involved beyond just board membership. Simply being a board member and putting it on your resume is not enough. Resumes do not generate new business. In addition, simply attending board meetings is not enough. That will not get you the type of exposure you need to start building relationships. If the board meets quarterly, that is definitely not enough exposure. However, if the board meets monthly, then this may be enough consistent face time to give you a foundation for building some relationships.

In any case, it is important that you get involved at a level beyond mere membership, which means getting involved with committees (ideally chairing a committee or event) and, ultimately, the goal should be to achieve a leadership role such as on the executive committee or a similar committee. When doing so, you must always keep in mind that it is still not about business development, but about your personal development. Clients and prospective clients want to do business with leaders, and anything you can do to further develop and enhance your leadership skills and your leadership profile will benefit you in your business development efforts. Therefore, as you get more involved with a nonprofit or assume leadership roles, always keep in mind that you are doing so first and foremost for the cause, second for your own personal development, and lastly for business development.

Another strategy that I want to mention relating to nonprofit involvement is to make sure that you take time to meet one-on-one with other board members. On a very large board, you may want to be selective about whom you meet with outside of the board meetings or committee meetings, but it is important to have these face-to-face meetings because this is where the real relationships are built. This is where you have the real one-on-one opportunity to sell yourself and to start exploring the topic of what your business is about and what the other board members' businesses are about. It is probably still not appropriate (at least early on) to try in any way to sell the other board members, but it is a great opportunity to start asking for referrals.

Once you have developed some level of trust, sit down with the other board members (just as you would with any other referral source) and ask them for opportunities to be introduced to other people they know. You may choose to do that with respect to looking for specific sales opportunities, or you may choose to just say something like, "I am always looking to expand my business network and I would love the opportunity for some introductions to other business leaders you know." Most people (and especially people involved with nonprofits) want to help people and are often willing (if not anxious) to serve as mentors. Looking for introductions to other influential businesspeople can be a win-win for both you and the person from whom you are seeking help. You must always build a relationship and trust level first, but this is one way that you can start to be more aggressive with the business development aspects of your nonprofit involvement without a significant risk of being branded as someone who is there just to get a sale.

Networking Groups

The next "be there" topic is structured networking groups. These groups can be formal (typically either local or part of a national organization that involves annual fees) or informal (organized by businesspeople and professionals) and meet on a consistent basis (typically weekly) for the express purpose of helping each other grow their businesses. They are also sometimes called referral or lead groups. The structure of these groups can vary, but common features are opportunities for the participants to let everyone in the group know who they are and what they do, educational presentations or information sharing, and opportunities for attendees to tell the group what they are looking for and to seek help with introductions in the form of a lead, a referral, or an introduction.

Frankly, I am amazed at how few lawyers are involved in these types of groups. In addition, many lawyers have very negative views of these groups, and there are two reasons for this (both of which are more about mindset than reality). First, lawyers are often frustrated by the fact that they get involved and they do not see immediate results. In these cases their expectations are unrealistic. Too many lawyers who participate in these groups somehow expect that they can overlook the relationship aspects and will immediately be fed high-quality referrals and introductions. While this does happen with certain business types in these networking groups, it is not realistic with respect to professionals.

Even in structured networking groups, it is still very much about relationships, especially with respect to any professional services (lawyers, accountants, engineers, architects, etc.).

For one thing, most businesspeople have a negative impression of lawyers, which makes it even more difficult for you to gain their trust and build a relationship in which they are willing to risk introducing you to a friend, business associate, or client. For another, they do not really understand what lawyers do or how they add value, which means you have to work extra hard at clarifying who you are, what you do, and what your value is to the members of the group. Finally, not everyone needs a lawyer today and not everyone is ready to talk about a new lawyer today, which means that you have to create the opportunities and in some respects be patient as you wait for them to develop. For all of these reasons, it is unrealistic for a lawyer to expect immediate returns from any sort of networking organization.

The second negative perception generally comes from the fact that lawyers do not want to be thought of as salespeople, and many of these groups are filled with either sales professionals or business owners who also function in the sales role. Frankly, many lawyers are intimidated by these types of people, either because they do not want to be viewed as salespeople or they are intimidated because these people are so much better at sales than they are. Being effective in these groups means learning and understanding what your real value proposition is and developing a strong 30- to 60-second commercial. Many lawyers do not like the idea that they have to actually start to think and act like salespeople and develop traditional sales tools such as a strong value proposition and a "commercial," and this causes them to have negative perceptions of these types of groups.

By the way, for a lawyer (especially a younger lawyer) there are valuable benefits to being involved in these types of groups. If you are committed to the process, you will gain confidence, you will become a better presenter, you will develop and use a strong introduction and 30- or 60-second commercial and you will clarify for yourself what makes you different and how you can bring value, and these are all tools, resources, and skills you can use in all of your business development efforts. Unfortunately, too many lawyers look at these groups as something that is "beneath them" either because they are not salespeople or they think that they have the wrong type of audience.

While it is very important to carefully evaluate the other members of these types of groups, most lawyers make the mistake of looking at the people in the room as potential clients, and then concluding that they are not the right audience. That is the wrong perspective. The people in these groups should not be viewed as potential clients, but as potential referral sources. The questions you should be asking are whom they do business with, whom they talk with in their businesses, and whom they typically sell to on a relationship basis. This is how you should judge the participants in any sort of networking group. The other issue is how committed the other participants are to the concept of helping each other, but that is a tough issue to judge based on attending perhaps one or two meetings. I cannot overstate the importance of looking at these groups as potential referral sources and as opportunities to make you a better business developer and, yes, salesperson.

Another benefit to these types of groups (which is often overlooked) is their consistency. Some lawyers do not like these groups because they think these groups meet too often (typically once a week), but this is where the real value is. Seeing these people consistently allows you to continuously remind them of who you are and what you do (so that you are top of mind) and allows you to accelerate relationship building. These types of groups force us to commit to a group of people with whom we are going to work hard to build strong referral sources. It may take some time, but if you commit to helping the group as well during that time, you will have gained valuable tools and skills to help you in all of your business development efforts and, with the right people in the group, you will have assembled a referral team that will help sell you throughout the business community. That is the beauty of leverage and the beauty of having a team of referral sources who are committed to helping you, and frankly, most lawyers do not have referral sources who are as strong as they need to be or should be.

Public Speaking

One business development skill that is often talked about, but rarely effectively implemented is public speaking. Public speaking is one of the most underutilized business development tools, and it is powerful because it gives you the ability to leverage your time (there is that powerful business development word again) by spreading some message or "selling yourself" to a group of people, rather than one on one. With our time being so valuable and time available for business development always at a premium, it makes good business sense to look for opportunities where you can "sell" to a group whenever possible. Public speaking is the perfect opportunity for that type of leveraged selling, even if you are not directly selling your services.

▼▼▼▼▼

Admittedly, not everyone is cut out to be a public speaker, but with a little practice and training most people can become good at speaking and thereby acquire another business development skill.

Obviously, one thing that prevents many lawyers from being more effective at using speaking as a business development tool is their hesitancy or even fear of speaking. It is well-known that public speaking is the number one fear among people (interesting, isn't it, that we fear speaking more than dying?), but much of that fear can be overcome with some training and development. I encourage every lawyer to take some form of speaking or presentation skills training because, even if you do not use it to develop into a speaker, it will make you more effective even in your one-on-one interactions.

In addition to overcoming a fear of public speaking, most lawyers also need to pursue better and more appropriate speaking opportunities. Most of the lawyers who do some speaking limit those opportunities to continuing legal education programs. Many lawyers believe this to be a very strong business development opportunity, but I am not convinced. Certainly, speaking to a group of your peers and demonstrating a high level of niched expertise (and not all continuing legal education situations provide this type of opportunity) can create the potential for you to receive referrals from program attendees. However, CLE programs often do not create very strong referral opportunities for several reasons.

First, if you are speaking on a specific area of expertise, many of the attendees already have that area of expertise or are seeking to deepen their level of expertise so that they can compete with you more effectively. Generally, they are not there seeking to identify someone to whom they can refer business. Obviously, there are always conflicts of interest that arise that might present an opportunity for you to be a referral source, but those opportunities are not as common as most lawyers assume. Second, many lawyers attend CLE programs solely to fulfill required compliance hours, and they are not there proactively looking for a referral source. Unless you make a powerful impact, the reality is that most of the lawyers will not even start to think of you as a potential referral source during the program. Once they leave, their natural tendencies take over, they get busy with their own activities, and they are even less likely to remember you as a potential referral source in the future.

When making referrals, most lawyers will do one of two things: (1) they will call someone they know (not just someone they saw at a seminar); or (2) they will call another lawyer they know to ask for a referral. Lawyers are typically risk averse, which means that they will more often focus on existing referral relationships, and they are unlikely to make referrals to someone whom they only heard speak. Certainly, you should continue to speak (or to start speaking) at CLE programs. It is great experience and certainly good exposure, but do not view such speaking engagements as strong business development opportunities.

Where should you be speaking? You should be seeking out and creating opportunities to speak to groups of people who are prospective clients or nonlegal referral sources. If you are going to invest the time to speak, why not speak to a group of potential clients in an industry or area that you are targeting or in which you already practice? What a great opportunity—speaking in front of a group of people who are your prospective clients. Whether it be trade associations, professional organizations, community organizations, or groups of businesspeople, these are the types of speaking opportunities that are truly leveraged business development opportunities.

▼▼▼▼▼

The great thing about some public speaking opportunities is that you are usually not selling your services at all, but rather you are selling yourself and your expertise *to a group that is interested in your expertise.*

Many lawyers think that these speaking opportunities are too hard to find, but that's only because they have not looked very hard. The fact is that organizations are always looking for people to speak (at no cost) on topics of interest to their group. They do not want people to come in and "pitch" their services, but they are looking for content that will be valuable and helpful to their members. The key is to develop something valuable to communicate, and then create a systematic plan for sharing that information with the types of organizations that might be interested in having you speak. As with so many aspects of business development, this is about targeting, creating a clear message, clearly communicating that message, and having a systematic approach to follow up. If you do this, you can develop great speaking opportunities where you can leverage your valuable business development time and speak to a group that is loaded with opportunities for you. It is just like fishing in a stocked pond, and that is where you should be spending your time.

Writing

Writing is another underutilized business development tool. Like speaking, fear can be an issue with writing, and finding time for writing remains a constant challenge. Like speaking, writing is a great form of leveraged business development, since a single investment of time and effort can give you access to a large number of people. Much like pursuing speaking opportunities, developing writing opportunities (the right ones) also requires a systematic and purposeful approach. Even those lawyers who do some writing tend to limit it to publications that are mostly read by other lawyers. Writing for other lawyers is much like speaking to a group of lawyers—there are no opportunities for direct clients and the referral opportunities are minimal for the same reasons we listed relative to speaking at CLE programs. Ideally you want to write for readers who are prospective clients or potentially strong referral sources. If you are going to invest your time in writing, you should invest it where the business development opportunities are greatest.

One example is trade associations. Most trade or industry associations have periodic newsletters, and, if you have ever produced a newsletter, you know that the biggest challenge is finding articles. Most publications of this type are looking for articles and would love to have someone write for them (ideally on a regular basis) to provide valuable information for their readers. Too often we assume that these publications have more than enough articles, when typically they are spending a great deal of time trying to track down material. The key is to have an article that is "right" or valuable for their readers.

Therefore, you must invest some time identifying publications that might be a good fit for you and your practice area, investigating those publications to find out what types of articles they typically feature, and figuring out what types of information that you could share with their readers. You can then take this information and develop and present a plan to show the organization how you can help with its publication by providing valuable information for readers.

When you have writing opportunities, it is also vital that you write with the readers in mind. Too often lawyers "write like lawyers" in very technical terms that might be appropriate if other lawyers were reading the information. However, businesspeople typically are looking for information in a different form. They want to get to the bottom line. They want to know how this information can help them in some way. They want to know how they can use this information to make better decisions or to improve themselves or their businesses. For all of these reasons, it is very important that you write with the mindset of communicating valuable information in a way that allows the reader to understand the information and to see and understand how that information can be useful to them. Writing that is focused on helping the readers, when written for the right audience, can be a very powerful business development tool.

▼▼▼▼▼

If your readers come away saying "This is great information, but how does it affect me?" then the article failed to accomplish its purpose. Instead you want readers to say, "This is great information and it was helpful to me."

Business development starts with being there, being active, and being involved in various ways. Each lawyer needs to find his or her path (and that is part of the planning process for individual and law firm business development programs). While you are conducting business development activities, always remember they are based on relationships and you need to seek out opportunities and strategies for accelerating relationship building along the way.

There are no special tricks or tactics when it comes to being there or being involved relative to business development efforts. There most definitely is a mindset that you must adopt that recognizes that business development time has significant value. You must commit to it and you must honor those commitments to yourself and to the future of your firm, but it is doable for any lawyer. Even if you have no skills or tactics for business development (and we are sharing many of those in this book), being there and being involved will ultimately deliver you some results and, at a minimum will get you on the road to being a business developer and creating a business developer mindset that will ultimately help you develop and refine the skills that will make you a rainmaker in the future.

Be Knowledgeable 31

When you saw this chapter title, perhaps you immediately thought that "knowledgeable" refers to knowledge of the law. For the most part it does not. It means being knowledgeable about businesses, particularly your clients' businesses. It means being knowledgeable about business trends, business industries, business practices, business pains, business solutions, business challenges, and business opportunities. It means thinking like a businessperson, not just a lawyer. It means reading business publications, not just legal publications. It means investing your time to learn how to be a businessperson and to understand business needs, rather than simply working hard at being a better lawyer.

Sometimes it means being knowledgeable about other people in the business community so that you can have a conversation with other businesspeople. It demonstrates that you are involved and that you are knowledgeable about what is going on in the business community. If you are not knowledgeable about the business community, then many people will assume (perhaps incorrectly) that you are not involved and that you are not knowledgeable about business.

> ▼▼▼▼▼
>
> People like to do business with other successful businesspeople, and sometimes they measure success by the extent of that persons' involvement in the business community.

It has often been said that there is no such thing as a stupid question, but sometimes there is such a thing when you are talking to businesspeople. If you ask a very naive question, people may think that you have not done your homework—that if you were involved and had even a basic knowledge of business you would not ask that type of question. So, in those cases, there is such a thing as a stupid question. However, if you are sincere in asking the question (and it does not come across as mere small talk), then you can benefit if the listener decides to share some important information with you. That is when you need to put both ears on high alert and listen, learn, and be genuinely interested.

Being knowledgeable also means continuing to educate yourself, whether by attending seminars, reading books, listening to tapes, or reading trade journals. If you say that you do not have time for these types of things, then imagine how that would sound if you were forced to admit it to a client, a prospect, or a referral source: "I do not have time to learn about business. I do not have time to learn about your industry or your business. I do not have time to learn the things that would make me a better lawyer and a better advisor for you and your business." Would you like to say that to your clients and prospects? Of course not, but that is exactly what you are saying to them (perhaps silently) if you choose not to invest some of your time in learning more, educating yourself, and making yourself a true advisor.

Lawyers often tell me that they are "seminared out," but when I ask them what seminars they have attended, the only seminars are continuing legal education seminars. CLE seminars will generally do one or two things for you. First, they will fulfill your CLE requirements. This is a must, but it does not enhance your value as an advisor. Second, you may learn some specific skills or acquire some knowledge that will help you be a better legal technician, and this adds some value to you as a lawyer, but not necessarily as an advisor. However, attending CLE seminars will rarely enhance your business development efforts, except in the rare case when you have an opportunity to meet or reconnect with someone who is a potential referral source. We will talk more about referral sources later, but for most lawyers, attending CLE programs is not a legitimate part of a business development plan. Instead, lawyers should be attending nonlaw seminars.

Attend seminars that are presented by business leaders and, perhaps most important, attended by business leaders or others who are your prospective clients. We mentioned this briefly with respect to differentiation. If you are a lawyer attending a business seminar, you will generally be one of the few lawyers in the room, if not the only one. That tells the businesspeople there that you are different, that you are interested in them, and that you are interested in being an advisor (a knowledgeable one), rather than a run of the mill technical lawyer.

Remember, being a better lawyer (a purely better technician) will benefit you to some degree, but it will not make you a better advisor, a trusted advisor, or the type of professional (notice that I did not say lawyer) that your clients, prospects, and relationships will seek out for advice and counsel. That is what we all really want and that is what business development is all about: being that trusted advisor, an outside counsel to the people who we know and who trust us. To achieve that status we need to make ourselves better by continuously striving to learn more (outside of our substantive legal areas) and by being engaged in the constant pursuit of enhanced understanding. One of the principal ways to accelerate relationship building is by investing in others, which is the topic of the next chapter.

Be an Investor 32

With respect to business development, you must be an investor: an investor in people, an investor in relationships, an investor in businesses, and especially an investor in your existing clients. When we talk about investing, we are not talking about investing dollars, but investing time, energy, attention, ideas, and resources in people and relationships. It is also about having the mindset of an investor or a giver versus the mindset of a taker. Most people will judge you quickly and accurately as to whether you are a giver/investor or a taker, and they want to do business with investors. The reason is simple—people gain great value from investor relationships, whether it is ideas, resources, information, or other valuable solutions, and most people recognize the value of working and associating with investor-minded people. Like so many of the topics we have discussed, it begins by developing, nurturing, and enhancing an investor mindset, which means that you must constantly think about others.

Constantly (or almost constantly) thinking about others is not easy, since we all have daily responsibilities in our own practice, within our firm, and within our own personal lives, but it can be done. In fact, it is not really about spending 100 percent of your time, energy, and attention on others, but it is about having a mindset that is open to investing in other people at any point in time. It does require that you keep other people and their needs top of mind so that when you see or hear of an opportunity to help them, you can take advantage of it and offer them some valuable information or resources. "Taker" minded people may not think that they are takers, but if they never give time, energy, and attention to others, then they are being selfish and they are being a taker because they are "taking" all of their time, energy, and talents and keeping them for themselves. This may seem like a fine point, but it is a very real difference in the value you can bring to others and, therefore, the value that they see in you as a relationship or as part of their sphere of influence.

Part of being an investor requires that you show interest in others, that you ask meaningful questions, and that you commit some amount of time, energy, and attention to trying to solve other people's problems. It means that you have to keep others and their needs on your mind enough to see the opportunities to help them and go out of your way to bring new ideas, new information, or new solutions to them, often without being asked. In fact, it is better if you do so without being asked, because it demonstrates that you are committed to their success, not just your own.

A perfect example of this is a habit or practice that lawyers have talked about for years, but rarely implement effectively—specifically, periodically sending articles or notes to clients and existing relationships just to show that you are thinking about them and trying to add some value. Lawyers say this is a good practice, but they rarely seem to get around to doing it. It just seems like too much work, but with a little bit of invested time (and with the assistance of a committed support team that can help you), it can pay huge dividends and build a great wealth of goodwill.

▼▼▼▼▼

Anything you can do that demonstrates that you are different and that you are thinking about your clients and relationships will help you to enhance, build, expand, and improve those relationships.

Make It Personal

One easy way to show that you are an investor is to personalize your communications. Certainly, e-mail has become an easy way to communicate (and I do not suggest that we stop using e-mail), but we often rely too heavily on e-mail (to the exclusion of other forms of communication), and we also forget to personalize e-mails. If you study any company that excels at customer service, they will tell you that one of the simplest ways to enhance customer service is to use the customer's or client's name as often as possible. Ideally, this means using a first name rather than a formal name. If you were to send a letter to a friend or business acquaintance, would you begin by saying "Dear Mr. Client"? Of course not—you would begin with "Dear Mary," using her first name because it is more personal. We all know this, but how often do we send e-mails that do not use the person's name at all? We simply fire away with whatever we have to say and forget the simple courtesy of using a name. In fact, it is not only a simple courtesy, but using someone's first name is a proven customer service improvement strategy.

I recently had this discussion with someone who said that they did not feel it was necessary because the person's name is already in the address of the e-mail. What do you think about that? What that person was saying (which I called them on) is that they wanted to do it the easy way, but I equated it to sending a letter with no name on it because there is a name and an address on the outside of the envelope. We seem to forget about the little things, which is why, when I send e-mails, I make it a point to always try and remember to use the person's first name. Even if I am in a hurry and firing off a quick response, I try (and I am not perfect) to remember to put the recipient's name in the e-mail. I also work to put my name in the e-mail beyond the e-mail signature, because it says that I went that little, tiny extra half step. They may not consciously notice the difference, but they will get the feeling that you are more invested in them because you take these little extra steps. In this aspect of business development, it really is the little things that can make all the difference.

Another great example of a business development strategy is the use of handwritten notes. I am far from perfect on this, but I do work hard at sending handwritten thank you notes to everyone I meet, whether it is a sales meeting, a referral or similar relationship meeting, or any sort of breakfast or lunch relating to business. Why is this important? Because it differentiates me and it tells people that I am willing to go the extra mile to personalize our communication. Everyone knows that our time is valuable, and if I take the time to write a handwritten note, that is an investment that I am making in that person. Ideally, you should use note cards that are *not* from your firm. Everyone uses their firm note cards, so being different means using some other type of cards. It is very easy with our busy schedules to try to find shortcuts or to use technology to make ourselves more efficient, but it is these little personalized touches that can make a big difference in whether a relationship is initiated, whether it is enhanced, or whether the relationship-building process is accelerated.

You may have already recognized this, but when it comes to personalized notes, there is a range of personalization. The most personalized is a handwritten note that is hand addressed and hand stamped. All of these things signify special treatment, additional time and attention, and additional interest. A metered stamp is easier, but it is less personalized. A printed label is easier than a handwritten one, but it is less personal. A typed note is easier, but less personal than a handwritten one (if you do type your notes, at least make sure that you personally sign them).

This personalization topic is the reason that every year in our firm every lawyer personally signed every holiday card. This typically involved a good number of lawyers signing 600 to 800 holiday cards. Yes, we did have our firm name printed on the card, but I insisted on this personal touch.

I learned this lesson from Jack Kahl, the former CEO of Manco (now known as Henkel Consumer Adhesives). Manco (now Henkel) sends out cards several times a year. They send out a St. Patrick's Day card, a Fourth of July card, a Thanksgiving card, and a holiday card, and every card that I have ever received was personally signed by Jack Kahl (they are now signed by his son, the current CEO, John Kahl). I once asked Jack about this and expressed to him how much time it must take to sign well over 1,000 cards at least several times a year. Jack told me that it did take a lot of time, but he believed it was critical to show that he was personally in touch with people and that he was willing to invest his valuable time in that communication. I listened and I learned well, and I have carried that over into my various business endeavors.

▼▼▼▼▼

It may seem like a simple little matter, but it is the simple investments of time that will differentiate us as lawyers and we will communicate the clear message that we are investors.

Make It About Them

One of the best ways to prove yourself as an investor is to help people. It is that simple. If you help clients solve problems, overcome challenges, achieve objectives, remove obstacles, and enhance their happiness or success, it is the surest path to great business development results and great business (and personal) relationships. One of the most important people (or groups of people) that we need to invest in is our existing clients, but we are doing a very poor job of investing in them. Often we do not understand our clients' businesses, needs, or goals. Many times we do not even understand what they are trying to accomplish or the types of challenges that they are dealing with on a daily basis. Why? Because we think it is not part of our job, and we are so very wrong about that. Our mission is and should be to help enhance our clients' success and even personal happiness.

Many lawyers have told me that they became lawyers because they wanted to make a difference, yet they found that they were just being lawyers and did not really see an impact. Part of the reason is that they have focused too much attention on just being lawyers, rather than seeking out the opportunities to help the people with whom they come in contact, especially their clients. It can be a little scary to start asking the deeper questions and to ask our clients to have a greater and deeper relationship with us, but it is such an important decision to make and it is the path not only to great relationships, but also to incredible success for you and your firm.

Many times we are so busy being lawyers that we do not even make time to see our clients face to face. We take the easy road, communicating by telephone and e-mail and actually avoid going out to see our clients face to face.

When we do need to meet with them, we often demand that they come to our place of business, compelling them to spend their time traveling, dealing with traffic, parking, and taking time out of their busy day to come seek our counsel. What message does that communicate? It tells them that we think our time is more valuable than theirs. One response I get from lawyers is that they are looking out for their clients by saving them money on travel time. That may be technically true, but maybe we need to think about investing in them by not charging them for our travel time because we believe that seeing them in person is important, we think their time is valuable, we value the relationship, and because we want them to know that their activities are very important and we want to be as effective and as efficient as we can as their advisor.

What impressions are we sending to our clients when we insist that they spend their time coming to see us and we charge them for our travel time when we come to see them? Maybe it is appropriate to charge for travel time in some cases, but as we have talked about before when it comes to client service, what message does that communicate and what more positive and investment-minded message could we send if we made it clear to our clients that we are willing to invest our time in them, their businesses, and their problems and needs.

By now we should all know the business reality that the cost of securing a new client is anywhere from six to nine times higher than the cost of securing new business from an existing client. Whether we are aware of this or not, in the business of law, lawyers and law firms seem to ignore it with most of their business development efforts, since business development seems to be limited to securing new clients, and little if any attention is focused on securing additional business from existing clients. Certainly, most lawyers and law firms experience increases in new business from existing clients, but it all too often seems to be by default rather than by design. If you ask a lawyer about his or her recent business development efforts, you will typically hear about efforts to secure new clients, but questions regarding efforts to secure new business from existing clients are met with blank stares.

One of the reasons for this lack of attention to new business opportunities with existing clients is due to an assumption (which is generally erroneous) that our existing clients know everything we do and that new business will automatically come to us without any effort on our part and without any attempt to ask for the business. This is the same mistake that most nonlegal businesses make, and the result is the same—new business from existing clients never comes

> ▼▼▼▼▼
>
> Assuming that your clients know what you do and what you are "looking for" is not only erroneous but dangerous to your business.

close to being what it could and should be. Many sales and marketing experts related to the legal industry believe that once you secure a critical mass of existing clients, you should be able to not only sustain but continually grow your business solely via new business from existing clients and referrals from existing clients. In other words, there should be no need to undertake any other business development efforts to secure new clients. Yet we all tend to spend a great deal of time and energy trying to drum up new clients while we basically ignore our existing ones.

Not only do we fail to seek out opportunities to talk with our clients about our firm (not just talk about existing legal matters) or to actually meet with our clients, but many lawyers actually avoid meeting with their clients. I gave an example earlier where a partner had specifically advised a lawyer to hand deliver some estate planning documents to a client, but that lawyer instead chose to put the documents in the mail. Here was a tailor-made opportunity to visit the client, but the lawyer was "too busy" to visit the client, even though it was on his way home. Why are we so afraid to meet and talk with our clients?

When assessing your business development efforts, it is very important to be honest about what constitutes business development efforts and what does not. A perfect example is telephone calls with existing clients. I have had many lawyers tell me about business development calls to existing clients, but when I asked what they discussed, the only topic was a pending matter. The lawyer was either asking questions, answering questions, or seeking additional information from the client. This is not a business development call. This is a "legal work" call, which relates solely to performing legal services. It may be about client service, but it is not a business development call. Business development calls to clients are the ones you make when you have nothing to ask them, nothing to tell them about a pending matter, and you do not need anything from them with respect to a legal matter. You are simply calling to touch base, to find out how things are going, and to see whether you can help them with anything. That is a business development call.

If you want to really stretch it, if you call a client regarding an existing matter and you start the call by asking them what is going on in their business and catching up on things in their business and talking about the types of things that you would on a business development call *before you talk about the existing matter,* then you might be able to argue that this is a legitimate business development call. Otherwise, recognize the difference and focus your time and attention on making business development and relationship-building calls, rather than just calling the client when you have to.

The final thought in this area of being an investor with your clients deals with the single most effective business development activity that any lawyer can undertake to grow his or her business. This is a proven method that has worked for lawyers everywhere and it works almost every time, yet it is underutilized by most lawyers. In fact, many lawyers ignore it entirely. Quite simply, visit your clients. Yes, it sounds like a "dramatic" step, but it is the best, surest, and most proven method of enhancing your client relationships and at the same time gaining additional business from your existing clients. Specifically, I suggest that you develop a plan to visit (in person) each of your existing clients at least four times every year. If you have so many existing clients that it is impossible to visit each one every quarter, I suggest that you identify a certain number of your top clients that you can visit face to face once a quarter. Rather than seeing more clients less often, I would shorten the list of clients you meet with so that you can meet with these key clients at least four times a year.

There are several key elements of these client visits that must be kept in mind. First and foremost, the meetings must be at the client's business location. The reason for this is that the meeting has to be about them. If you make them take their time and energy to come to your offices, the meeting is about you. The only way to make the meeting about them is to meet at their place of business. In addition, meeting at their location is a great opportunity to have them show their business to you. If you have not asked your clients to show you their businesses, then you have not yet shown your clients that you are really interested either in them or their businesses.

▼▼▼▼▼

Business people are very proud of their business. They love the opportunity to show it off and to tell people what they do, how they do it, and where they do it.

Visiting your client's location also provides you with the unique opportunity to ask specific questions about the business, to better understand it and to be able to be a better advisor when you talk to them on the phone (because you can visualize what their operation looks like and even feels like). You can potentially identify other areas where you can help the client based on what you see, hear, and observe. Visiting your client's location and taking a tour can pay huge dividends to the relationship and to your business development efforts, but few lawyers ever do it once, let alone do it throughout the year.

Second—and this is big—you must not charge for the meeting. This meeting is not about providing legal advice (although if the client gets some free legal advice during the meeting, then more power to them). What a great investment for you to make in them and in the relationship. For these meetings to be an investment, you cannot charge for your time. Charging for your time makes it about you, and it will make your clients more likely to say no to the meeting and to see you as nothing more than a time biller. Bottom line: If you want to make it about them, you cannot charge for your time.

Now let us talk about what the meeting is about other than you being at their place, at no cost, and having an opportunity to see their business and operation firsthand. While some of you may abhor the concept of a script, the following is a fairly specific overview of what these meetings should be about and what you need to tell the clients that they are about. As you plan your first rounds of meetings with existing clients, you need to contact them and indicate that you want to get together at their home or place of business (at no charge—make sure that is clear) with this agenda:

1. I want to find out how we are doing. It is very important to me to know that we are delivering the type of services and experience that you expect. I want to take this opportunity to find out how we are doing.
2. I want to find out what is going on with you and your business. I want to find out what you are working on, what you are looking to accomplish, some of your goals, and some of the specific challenges that you are dealing with. I want to better understand you and your business so that I can be a better advisor to you.
3. I want to find out whom you are working with, whom you would like to work with, and any other information that I can use to try to help you improve your business. It is important to me that I take an active role in working with you to help you achieve your goals, and I need your help to do that.

The exact words are not important, but the concepts are.

First, I need to know how we are doing. Second, I need to know what is going on with you and your business and what you are trying to achieve. Third, I need to find out specific ways that I might be able to help you achieve your goals beyond just being your lawyer. The power in this is incredible. Not only is it a relationship builder, but the lawyers whom I have talked to about this strategy (and those who have implemented it) have consistently told me that they typically come back from these meetings with new business. So, it is not only a relationship builder, but a way to develop new business.

It is not about churning a client for new business, but it is about being so in touch with your client and so knowledgeable about their needs and goals that you are able to identify ways that you can help bring more value to them or their business. It is about delivering the type of services and advice that they need to achieve their goals, and nothing you can do can make a more significant and positive impact on your clients and on your client relationships. This strategy will work, but it will work only if you commit to it and follow through on it. Remember, investors make the best advisors, and you need to continually show your clients, your referral sources, and your other business contacts that you are invested in them and their success.

Be Specific 33

Being specific (or intentional) is a concept that can make the difference between business development efforts and wasted time. In a profession where time is always at a premium, we cannot afford to waste time on business development activities that have little likelihood of succeeding, particularly when we control the quality of the opportunities. Certainly, many aspects of business development are outside of our control, which can result in time being wasted, but shame on us if we knowingly engage in activities without being specific and intentional and thereby minimize potential value from our activities. One of the key ingredients of business development efforts (versus activities) is being specific and intentional, especially with referral sources.

Just Plain Lunch

Meals (breakfast, lunch, or dinner) are a perfect example of how a lack of specificity and intention (and also clear communication) can minimize the value of the time you spend. Let us use lunch as an example. Although many of us commonly refer to lunches as being "business lunches" (for purposes of this discussion we are referring to lunches with business associates or potential referral sources), there are actually three different types of lunches. First and foremost is a true business lunch, where there are specific, intentional, and targeted discussions about how you can help each other, including (ideally) discussions of specific referral opportunities. This is a true business lunch. The second type of lunch is "lunch with a friend." Lunch with a friend occurs when you have lunch with a business associate or referral source, but you never really talk about how you can help each other, you do not discuss specific referral opportunities, and, in fact, you barely talk about anything that might help either of you improve your business development results. You may have framed it as a "business lunch," but you never discussed business (at least not with any degree of specificity or intention) and, therefore, it is nothing more than "lunch with a friend."

Actually, "lunch with a friend" applies to many business development activities. In talking with many law firm partners and marketing directors, there are countless examples of lawyers engaging in so-called marketing activities such as dinners, drinks, ball games, events, and so on, where even the law firm personnel know that it really was not a true business gathering. Taking your friends to a ball game is not business development, especially if you have not (over some period of time) developed any business opportunities or referrals from those friends and you cannot point to any specific likelihood of that occurring in the future. Law firm expense accounts are filled with examples of lawyers going to ball games and incurring expenses for drinks, dinners, and other items with the same small group of people over a long period of time with little or nothing to show for it in terms of new business opportunities.

▼▼▼▼▼

If you cannot specifically demonstrate the opportunities created or likely to be created with people, then they are not business contacts. They are friends.

Please note that I continue to refer to opportunities (true opportunities), rather than limiting it to new business. Certainly, the goal is new business, but it all starts with opportunities, and business development efforts should be judged in significant part by the number and quality of the opportunities, not just new business. If you are consistently generating quality opportunities, but not securing what you believe to be an appropriate amount of new business, then you can start to evaluate what you are doing and how you are doing it with respect to turning opportunities into new business. However, the focus should generally be on the types of opportunities that are developed. If you are not developing opportunities from or through some of your business contacts, then lunch, dinner, or any event with them is merely an outing with a friend, rather than a business development activity.

Finally, there is "just plain lunch." This is the worst of all types of activities because it is not focused on specific and intentional business discussions and opportunities and it is not even with someone that you would consider a friend. This is a monumental waste of time—spending time with someone who is not a friend (and who you may not even like) without any realistic opportunity to develop new business opportunities. You must eliminate this type of activity immediately. These are the types of "time bandits" that will steal time from valuable business development efforts and delivering your services.

These are the types of activities that will tire you out and may discourage you, since you will feel (very quickly) that you are wasting your time if all you are doing is engaging in "just plain lunch" or "just plain getting together." Spending time with friends is certainly an important use of your time and, obviously, investing time to meet with business associates and referral sources with specific and intentional discussions about opportunities is a great investment of your time, but meeting with someone under the guise of business development is a waste of time.

"I'll Keep You in Mind" Does Not Work

We should now talk about some examples of specific and intentional business development meals, events, or even telephone calls. First, you can accomplish a great deal by telephone, especially ensuring that you have consistent and continuous contact with your key business associates. Certainly, "face time" is very important, but it is unrealistic to think that this is possible on a consistent basis with all of your business relationships. Rather, you can use the "face time" for periodic get-togethers, and use telephone discussions in the interim.

By the way, you should spend some "face time" with your key business relationships every six to eight weeks. This type of regular time together is one of the most effective ways to enhance your business development results. It allows you to continuously keep each other up to date on what each of you is doing and what you are trying to accomplish. It allows you to continually share ideas, educate each other on how you bring value to clients, and accelerate and expand the relationship-building process. Frankly, if you are not in regular contact (especially with your best contacts), despite everyone's best intentions, many opportunities will be lost because everyone is busy and they forget about each other, except for the most obvious opportunities for referrals.

One of the most important steps to becoming more effective in our one-on-one business development efforts is to recognize that the concept of "I will keep you in mind" is almost worthless and can be the kiss of death to new business opportunities. We have all had conversations with people we have just met or people we have known for some time in which the meeting or discussion ends with, "I will keep you in mind." More often than not this means just the opposite. Actually, they will not keep you in mind and that is just a polite way of saying that you should not expect to see any opportunities coming from this person. This sounds harsh, but if you think back to similar conversations you have had, you may have had the feeling when you heard that phrase that you were getting the polite brush off. It does not mean that the person does not like you or does not think that you are valuable. It may mean that they are not the type of person that is really committed to engaging in proactive and intentional sharing of business opportunities. Not everyone is. Some people are being polite when they say, "I will keep you in mind," and others actually mean it, but they may not have the skills and the mindset to actually follow through. The other problem is that we may not have done what we need to do to allow them to effectively help us.

▼▼▼▼▼

Unfortunately, we assume that everyone will do what they say they are going to do, but the reality is, many people are not that committed and are not willing to do what it takes to help others succeed.

Tell Them Early and Often

One of the first and most important lessons that I learned (almost the hard way) about referral sources is that you can never educate your clients and referral sources too often or too well with respect to what you do, whom you work with (or want to work with), and how you bring value to your clients. Unfortunately, we all tend to make the mistake of believing that the people who know us are as interested in what we do as we are. We certainly know what we do (although we may not know whom we want to do it with), so we tend to assume that everyone else does as well. We believe that we only have to tell the story once and it will be remembered by everyone who hears it, but there are many reasons that the people we talk to cannot and will not remember the entire story or the correct story. Remember, when we talk about what we do, that is about us, it is personal to us, and it is important to us. However, when we tell that story to others, it is not about them, it may not be that important to them, and they are very busy with all the things that consume their thoughts, time, and energy. Therefore, it is up to us to make sure that we continually, clearly, and repeatedly let people know who we are, what we do, and how they can help us.

Obviously, we also have to do the same for them. While it is certainly their obligation to make sure that we know what they do and how we can help them, if we are an investor in the relationship, we should continually ask them to clarify and to make sure that we fully understand what they do and how we can help them. While quality relationships (especially referral relationships) are *not* based on a *quid pro quo* concept (you give me a referral and I might think about giving you one), all of us are looking for a mutually beneficial relationship. Given that fact, it is up to us to work hard to help the people whom we would like to have help us in return. Rather than failing to perform because the other person failed to do their job in helping us to know and understand how we could help them, we should be taking affirmative steps (if we believe that it is a quality relationship with strong potential for future opportunities) to help the process along.

I can remember very clearly when I learned the lesson that you can never communicate too often or too much regarding what you do. I had a very strong referral relationship with another lawyer. In fact, this lawyer had referred several pieces of business to our firm, and we had in turn referred business to him. One day I received a telephone call from this lawyer and he asked me to give him a referral for a domestic relations lawyer. I paused for a minute (if he had seen my face he would have seen a questioning look in my eye), then I told him I would be more than happy to make the referral and, in fact, I would walk down the hall to make the introduction. He then asked me what I was talking about and I explained to him that we had had a domestic relations practice in our firm for the past 18 months. He said that he did not know that and I, of course, was very diplomatic and said something to the effect of shame on me for not letting him know.

In my own head, however, I was saying something to the effect of "How in the world could he not know?" After all, we had done a special mailing about the addition of the practice. We talked about that practice in each of our quarterly newsletters. I thought we had done all of the right things to get the word out, but here was one of our best referral sources who did not know we did this type of work. Frankly, I was thankful that he had called me for the referral. Imagine if he had given the business to someone else because we had not done a good enough job of educating him. This taught me the valuable lesson that you can never educate your business associates too much about what you do.

I am always amazed when I hear lawyers or anyone tell me that they do not have to do anything more to educate their clients and their business associates about the scope and depth of their products or services. No matter how much you have done, there is always more that you can do or something that you can do better to make it clear and memorable for your clients and your associates. People are always amazed to find out what their clients and associates do not know. Instead of being amazed, we need to focus more of our time and energy on doing a better and more consistent job of educating those around us. This brings us to another key area relating to referral sources—that we must make it easy for people to help us.

How Good Are Your Referral Sources?

As we discussed earlier, our clients and others with whom we have relationships are busy with their own businesses, their own lives, and their own distractions, and this makes it very difficult for them to help us in any consistent and productive manner. The key is to make it easy for them to help us. If it is at all hard, they will not help us. They may like us a lot and they may even have a sincere and genuine desire to help us, but most people will not help others unless it is easy. Sure, there are situations where the relationship is so good or the opportunity was so clear and easy to identify, but those are few and far between. More important, those types of situations are not enough for us to depend on to help generate the types of new opportunities and results that we want and need. We need more reliable and consistent methods to create better opportunities and deliver different and better results, and making it easy for people to help us is vital to that process.

▼▼▼▼▼

We cannot depend on referrals that fortuitously occur or the easy ones that will happen, because that is not enough to give us the comfort level we need to allow us to focus our time and energy on the important things in our businesses and practices.

So how do we make it easy for others to help us? We have already talked about the importance of clearly, consistently, and regularly communicating what we do as a key ingredient. Another key element is being specific. Actually, being specific is critical for all parties who are trying to find ways to help each other. If you meet or talk on the phone with someone and all you say to each other is something like, "If you ever see anyone who might be able to benefit from our services, please let me know," that is not specific enough to help make it easy for either party. While they may be able to keep you in mind, they do not really know what to look for and, most importantly, you have lost the advantage of having them at their most focused—when they are sitting in front of you or when they are talking to you (and it works for you as well).

When you are together or talking, each party (we hope) is at their most focused on helping the other person, but every minute after you leave the meeting or end the telephone call, people will naturally start to shift back to their own priorities, needs, and challenges. While there can always be shortcomings or failures on follow-up, if you come away from a meeting or telephone call with a specific action plan regarding specific opportunities, then you have created some accountability for each of you and you have something specific to follow up on.

For example, if you end a lunch with both of you saying that you will keep the other in mind, how do you follow up on that? Do you call the other person and say, "Are you keeping me in mind?" Do you call and ask, "I know you have been thinking about me, but have you stumbled across anyone that you can refer to me?" Of course not. Although it does not make sense, that is essentially the environment we create when we have only general discussions about helping each other.

You must keep in mind that how you become specific is not important. What is important is that you are specific. For example, just as we discussed with respect to creating niches and specialization (which helps us focus), doing the same thing with our clients and referral sources also helps them to focus. While you may be open to doing work for any type of client, you may tell a client or referral source that you are currently targeting manufacturing businesses. This is still pretty broad in nature, but it is certainly a lot narrower than the "anyone" or "any business" approach. The way our minds work requires creating a sort of funnel or filter system for people by being more specific. If I say that I am looking for introductions to any small business, this is too hard for most people. They start to think about small businesses and, for most people, they know so many that they are immediately overwhelmed and they consciously or unconsciously conclude that it is too hard to try to come up with an answer. However, if you use specific references or descriptions to help their mind start to break it down into smaller pieces, you are making it easier for them to think of opportunities and, therefore, easier for them to help you.

For example, if you said that you were currently targeting businesses that manufactured parts for or distributed parts to the automotive industry, the listener can very easily process that information and determine whether they know anyone in that industry. If they know just a couple, you can then focus on how they can make an introduction for you to these types of businesses. If they do not know anyone in those industries, you can then move to another specific area until you come up with a very short list of opportunities where they may be able to make an introduction. Specificity will make it easier for both of you.

> ▼▼▼▼▼
>
> You are not trying to build your entire practice or build your entire firm's revenue in one meeting or one phone call. Rather, you are trying to discover some specific opportunities to help each other.

A different type of example would be to talk about specific companies. You may even talk about companies in a particular city or on a particular street in a particular city. It may seem like nonsense, but this works across a wide range of industries. It all relates to how our minds process information and the fact that people will be most effective at helping us (and we at helping them) only when it is relatively easy. We do not have the free time and the free mental capacity to spend our days driving around or sitting around an office thinking about opportunities for another person. We are most likely to help each other only when it is easy.

Another example of being specific or, in this case, a little more focused on being intentional, is to focus your meetings and/or telephone calls on identifying for each party one or two opportunities to pursue. Being specific in coming up with these opportunities can be helpful, but in any case, you set a goal for the meeting to walk away with just one or two follow-up opportunities that each person will pursue for the other. You may talk about some things that each of you are doing, or examples of clients you have been working with, with the goal of stimulating or triggering a thought about a new opportunity. You then should adopt and develop some sort of action plan such as, "I will commit to introducing you by telephone or scheduling a meeting for you with this person within the next three weeks." Now, you have specific goals with respect to specific opportunities with specific timetables. Both parties are now accountable and it is relatively easy for both to know what they need to do to follow through. If either side fails to follow through, it is pretty clear and they have very little to hide behind because the expectations were clear. This is an example of combining specific discussions with specific goal setting, and intentional efforts geared toward helping each other.

One way to deal with these challenges is to have an up-front discussion with people you meet (especially your best contacts) and create an expectation that you will meet or at least talk on a regular basis, and you mutually agree that you will be specific when you get together or talk. You make a commitment that you will not just "keep each other in mind," but that you will both commit to seeking out specific opportunities for each other. These mutual commitments (with consistent follow-through by both parties) will lead to the development of better and more consistent opportunities.

Building Your Tool Kit

One challenge for us as lawyers is that we are notoriously bad at giving referrals, unless they relate to legal services. Our comfort zone is legal services, so if someone has a need for legal services that we cannot fulfill for any reason (i.e., a conflict or a different practice area), most of us are more than willing to make a referral. However, we tend to fall short when it comes to making introductions and referrals that do not relate to legal services. First, we are not doing a good enough job of asking questions, understanding needs, and becoming trusted advisors in order to discover opportunities to make nonlegal introductions or referrals. Second, and here comes that word again, it is outside our comfort zone. Legal services are what we know, and it can be a little risky to think about making introductions or referrals that are outside our areas of expertise. Third, we may have done a poor job of assembling a "tool kit" of other resources that we can refer and introduce to people to help them with their needs and challenges. This is a very important topic, since it is one of the easiest things to do and is a great way to get started with business development, especially if you are a newer lawyer.

In the business world, one of the biggest complaints from professionals and business resources is that they are referring business to lawyers, but lawyers are not referring business to them. Typically, their conclusion is that the lawyers are selfish, but many lawyers simply do not know how to do it and are not comfortable doing it. Most of the lawyers who are called "selfish" are not selfish and have no idea that they are being thought of that way. This is a major disconnect because, as we can all guess, if people do not believe that lawyers are working to their mutual benefit, they will stop giving referrals to the lawyers, and the lawyers may never know why.

Like so many things relating to business development, we need to make the giving of referrals (especially nonlegal referrals) a top priority. We need to do this first and foremost because it is one of the best, easiest, and most powerful ways that we can help our clients and business relationships. You can perform no greater act than to help one of your relationship partners, which is why it is so important to make it a top-of-mind subject. Second, the reality in the business world is that people are looking for mutually beneficial relationships. If you are only a receiver of referrals, and you do not aggressively work to give referrals and introductions, your referral sources will "dry up." For all of these reasons, we need to do a much better job of thinking about referrals and introductions with the goal of helping our clients and business relationships, as well as helping to improve our own direct business development results.

Unfortunately, people in a business relationship do not always have the best and optimum level of communication, which can result in the flow of referrals and introductions stopping with neither party knowing why.

One key aspect of your business development efforts should be to figure out and plan for the types of people that you need as referral sources (to give you referrals) and the types of people and business resources that you need to have available to give referrals to. This is what we refer to as your business "tool kit." With respect to those whom you want to receive referrals from, you need to develop a list of those industries or professions, figure out in which areas you already have a good referral source, and, develop a plan to meet and develop a relationship with someone in an area where you do not already have a good referral source. Similarly, you need to do the same thing with respect to resources that you can refer to others.

Certainly, your referral sources may also be (and probably should be) part of your business resources "tool kit," but there are probably other areas where you need resources that may not necessarily be a target as a referral source for you. In fact, I encourage you to continually build your "tool kit" because it will make you a much more valuable advisor and resource for your clients and your own relationships if you can be the "go to" person for nearly anything that they need. I continually refine and expand my "tool kit" because I want to get to the point where I can be a resource for just about everything.

Whenever someone calls me looking for a product or service that I cannot give them a referral for, I am disappointed and I make it a point to identify a resource in that area. Obviously, you will never be able to cover every conceivable product or service, but you can develop a range of resources that is so expansive that you are never more than one phone call away from the product, service, or solution your clients and relationships need. That is my goal and I encourage you to make it yours as you develop your business resources "tool kit."

Let's go back and talk briefly about that list of referral sources you need as a lawyer. This list will vary depending in part on your practice area. In fact, there will always be specific resources that are a match (or a better match) based on your unique practice area or particular niches that you have. However, most business lawyers consider certain areas to be core referral sources: accountants, financial planners, bankers, investment bankers, business brokers, and so on. The list may vary, but what is important is that you invest some time figuring out whom you already have as referral sources, whom you need as referral sources, and how you are going to go about identifying and developing the needed referral sources.

As with clients, you also must continually evaluate your referral sources. So many people tell me that they have referral sources, but when you ask them about referrals from those sources, they have either never had a referral or have not had a referral for a long period of time. How you judge your referral sources is up to you, but it is important to continually monitor and measure the productivity and effectiveness of your referral network. Have you done a poor or ineffective job of communicating to them what you are looking for? Do you need to do a better job of being proactive in educating them and in asking for referrals? Do you need to be more specific? Do you need to be more systematic? Whatever the reasons, you must continually evaluate your referral sources so that you do not waste your time relying on referral sources that are not likely to deliver the types and quantity of opportunities you should expect.

Two questions I often hear relating to building a tool kit of resources are "How do you do it?" and "Doesn't that take a long time?" Regarding how long it takes, it is true that it can take time unless you take advantage of some great shortcuts. It would take quite some time to develop a list of resources you can trust and with whom you have some level of relationship; however, a great way to accelerate this process is to work with others. Instead of starting from scratch, go to your existing referral sources and ask them whom they use. You may ultimately decide that you want to find a different or an additional resource, but if a trusted referral source introduces you to another resource, that can result in some giant leaps in terms of the relationship and trust level with that resource.

Likewise, talk to other people around you. Who are their resources? Who do they look for and who do they refer when someone needs a particular product or service? Whenever I talk about this approach, I always get this question: "What if the people I know do not want to introduce me to their referral source, believing that it will potentially hurt their opportunities for referrals?" First, we need to understand that working together will ultimately help everyone win more and more often. In addition, we often forget that another person's resources or referral sources may know someone to whom you can be introduced.

For example, I have often been told something like, "Most of the good accounting firms [great referral sources potentially] are taken by the other lawyers in our firm." That does not make any sense. Most accounting firms have several accountants, and someone else in your office may have a good relationship with one or two of the accountants, but not with all of them. Like many law firms, accounting firms are not known for consensus decisions. In other words, the fact that one accountant has a relationship with one lawyer does not mean that the entire firm will work with that same lawyer. If you are a younger lawyer just getting started, you ought to be meeting and talking with younger accountants who are likewise looking to create relationships and to find people to work with on business development efforts. While

▼▼▼▼▼

Relationships are personal and, most often, one-on-one. Therefore, there are plenty of opportunities to develop multiple resources and referral sources within a single company or firm.

there is nothing wrong with a young person trying to create a relationship with a senior resource or referral source, that is rare for obvious reasons.

As we have said many times, too often we want to do everything ourselves rather than looking to others for help. Even if you do not have a single strong relationship in business (although I suspect that everyone has a few), as you develop your first one you can then look to that person and ask them whom they look to for various products and services. In this way, you can very quickly and relatively easily build your resources and tool kit. Then, as you move forward in your business development growth, you can keep your eyes open for new or different resources. So often we hear lawyers say that business development is too hard and that there is not enough time for it, but we do not have our eyes open to the opportunities to work together and to do it more efficiently and more effectively just by doing things a little differently. If you are doing nothing, certainly you need to start engaging in business development efforts. However, you will usually find that different results flow from different activities and different efforts, not necessarily from more work and more effort. Ultimately, business development is about being different, and this includes doing things differently.

Another great way to enhance your opportunities with key relationships is to create certain systems that will help you consistently refer them. One strategy is to identify your very best relationships (those people whom you will unequivocally recommend and endorse to others), and then assemble a set of business cards from them to carry with you everywhere so, when the opportunity presents itself, you cannot only say to someone, "You ought to talk to this person," but you can reach into your bag and hand them a business card. This is a powerful endorsement. If you are carrying their business cards with you, then you are strong believer in these people, which makes it even more likely that the person you are speaking with will want to at least talk to someone you are recommending.

It seems like a very little thing, but remember, it is the little things that make all the difference in business development success. Similarly, being specific and being intentional is a relatively little thing that can enhance the quality and quantity of your opportunities and the results you achieve.

Be Systematic 34

Let's be clear from the beginning—systems and being systematic are key ingredients in business development success. We have already discussed numerous examples of different systems you can use not only to help you do what you know you need to do (and want to do) in the area of business development, but also to help you be more successful at it. As we discussed earlier, committing to a plan of meeting with your key clients at their offices at least once a quarter is part of a system. It is easy to follow and easy to track. It certainly does not guarantee that you will do it (that is up to you), but having a system that can track and measure your activities and progress makes you much more likely to follow through. Even our discussion about being specific is really a part of being systematic, since it depends in large part on you doing certain things to arrange the meetings or phone calls and having a system for what you do when you have them.

For most people, especially those who rely on billable hours and are always challenged to find time for business development, creating and following systems is probably one of the most important steps to help you actually implement your ideas, plans, and activities. Remember our earlier discussion about how easy it is for professionals to fall back to what comes easily and what is most comfortable (billable time), especially when the alternative is business development. That is the reality for most lawyers. However, if you can create a system or process to help you in

> ▼▼▼▼▼
>
> If you do business development only when you have "free time," then you will generally do little or no business development.

your efforts, you are much more likely to invest the appropriate time in those efforts.

A great example of how systems can support you in your business development efforts and activities is the use of technology. There are numerous technological tools such as contact management or even sales management programs that will allow you to not only track information, but also to help you to schedule events and follow ups, to help you keep track of activities, to help you keep track of important information with respect to clients, prospects, and relationships, and allow you to be accountable for the activities that you are seeking to implement. Traditional salespeople—yes, this is the place to look for resources—rely heavily on technology and related systems to help support and enhance their sales and business development activities. These are recognized tools that cross many sales professions, but professional service providers, including lawyers, have been very slow to adopt them.

One of the primary reasons, as stated earlier, is that lawyers are reluctant to acknowledge that they are salespeople and, therefore, that sales tools could be of value. For some reason we think that these types of tools detract from the relationship nature of our business and our sales efforts, but in fact they are a perfect complement. Contrary to popular belief, relationships are not just about getting to know someone. In many cases, relationships are built and accelerated based on following specific steps. As we have said over and over, it is often the little things that create, accelerate, or enhance relationships, and processes and systems help us with these little things.

Systems may also go beyond technology—actually, they can be much simpler than technology solutions. For example, assume that you have decided that you want to send a handwritten thank you note to every person you meet with. That is a terrific goal, but you will be more likely to actually follow up on and achieve that goal if you build a system around it. Here is how that system might work:

1. After every meeting, you give the business card with the name and contact information to your assistant.
2. Your assistant is instructed to bring you the appropriate number of thank you notes with the business cards or the names of the people who are to receive the notes.
3. Your assistant is instructed to follow up with you within a designated period of time to ensure that you have written the notes.
4. Either you or your assistant addresses the envelopes by hand.

There are various ways to create a system around thank you notes, but the important point is that you create a system that helps ensure that you will actually do it. It is even better if you have a follow up or support system to ensure that you do it. The key is to make it easy, traceable, and accountable. That is the beauty of a system. It can be very simple and can apply to the most simple tasks or activities, but building a system around business development activities can be the critical difference between actually doing them and not doing them.

Another great system to help you with your business development efforts, as well as to help you better manage your time for all of your efforts, is to schedule business development time on your calendar. In other words, decide how many hours every week you intend to devote to business development efforts and schedule that time on your calendar. For example, you may designate two hours every Tuesday and Thursday from 3 to 5 P.M., which would be in addition to any other business development time in the form of meals or after-hours activities. Certainly, there will be times when you are literally forced to do something else during these designated business development times (e.g., if you are a trial lawyer, a pretrial or other hearing may be scheduled or you may need to meet with a client during these times), but when this happens, you should move that business development time to another day during the week. It is very important that you commit to this amount of time every week so that these business development blocks of time are moved, not canceled.

When you schedule these blocks of time, it is also vital that you treat them as nearly always inviolate. You must treat them like any other meeting—a client meeting, for example—so that you can honor your commitment to invest this time in business development. How inviolate is this time? When someone asks if you can meet or do something during these times, you would tell them that you are already committed to a meeting. If a judge is trying to schedule a hearing, unless the delay is detrimental to your client, then you are unavailable due to a prior commitment.

These blocks of business development time are your time to invest in yourself, in your practice, and in your firm, and this is valuable time that must be preserved and protected. How much time you invest each week (during business hours and after business hours) is ultimately an individual decision, but I encourage you to schedule more time, rather than less. In terms of guidance, even if you are just beginning, I suggest that you find a way to invest eight hours a week in business

▼▼▼▼▼

Your business development time must be considered just as important as your billable time. Otherwise, you will not do it and you will not only allow it to be moved or canceled, but you will actually look for ways to move or cancel it altogether.

development efforts. Some of you may be thinking, "I do not have an extra eight hours every week." That may be true right now, but you need to find a way to convert some of your other time into business development time.

First, nearly every one of us already wastes plenty of time that can be devoted to business development efforts. How much time do we waste during the day? How much more efficient can we be with a better plan every week and every day? How much more could we accomplish if we got up just 30 minutes earlier? How many lunch times are wasted during the week that we could use for business development efforts? How many times do we work longer than we need to because we were not committed to leaving the office at a specified time? Being busy is not an excuse for avoiding what you know you need to do to grow your business.

If you are too busy to invest in the growth and future of your law business, then it is at risk. The size and scope of that risk may vary, but it is very much at risk, and your law business certainly will never be able to achieve its full potential without your commitment to do what you must to achieve financial stability and success. Systems are one of the main ways that you can take back some of that lost time so that you will have the time to not only do the business development things that you must, but also to be most effective in those pursuits.

Big businesses recognize not only the importance but the great value of systems. Systemization creates consistency, efficiency, and profitability. That is a given in the business world, which is why it is so important that you not only focus on systematizing your law business, but also on your business development activities and efforts. As we have said before, systems help you do what you already know you need to do, and they also help you create better habits—in this case, business development habits. We have mentioned several times how easy it is to fall back to our comfort zone of billable hours, which makes it even more important that you develop systems and habits that will help you make business development something that you do naturally and without even thinking about it.

If you have to think about it, then you are wasting that time thinking about it rather than doing it. If you have to think about it, you are more likely to revert to what comes easiest and most naturally, which is billable time. Hopefully, we can all recognize the value and significance of business development activities, and being systematic and intentional can help each of us put our activities and efforts in line with the recognized value of these efforts.

While it is true that "I will keep you in mind" generally does not work, there certainly are lawyers who develop strong opportunities and results with relationships by relying on that concept alone. I am not suggesting that "I will keep you in mind" never works, but I am suggesting that for most lawyers it will not be effective. There are some lawyers who do a terrific job of business development without using some of the specific skills and tactics discussed in this chapter. For some lawyers business development and generating referrals (and even giving referrals) is so natural—either because it is natural or because they have developed the habits over the years—that they do it without thinking about it, they are good at it, and "I will keep you in mind" delivers the types of results that they want. However, this is not the norm.

For most business professionals in any industry (and especially for lawyers) you need to develop systems to help you to follow through with your business development activities, you need to be more specific to help stimulate the referral process, and you need to be more intentional with and about your efforts to achieve your desired results. The goal of the strategies and tactics covered in this chapter is to help us make business development a habit—something that we do without thinking about it. The trouble with business development for most lawyers is that if we have to think about it, we either will not do it or we will be ineffective at it. That is why being systematic and intentional is so important to the entire business development process.

Be Purposeful 35

We have talked about the concept of being purposeful several times in this book, but it is critical to re-visit the concept as it relates to business development efforts. While being purposeful has some impact on the quantity of your business development efforts, the real value comes in improving the quality and effectiveness of your efforts. With time at a premium, it makes sense for all of us to invest our time wisely by making sure that everything that we do in business development is done with a purpose and with a plan. All too often, the focus is on quantity (i.e., meeting as many people as we can) versus quality (focusing on the right people, the right relationships, and the right strategies for building relationships). Contrary to what you may see on your next visit to a chamber of commerce meeting, business development is not about collecting business cards, and certainly not about collecting as many business cards as you possibly can. In fact, networking is a great area in which to discuss being purposeful and how networking with purpose can dramatically improve your results.

One example of networking with purpose relates to the business card "dance." Our goal in networking should not be to collect business cards (by asking for them), but to conduct ourselves in such a way that people offer their business cards to us. We want to do and say the right things so that the person we are talking to wants to stay connected to us and, as a result, offers us a business card. If we have to ask for a business card, then it generally means that we have not built a sufficient level of trust or interest for that person to want to volunteer their business card to us. Ultimately, business cards should be exchanged based on a mutual interest in exchanging them or offered by one person to another because they have an interest in connecting with that person on a level beyond just conversation. Exchanging business cards is *not* about wanting to make a sale or to garner a new client. This is one of the biggest mistakes people make when they are networking because they engage in "net selling" where they are trying to sell someone the first time they meet and before they build up any level of credibility, trust, or relationship.

Over the years, I have developed a concept that I call the three "knows" of networking, which relate to the concept of "who you know" that we have heard is so important. In fact, "who you know" is really not that important, as evidenced by the three "knows" of networking:

- Who you know
- Who knows you
- Who they know

The first level—who you know—is the bare minimum level that most people seek to achieve and, in general, it will deliver few (if any) opportunities to you. The second level—who knows you—is a step closer to the desired relationship-building level, and it may deliver some opportunities and some results, but not the types of opportunities and results that you want and need. The highest level—who they know—is the ultimate in relationship building, trust building, and credibility building, and this is the level of networking and relationship building that will bring the right opportunities to you and your firm on a consistent basis. Let's explore each of these levels in more detail.

The "who you know" level is epitomized by the tactic of attending lots of networking or other events, collecting lots of business cards, and meeting lots of people. At the end of the day, you have collected lots of business cards, you have met lots of people, and you can now claim to "know" lots of people. But, generally, there are no relationships and those people do not "know" you. You may have built up a large database of names and contacts, but there is no foundation upon which you can take those names and build a referral network or a client base. Generally, what you have accomplished is that you are very tired (from attending so many events), and you will have a hard time even remembering the names of all the people that you "know." This level—who you know—is how most salespeople engage in networking, which is why networking often has such a negative and unfavorable reputation. This is absolutely not what I recommend for your networking and business development efforts. It will tire you out, it will likely offend many people who do not appreciate having your card thrust upon them and having you demand their business card, and you are unlikely to have any foundation for establishing sources of new business from your networking activities.

The second level—who knows you—will definitely deliver business results for you, and it is certainly a much higher level of networking and relationship building than the "who you know" level. The fact that you know someone is not significant—what is significant is that you have made such an impression on them that they remember you (favorably) and they have an interest in remaining connected to you. This means that they will remember you, they will be open to an ongoing connection and relationship, and they will speak highly of you when your name comes up with others. Achieving the "who knows you" networking level is certainly not about collecting business cards, but about doing and saying the right things, and being the right type of person, so that others will remember you and want to "know you."

To put it simply, the "who knows you" level of networking is based on the positive impact you have on the people you meet, associate with, and begin to build relationships with.

At this networking level, the people you have met, continue to stay in touch with, and begin building relationships with can become prospective clients and may occasionally refer someone to you, but the referrals will typically be reactive (only occurring when someone asks for specific help that he or she believe you can deliver). Certainly, these are quality relationships that are worth having and nurturing as part of your network or sphere of influence, but the "who knows you" networking level is not the ultimate goal.

The holy grail for anyone, including professionals, is the "who they know" networking level. This level is achieved once you have surpassed the "who knows you" level and you have built such trust, credibility, and good relationships that someone is ready, willing, and able to consistently, regularly, and emphatically refer you. Not only will they reactively refer people to you when the perfect situation arises, but they will keep you in mind, they will introduce you, they will proactively market you and your services to others, and they will effectively be your "raving fan." Achieving this relationship level is not easy and it usually does not happen overnight. It requires an investment in order to make the other person comfortable being your zealot or raving fan. Most of us are hesitant to unequivocally recommend someone unless we are very sure about that person, which is why it requires additional and different effort to achieve a relationship whereby another person is willing to introduce you, refer you, and endorse you to "who they know."

The significance of this highest networking or relationship level is that it is where the greatest degree of leverage occurs. If you spend all of your time building relationships focused on achieving a new client from the person who you are networking with, then your best result is a single new client. However, if you can achieve the "who they know" networking level with any person, that person can now refer you to dozens of new client prospects and opportunities. One relationship can potentially open the door for you to almost limitless new business opportunities, which is a perfect example of leverage. Selling one-on-one is hard work and time consuming, but investing in relationships can deliver exponential returns in terms of new business opportunities and new business. The "who they know" networking level is the path to leverage and great revenue growth.

Who, What, and Why of Business Development

As we have said before, it is critical that we not confuse activity with productivity. In assessing your activity versus your productivity, there are several key areas that you need to evaluate:

- What meetings do you attend?
- What publications do you read?
- What seminars do you attend?
- Who else attends these seminars?
- What books do you read?
- Do you do anything with what you learn?

Everything you do and intend to do needs to be part of a plan and a purpose consistent with your plan. You need to ask yourself what you can do with what you learn. You need to ask yourself whether the people you are meeting are the people who can help you to grow and improve your business. If they are, then you need to focus on improving your relationship building skills. If they are not the right people, then you need to start meeting the right people.

For every activity you need to ask yourself why you are doing it, what you expect to achieve, and how you expect to achieve it.

So many lawyers attend meetings without having any idea why they are there (other than vaguely "marketing"), and they do not know what to do once they get there. Likewise, many lawyers read legal publications (to improve their legal skills), but they never read the publications that their clients and prospective clients subscribe to and read. Trusted advisors read what their clients read. Lawyers attend only continuing legal education seminars, and not business seminars. Here is a little hint. . . . business owners and executives attend business seminars, and you will rarely find lawyers at these business seminars. Imagine the impact and differentiation if you are the lawyer (perhaps the only one) who attends a business seminar.

When an attendee at a business seminar asks why you are there, you can answer, "because I want to make sure that I am a good business advisor for my clients, and this is a way for me to better understand the business issues that my clients deal with every day." Wow! What message does that send to the people you meet at these business seminars? By the way, it is also highly unlikely that you will find any new clients or prospects at a CLE seminar. The room is filled with your competitors, not your prospects. The bottom line is that you need to have a plan and a purpose, you need to make sure that everything you do is consistent with your plan and your purpose, and you need to make more and better decisions about who you are meeting, what you are doing, and what type of message you are communicating.

Before we move on, here are a couple of final legal marketing keys. First and foremost, you need to market and sell all the time. While you may designate time for business development efforts, you need to have a business development mindset all the time so that everything you do is driven by a focus on business development. The reality is that almost everything you do as a lawyer is ultimately about business development. The services and the service experience that you provide to your clients is a part of business development. This does not mean that providing good legal services or even great service experiences for your clients is all you need to do to accomplish your business development goals, but your services and your service level are certainly part of business development.

Similarly, how you bill and how you collect for your services is ultimately a part of business development. Likewise, every person in your firm is part of your business development team. How you work together (or not) and how you interact with clients will have an impact on your business development results. Remember, your clients' entire experience and the message that you communicate to prospective clients are vital to your business development efforts, but you still need to expend effort toward specific, targeted, and intentional business development if you want to achieve different and better results. We have already talked about how important it is to focus on your activities and to set goals for those activities, but if you do not track what you do then you will never know how you are doing. This

> ▼▼▼▼▼
>
> In addition to having a plan and a purpose, a key ingredient in being purposeful is tracking your activities, as well as your results.

type of measuring is vital if you are to sustain the right business development activities.

What should you track? Everything! You need to track your phone calls—who you call, and what you discuss. You need to keep track of the organizations that you are interacting with—how and when you interact and the results of those interactions. You need to keep track of the meetings you attend, the events you attend, and the opportunities you have to speak. You need to keep track of your writing opportunities. You need to keep track of who you have breakfast, lunch, or dinner with and the results of those get-togethers. You need to keep track of the seminars you attend and who you spoke with at those seminars. You need to keep track of every single networking opportunity that you create or take advantage of.

In short, you need to track absolutely everything that you do because it is the only way that you will be able to see what you are doing, assess the results of your efforts, and ultimately make adjustments to improve either the quantity or the quality of your efforts. Without specific and measurable activity goals, and without tracking your activities against those goals, you will never know how you are doing or how you can improve.

I read many years ago that the space flights to the moon were only on course 1 percent of the time, which means that they were off course 99 percent of the time. The key is that they constantly readjusted their flight pattern to get back on course. In other words, their flights were a constant series of adjustments to stay on course, and you need to do the same thing with your business development efforts. The path to success in business development is not a straight line, but a series of twists and turns, improvements and setbacks, successes and failures, good days and bad days, and times of being on track and times of being off course. The key is to be so focused on your activities and your results that you can make necessary adjustments quickly before you get too far off course.

Despite the ups and downs, if you constantly track and assess your activities and results, you can continue to make adjustments and thereby stay relatively on course. However, if you fail to track your activities and your results, when you go off in the wrong direction, it may be easy for you to go so far off course that it will be very difficult or impossible to get back on course because the adjustments needed would be too significant.

Tracking your activities and your results on a consistent basis will give purpose to your business development efforts and help improve the quantity, quality, and consistency of your results. Ultimately, consistent business development results will give you and your firm the greatest level of security and confidence in the future.

To Achieve We Must Do

In the movie *The Untouchables*, Sean Connery's character is ambushed in his home and Kevin Costner's character (Elliott Ness) finds him bleeding and near death on the floor. With his dying breath, Connery asks Costner this defining question: "What are you prepared to do?" In that case he was talking about what Costner was willing to do to avenge Connery's death, but what he was really saying is are you up to the task? Are you willing to do what needs to be done to achieve the goals that you have established? Are you willing to risk it all to do what is right and that which must be done? These are the same questions that we must ask when it comes to business development.

We may think that business development is not a matter of life and death, but it actually is about life and death—the life and death of a law firm. Clients and revenues are the lifeblood of any business, including law firms.

Too often we are tempted to let others do what must be done for the future and financial stability of the firm, but it is really up to each lawyer in the firm to do what must be done. They may have different skills, abilities, and connections when it comes to business development, but all lawyers can do better than they are already doing. Imagine the opportunities that would exist if everyone was fully engaged and committed to the business development process. Imagine the firm's success if everyone improved their business development efforts and performance by just 10 percent more. All of us can do a little better. All of us can do a little more. All of us can make a difference in the future of our law firm. The question we must ask is—are we prepared to do what needs to be done, what we know we should be doing, and what will help secure the financial strength and future of the law firm? As Sean Connery asked Kevin Costner, "What are you prepared to do?"

Ultimately, we all recognize that our opportunities and results will be determined in significant part by what we do, but we have several problems. In some cases we do not know what to do or how to do it. In other cases we know what to do, but we somehow never find the time to do it, and sometimes we waste our time on activities that never really had any significant likelihood of success. Our focus in this chapter has been on all of these challenges. We all need to do a better job of being honest with ourselves and assessing the effectiveness of our activities, recognizing the difference between focused, effective business development efforts and activities that allow us to feel like we are doing something when they are really not likely or even intended to be productive.

While it certainly is important to "just do it" when it comes to business development, we need to get our focus back on productivity and effectiveness and not just on being active. There are many ways and strategies for us to improve our business development opportunities and results, but we must make the commitment to the value of those efforts and to the process of improving our skills. The purpose of this chapter has been to work through some of the various ways that we can improve not only the quantity, but the quality, of our business development efforts all with the single-minded focus of improving our opportunities and our results.

PART VI

Law Firm Path to Success

36 Sales Is Not a Four-Letter Word!

When it comes to sales—yes, selling legal services is sales—the key to success is our ability to sell products or services. We talked earlier about the relative value of rainmakers versus technicians, but it is difficult (or impossible) to ignore the reality that without clients there is no business, there is no one to provide services to, and there are no hours to bill. Without clients there is no business. We must keep this fact in mind as we start to assess and evaluate the role of sales in a successful law firm, acknowledging that the key to that success is building relationships. Remember, we are all capable of achieving periodic, occasional, and one-time sales, but one-time sales simply pay the bills. Long-term relationships, repeat customers, and raving fans who refer new clients to us are the heart and soul of what will grow your law business.

Most lawyers do not like sales, avoid the word, do not want to be salespeople, and will claim that lawyers are not ethically permitted to sell. Wrong, wrong, wrong. First, sales are essential to any business, including the business of law. Therefore, it is critical to get past any discomfort with the word "sales" so that we can become better sales professionals. Second, the reality is that we all sell all the time, but we need to take those selling experiences and skills and carry them over to our business development efforts. Third, we need to demystify the selling process and recognize that selling is really nothing more than asking questions—it is not cross-examining, but asking questions of people. Finally, recognizing that we are sales professionals will allow us to pursue the right type of training and systems to help us to be more effective. Until we get past these obstacles we cannot fully engage as sales professionals.

First, I want to deal with the issue of "comfort level." When we talk about selling legal services, we are not talking about turning every lawyer into a used car salesperson (no offense to that industry, but that is one perception). We are talking about relationship-based and consultative selling designed to let people know how we can help them and match a need with a solution. We are not talking about the sales activities of Paul Newman in *The Verdict,* where we hand out our business card to the grieving widow at the funeral of her husband. We are not talking about handing out business cards at automobile accidents. We are not talking about sending letters to the families of victims of airline crashes (which, by the way, is permitted if the applicable guidelines are followed). We are not talking about telemarketing. We are not talking about going to business events and shoving a business card into the hand of every person we meet. We are not talking about "selling" anyone on anything. We are talking about letting people know (clients, prospects, and referral sources) what we do and how we can help them. This is neither sleazy nor unethical.

Let's talk a moment about the ethics question. We are not going to evaluate every potential ethics question relating to business development efforts, but we need to address the misconception that selling legal services is unethical. I cannot tell you how many times lawyers have told me that they cannot sell their legal services—that it is unethical. Frankly, that is an absurd statement. The rules of ethical conduct tell us what we can and cannot do, and I am in no way suggesting that any of you violate those codes of professional responsibility. What I am suggesting is that you decide what you want to achieve and develop a plan that allows you to achieve those goals consistent with the rules of professional responsibility.

In contrast, many lawyers approach the process with the view that selling legal services is unethical, and they need to somehow be convinced that they can do it. This is the wrong approach. As you may be aware, several law firms in this country have hired nonlawyers to serve in the role equivalent to a "director of sales." These people sell legal services for the firm, and they are not lawyers. Several lawyers have told me (when they have heard of these types of roles) that it is unethical. The fact is that there is nothing that says that only lawyers can sell legal services—absolutely nothing. Now, there may be a challenge in compensating these individuals without violating ethical rules with respect to the sharing of legal fees with nonlawyers. That may require creative compensation structures, but anyone can sell legal services, and there is no ethical restriction on doing so.

In fact, I firmly believe that this is the future of business development for law firms (especially larger law firms)—hiring someone who has no billable hour requirements whose responsibility is to sell and market legal services. The reality is that these people will almost never actually close new legal business, but they are essentially opportunity creators. Their role is to create new opportunities, enhance existing opportunities, and develop better opportunities for new business with existing clients or new clients. These opportunity creators do not violate ethical rules (assuming that their activities are consistent with the Code of Professional Responsibility), and they are perfect examples of how law firms can be more creative, more businesslike, and more effective in business development efforts.

> 
>
> It is vital to remember that we cannot move forward and achieve better opportunities and results unless and until we overcome our discomfort level with the concept of "selling" legal services and move past the perspective that anything involving "selling" is unethical.

One of the biggest steps for lawyers to take in overcoming their own negative perception of selling is to recognize that we already sell . . . and we do so all the time. In everything we do (personally and professionally) we are selling ourselves. Some lawyers think this is something very different from selling legal services, but in reality it is very much the same. As we've already established, most clients and prospective clients are not knowledgeable enough to understand and "buy" legal services, which means that they are "buying" the lawyer. In other words, we sell legal services by selling ourselves. Since we are constantly selling ourselves in all parts of our lives, the selling of legal services is just another way that we sell ourselves. Similarly, and especially in our day-to-day practice of law, we are regularly selling our ideas, perspectives, and theories. Lawyers are called on almost daily to sell some idea or concept to their clients or to their fellow lawyers in their firm. It is what we do nearly every week—if not every day. The "sales" reality for lawyers is that we sell constantly as lawyers and as people, and it is just a small step to start thinking and functioning like sales professionals in selling our legal services.

Part of the problem is that there are so many negative perceptions of and about salespeople that lawyers (who are already working almost constantly to "be different" from everyone else) are spending time and energy claiming to be different from salespeople. The fact that some salespeople are unprofessional and engage in offensive practices does not mean that lawyers have to be unprofessional or engage in the tactics or practices that have given traditional salespeople a bad name. The whole point here is for lawyers to simply admit that their role in developing new business is the role of a sales professional and, therefore, they should adopt and implement systems and strategies that work for other sales professionals (many of which we have already discussed).

In fact, most lawyers are already on the road to becoming true sales professionals, but they limit themselves and their results by putting up mental roadblocks that keep them from fully functioning like sales professionals. As we have said before, many lawyers know what to do, but they do not do it, including adopting the types of tactics, skills, and practices that make sales professionals successful. In my many discussions with rainmakers in law firms, they all acknowledge that selling legal services is just that—sales—and that there is nothing really unique or different between selling legal services and selling anything else (especially services). Most of these rainmakers long ago recognized that even as lawyers they must function as sales professionals by doing what sales professionals do to develop more opportunities and to convert those opportunities into new business (whether from existing clients or from new clients).

A perfect example of this recognition comes when you ask rainmakers whether it is appropriate and necessary to "ask for the sale" with respect to legal services. Without exception, the answer is absolutely, yes—you must ask for the business when you are talking with clients, prospects, and referral sources. Why? Because the same statistics that apply to every other salesperson or sales professional also apply to us as lawyers—if we do not ask for the business, we will not get it.

How Do We Sell?

We should also spend some time considering the four key ways that lawyers sell or should sell:

1. Lawyers sell directly . . . usually by asking questions.
2. Lawyers sell indirectly via referral sources (which is the best and most leveraged way for lawyers to sell).
3. Lawyers sell themselves by *showing*, not telling.
4. Lawyers sell the overall firm via cross-selling (another one of the best and most leveraged ways for lawyers to sell).

▼▼▼▼▼

Why referrals? With all of the reluctance lawyers have about selling their services (especially directly), selling through referral sources is a great way to sell without dealing with some of the hurdles (real or perceived) in direct selling.

We have already talked about how we sell ourselves (and therefore our services) as lawyers along with various strategies for directly selling services to new clients, but two of the easiest ways for lawyers to sell their services are via referrals and by cross-selling within the firm.

The best thing about referral selling is that it offers much greater opportunities, especially for leveraged selling. If you are trying to sell one-on-one to a prospective client or to an existing client, two things can happen. Either you get the new client/business or you do not. Therefore, for all of your invested time, energy, and effort, even if you are successful you have only secured one new client or matter. Certainly, the size of the client or matter is significant in assessing its value, but it is only through referrals that you can sell yourself "once" (to the referral source) and thereby create multiple and ongoing opportunities.

Yes, you must still "close" the new business even with a referral, but the opportunity came to you with little or no time or cost investment and, as we all know, referrals are much more likely to close than direct sales (because of the strength of the referral and endorsement from your referral source). This does not mean that you should only invest time and effort on referral sources, since we should all diversify our business development efforts (including direct efforts to secure new clients and working with referral sources to develop new clients). However, for all of the time and effort that you invest in pursuing a new client directly, your net return is, at best, one new client, while you can invest the same amount of time in a referral relationship with the potential to achieve any number of new clients. This is one of the best examples of leveraged business development efforts.

Likewise, cross-selling within the firm is another great form of leveraged business development. Obviously, these opportunities exist only when the firm has more than one area of expertise or practice area, but in such firms cross-selling is a tremendous business development tool. The leverage exists because it allows every member of the firm to sell not only their services but the services of the entire firm. Sadly, many firms fail to take full advantage of these opportunities. This is unfortunate because cross-selling is the means to deal with the "no current need" challenge in selling anything. A business reality is that most people do not have a need for what we are selling at a particular point in time. For this reason, it is vital to stay in front of people so that you are "there" when they have the need. However, if you are selling a wider range of services (beyond your own practice area or expertise), it increases the likelihood that you can offer something where there is an immediate need.

Despite all of the advantages of cross-selling, most lawyers and firms do a poor job of it. Part of this is due to the misconception (common in many professions) that you can sell only what you know or are an expert at, when the reality is that you only need to create the opportunity for the other experts in your firm. Another failing is the tendency for lawyers to focus on selling their own services and limit cross-selling to their spare time or when their own plate is full. This is sometimes driven by the firm's compensation system failing to give adequate credit for cross-selling. If the compensation system is heavily weighted toward business that you do yourself, then lawyers may think about cross-selling other services only when their plate is not full and when they feel that they do not have current opportunities to sell their own services (which, of course, is never). What we should be doing is constantly thinking about the full range of the firms' services and selling the firm first, whether it is your practice area or not. This mindset can significantly enhance and improve a firm's cross-selling efforts, opportunities, and results, but it all begins with changing the lawyers' and the firm's mindset to one that not only accepts selling, but embraces it.

One important sales strategy for lawyers (and another reason to recognize that sales is not a dirty word) is the art and skill of asking questions and, most critically, actually listening to the answers. This is not about cross-examination or leading people to our pre-determined conclusion, but about asking questions that tell the client or prospect what we and our firm are about. Thus, questions are an important part of individual and law firm differentiation. Too often we want to jump ahead and want to know from a client or prospect "what happened" or ask them to "tell us the story," when we should first focus on what is important to the client in terms of goals, results, and impact. How often have we talked to clients or prospects and never asked or understood how the situation affects (or could affect) them, their families, and/or their businesses?

> ▼▼▼▼▼
>
> Questions are a great tool for communicating to clients and prospects that it is all about them and that you are genuinely interested in them and in their results.

Some time ago I conducted a workshop for lawyers on business development skills. One of the younger lawyers raised his hand and shared with the group that his biggest frustration or challenge was that he did not know what to say to clients or prospects. He felt like he was "on stage" and had to perform, and was very uncomfortable and insecure interacting with clients and prospects. My advice to him (and the assembled group of lawyers) was to stop talking (and worrying about talking) and to start asking questions. I suggested that he concentrate on asking questions to help him better understand their business, needs, goals, and interests. I told him to make it fun because getting to know people and their businesses is fun and interesting. He was so worried about "presenting" himself and his firm that he had forgotten the basic skills of interacting with people.

Two or three days later I received a voicemail from this lawyer. He said that he met with a prospective client shortly after the workshop and had consciously thought about simply asking questions, instead of worrying about what he was going to say or how he was going to "present." As you can guess, he told me that it was "easy," "comfortable," and successful—he secured a new client. He emphasized how easy it was and how he could not believe that he had not done it before, but that is so typical of many aspects of the business of law. We know what we need to do and should do, and it may not be that difficult, but we often fail to do it because of so many self-imposed misperceptions about our profession and our role with clients. As lawyers, we sell solutions and the only way to identify the needs so that we can find the right solutions is by asking questions.

Sales Systems for Lawyers

One of the most significant things that "sales recognition" can do for lawyers and law firms is to open the door for the firm to develop and implement effective sales systems. Lawyers may not see the need for sales systems, but sales professionals definitely do. Similarly, "sales recognition" is the first and most significant step toward developing a sales culture within a law firm. A sales culture exists when the firm and its lawyers recognize that sales are an integral part of their operations; when they recognize that everything they do must be viewed as a part of business development; and when they commit to implementing processes and systems that will help everyone do a better job of enhancing client relationships, improving new business opportunities, and making referral relationships more productive.

One key type of system that sales-focused lawyers can implement is a "touch" or "drip" campaign. We have talked several times already about the need to develop systems that help lawyers and law firms better and more consistently communicate with clients and others, and a touch or drip campaign is precisely that type of system. Touch or drip campaigns are designed to keep your name and relevant information in front of clients and business relationships.

A simple example of one part of a touch campaign is a firm newsletter. Whether it is monthly (better) or at least quarterly (at a minimum), a well-written newsletter is a systematic and regular way for a law firm to communicate with its clients and, ideally, other business relationships. The key word here is well-written, but this is more about focus than quality of writing. One big failing of law firm newsletters is that they are written more for lawyers than clients. While some of the topics might be of interest to clients or other readers, they are written in "technical" terms by lawyers, as if the readers are other lawyers. Clients and other contacts need and want helpful information that they can easily use for their benefit. This is all part of making certain that what you say, do, and write is client focused. That is why newsletters (as an example) should be designed and produced based on what the readers want, not what the firm wants to tell them. The problem is that many law firms rely on their newsletter as their only systematic touch program. Touch campaigns can include everything from newsletters, to letters, to postcards, to e-mails, to gifts, to notes, to articles, to telephone calls. Touch campaigns are often called "drip" campaigns because they involve dripping (one drop at a time) on clients, prospects, and others. These others are often overlooked by law firms. They send their newsletters and other firm communications to existing clients but forget to include many others who can or should be helping to generate and enhance opportunities for the firm. Whatever the vehicle chosen, the key is consistency—and systems drive consistency.

▼▼▼▼▼

The challenge is that without a systematic approach to a touch campaign, the contacts and "touches" are sporadic and inconsistent, which nullifies their value and impact.

The value of systems for law firms is that they help motivate us to do what we know we need to do, and they help us so that we do not forget what we want to do and have planned to do. We may want and need to stay in regular contact with our clients, prospects, and others with whom we have key relationships, but busy work schedules sometimes make that a challenge. A good sales system will help remind us of what we need to do to keep our business development goals on track. We talked about one such system of making notes on business cards when you meet someone new and recording that information in your contact management or similar software program. Even better, law firms could further improve their sales efforts by actually implementing a true sales-focused technology program.

There are basically three types of contact management programs:

1. A program that is primarily a place to store and retrieve information and to maintain a calendar;
2. A program designed to support customer or client service; and
3. A sales system.

There are big differences between them and only a system that is specifically designed and intended to serve as a sales system can bring the best and highest level of sales and business development effectiveness to a firm and its team of sales professionals.

We have already talked about being systematic when it comes to your individual and firm business development efforts, and such systems are most often implemented when lawyers embrace the idea that they are all sales professionals, that there is nothing wrong or unethical about lawyers functioning as sales professionals, and that law firms with a sales culture will be more successful and stable than other law firms. To achieve its greatest potential, a law firm needs to commit to and invest in building a sales engine and processes within the firm . . . just like every highly successful business.

The Path to Trusted Advisor

37

Riddle me this: What does every lawyer desperately desire to be, yet already claim to be? Answer: A trusted advisor. We've already talked about the fact that nearly all lawyers "claim to be" trusted advisors to their clients (and the fact that this statement is not an effective differentiation point since everybody says the same thing), but the truth is that being a *true* trusted advisor is a path to great success in the business of law. The problem is that lawyers spend most of their time claiming to be trusted advisors, but they are not investing much time, energy, or resources in *being* a true trusted advisor. As in so many things in life and in business, saying it is so does not make it so. Claiming to be a trusted advisor is nothing more than words—empty words if you are not walking the talk and *doing* the things that demonstrate that you are in fact a trusted advisor to your clients.

Do clients want to do business with lawyers who actually add value and function as trusted advisors? Absolutely, but how do you become a trusted advisor beyond just claiming that status in your promotional materials or on your Web site? While the path to trusted advisor may not be easy or quick, it is relatively straightforward and open to virtually every lawyer. Incidentally, if you want to read more about the path to trusted advisor status, a terrific resource is Dave Maister's book, *The Trusted Advisor* (Free Press, 2000), which is devoted to the trusted advisor role—what it is, what it is not, the client's perspective of a trusted advisor, and how professionals must think and act to achieve trusted advisor status.

Before we talk about my steps to trusted advisor status, we should first take a look at the person or profession that currently possesses the trusted advisor status for most people, especially business owners. This is not a secret, and whenever I ask a group of lawyers to name the profession that is most likely to be the trusted advisor to a business owner—the first person called when the business owner has a problem or a need—the answer is always the same . . . the accountant.

Before I go any further let me make one thing very clear. The following discussion about accountants in the role as trusted advisor is intended to highlight what accountants do very well, and I in no way intend to imply (or suggest) that accountants are not good at business development. However, accountants and lawyers have many things in common, including the fact that they both typically are not natural salespeople, most do not take a systematic approach to sales and business development, most are compensated on an hourly basis, and most are the primary deliverer of services for their clients. With all of these things in common, why do accountants (rather than lawyers) tend to be the trusted advisor to their clients? For the answer we need only look at what accountants do with and for their clients rather than at some grand and glorious sales and marketing initiative.

I was very curious about why accountants tend to be the people who other people (especially business owners) call when they have a problem or a need, so I took the direct approach and started asking business owners this question: Who do you call when you have a problem or need in your business? As expected, most of the time the answer was their accountant (while occasionally the answer was financial planner or lawyer), and I then asked them why they called their accountant. By the way, I did not ask who their trusted advisor was or why their accountant was their trusted advisor, since most people do not think in those terms. This is part of the problem I have with lawyers who are always "marketing" themselves as trusted advisors, since being a trusted advisor is something you are and do, not a badge of honor that you wear or a title that you attain. Yes, some clients refer to their accountant or lawyer as their business advisor, but you rarely hear a reference to them as their trusted advisor.

> ▼▼▼▼▼
>
> Trusted advisor is a status that you achieve based on what you do and how you think—it is not a title.

In any event, I asked many business owners why they tended to call their accountants when they needed advice, and their answers spoke volumes about the simplicity of the path to trusted advisor. Some of their answers varied (e.g., I am related to the accountant or he or she is my business partner), but the common theme consisted of three simple and basic points:

1. The confidential relationship between accountants and their clients;
2. The fact that accountants typically have regular contact with their clients throughout the year (typically, quarterly or at least several times a year), which is just a part of the accountant's duties; and
3. The accountant's role of helping clients either make money or save money, whether it be via tax advice, tax preparation, tax planning, financial analysis, benchmarking, and so on.

Pretty simple, isn't it? Three little things, but they make a big difference when it comes to achieving that highly coveted trusted advisor role.

Obviously, we need to abandon our quest for trusted advisor status, since we cannot possibly compete with the advantages held by accountants—or can we? Let's take a look at these steps for accountants to trusted advisor status. Yes, accountants do have a confidential relationship with their clients, but so do lawyers. I will not debate here the relative value or sanctity of this confidential relationship, but it is safe to say that the confidentiality of the attorney-client relationship is at least as sacred and inviolate as the accountant-client relationship. Isn't that interesting—we have just as significant a confidential relationship with our clients, which means we have satisfied one of the three steps to trusted advisor status.

The second step is regularly scheduled meetings with your clients throughout the year. If you are thinking that the accountants have an advantage here (because their work usually requires them to at least have quarterly meetings with their clients), then you missed the boat. While your legal practice may not require you to regularly meet with your clients throughout the year, it would be a simple matter to make that part of your ongoing client development and client service system. You simply schedule quarterly meetings with each of your clients (or least each of your best clients) throughout the course of the year. So now, without much effort at all, we have suddenly achieved two of the three steps toward trusted advisor status, but what about that final step—having a mission to help our clients make money or save money.

Some of you are probably reading this and saying, "This is where we cannot compete. It is the accountant's job to help clients make or save money through advice and tax work, and this is what allows an accountant to more often be the trusted advisor instead of lawyers." It is precisely that narrow and limited view of our role as lawyer that is keeping us from achieving trusted advisor status. I will grant you that it may be a little easier for clients to see their accountant's role in making money for them or saving them money (because it is almost an inherent role in the position), but it absolutely is and should be your role (as the lawyer) to help your clients make or save money. You just need to change how you view your role (and how you communicate with your clients), and recognize that you are in a position to help your clients make or save money, which also includes reducing risk.

We have already talked about these different ways to look at the value of what you do for clients including the fact that it is up to you to show your clients throughout the process how, when, and how much you are making them or saving them, or reducing risk. The opportunities are already there, but it is up to you to do a more effective job of focusing your advice and efforts on the client's real interests (typically financial or risk related) and to communicate a clear, consistent, and repeated message to your clients on how (and how much) you are impacting their financial results and financial health.

There it is. The accountant's (and now the lawyer's) path to trusted advisors status:

- Maintain a confidential relationship, which already exists;
- Meet with your clients regularly throughout the year (ideally, on a quarterly basis); and
- Advise and represent your clients with the goal of helping them make money, save money, or reduce risk; make sure that they are aware that this is where you are focusing your efforts; and show them the fruits of your efforts.

It really is that simple, but most lawyers are missing this opportunity to achieve that holy grail of business development in client relationships . . . trusted advisor status. If you take nothing more from this book than these three simple steps to trusted advisor status (and take the affirmative steps to implement them), you can be assured of better client relationships, more clients, better business development results, and a more successful firm. Now, let's take a look at some different ways to help you enhance your clients' success as part of the process of becoming their trusted advisor.

The Most Powerful Question

38

I have always believed that the best way to enhance your business development results and, thus, your business success is to stop selling legal services (or any services for that matter) and to start helping your clients and others with whom you have key relationships. I have talked about the sales philosophy of focusing on connecting people as the path to outstanding business development results, which is an important part of the overall philosophy of helping others. You will note that I did not call helping others a business development strategy, but rather a philosophy, because helping others has to be a personal and professional philosophy that you believe in. You cannot fake it because people will see you as being less than genuine if you are either pretending to help others or helping others clearly with the hope of a direct benefit. This type of quid pro quo "marketing" turns most people off, and frankly I have always avoided it when anyone has approached me about forming a so-called relationship that is ultimately based on a *quid pro quo* type of understanding.

What does *quid pro quo* marketing mean? The best way to describe it is visually. Picture yourself at a meeting (perhaps a lunch or breakfast meeting) with a so-called referral source or at least a potential referral source. This so-called referral source is sitting across the table from you with a strong lead tightly held in his fingers, but instead of giving you the lead (the opportunity), he is holding onto it with his other hand outstretched and open . . . waiting for you to deliver a lead or referral first (or at least simultaneously). Do you have this picture in your mind? Can you see the two of you sitting across from each other in a position to help each other, but holding out so that the supposed help is really more of a trade of leads? This is the *quid pro quo* approach to networking and referrals, and it does not work.

Yes, if you are going to help others in a meaningful way, it is reasonable to expect their help in return, but it may not be a one-for-one return, and it may not happen on the same timetable. Admittedly, you cannot wait forever for reciprocal help, and you may at some point have to make a business decision that a relationship is not strong enough for you to continue investing your time and your leads or other help for the other person. But that decision is going to come down the road. And you may get hints that this person is not really as committed to helping you as he or she suggests. We all will generally get a feeling or a gut instinct as to whether someone is genuinely interested in helping us, and those are the people for whom we need to invest our time, attention, and resources to build a better and mutually beneficial relationship.

This is why I am talking about a genuine commitment to helping others as the path to enhanced relationships and, ultimately, improved business results and success. I will assume that you have this philosophy and are genuinely committed to finding ways to help others. As I said earlier, this giving philosophy is something that I have held and practiced for many years, but in recent years I came upon a resource that crystallized the concept perfectly. I am sure that most of you know the name Thomas Stanley. He is the author of *The Millionaire Next Door* and *The Millionaire Mind,* both of which are very well-known books. While both are outstanding, it is another work by Stanley that I believe is his best, especially when it comes to professionals and business development.

Networking with Millionaires (Simon & Schuster Audio, 2001) is the title of the audio version of the book; the written version of the book is titled *Networking with the Affluent* (McGraw-Hill, 1997). In it Stanley talks about various strategies for becoming a trusted advisor to your clients and others with whom you have relationships. Stanley explores many different ways in which you can become a true "trusted advisor" not only to your clients, but also to business associates who can help you develop more clients and more business. In short, to be a great networker and to develop referral sources that will drive your business to success, you need to constantly and creatively look for ways to help other people be more successful themselves. Stanley puts forth a concept that is one of the most insightful and effective in the business development arena—it is called the most powerful question.

In fact, it is the *most powerful question in business development.* It is *not* "What pain do you have that I can make go away?" It is *not* "Which of *my* products or services do you need today?" The most powerful business development question is *"What do you need?"* Let me say it again: "What do you need?" It is profound in its simplicity. While it appears to be too easy and too simple, its power becomes evident when you think about what it really means. By the way, the question is not limited to business needs. It expresses a genuine and sincere interest in finding out what the person across the table from you needs in business or in life. This is not about selling your legal services. It is not about necessarily telling prospects, clients, or others that your services can help them with a need. Rather than approaching clients, prospects, or business associates from the "I" perspective ("What do I need?" or "What can I do for you?"), look for ways to help them. There are many ways to help, but one very powerful way is to be a resource.

When you talk to a prospective client or even an existing client, you typically start asking questions to discover a legal need that you believe you can solve. Then, once you've discovered the need, you offer up your services as the solution to the need. But no matter how good you are, that person knows that you are there to sell them something. Imagine if, instead of focusing on services, you simply asked the prospect "What do you need?" And when that prospect identified a need that your services cannot fulfill, you still offered up the needed solution. When you do this, you become a trusted advisor, not just a salesperson or vendor of legal services. You clearly differentiate yourself from the rest of the industry. In fact, you become something special and unique. You may not get new business that day, but the credibility you create and the relationship you build will deliver in the future. Not only will you likely have the opportunity to do business with people when a need for your services arises, but they will become your "raving fans" to drive other business to you. So just keep it simple: "What do *you* need?"

When you ask people what they need and then seek solutions and answers to their needs, you can see the power of the question. Remember, we are not talking about what they need in the way of legal advice or services, but rather what they need help with. Often the help they need will have nothing whatsoever to do with you, your firm, or your services, but this is how you differentiate yourself from other lawyers and, frankly, other business professionals. If your mission is to find out what your clients and associates need help with, and you are committed to trying to

▼▼▼▼▼

When you ask clients what they need, you are no longer the lawyer; you are the person (and typically the only one) who has stopped worrying about your legal services and fees and is focused entirely on helping that client.

help them with these needs, you are well on your way to becoming a true trusted advisor. While it is obviously your goal to provide some form of substantive help, success in helping them is rarely necessary in order to proceed down the path toward trusted advisor status or even to achieve it. If you are making the effort (and clients know when your effort is genuine), you will typically be rewarded.

39 Stop Selling and Start Helping!

When it comes to business development efforts (also known as sales efforts), many lawyers convince themselves that the process of getting new clients or additional business from existing clients is akin to direct selling (i.e., find a prospect, find a need, and close the sale). When selling professional services, however, the formula is much different, particularly because many prospective purchasers of legal services do not typically have a need at the exact time a lawyer is talking to them (obviously, when a person or business is seeking legal counsel for a known need, the formula is much different). One element of selling certainly exists in all sales situations—that of asking for the sale or at least making it clear that you want the opportunity to work with a prospective client.

Rather than focusing on direct selling methods, the most effective way for all professionals (especially lawyers) to sell themselves is by helping others. You can become a trusted resource and advisor for your clients in a number of ways, all focused on being their resource for everything. We talked about the path to trusted advisor in Chapter 37, but this chapter will explore some of the specific ways that we can help clients and others. I refer to this as "selling by connecting" business development, and it is a skill that lawyers must learn in order to be effective and that most current rainmakers have already mastered (sometimes without even realizing it).

Many of us are uncomfortable with the direct approach to selling legal services. Whether we are attempting to sell legal services to prospective clients or additional services to existing clients, many of us have a significant level of discomfort in this process. We may be uncomfortable selling ourselves or our services or we may be uncomfortable with the "risk" that the client or prospect will say no, or will not have a need, or will not recognize the need. This is a challenge familiar to anyone in sales in that there is always a risk (and potentially a fear) of some form of rejection, and many times this discomfort results in not making the effort.

> ▼▼▼▼▼
>
> One of the potential problems with a direct sales approach is the risk that it can create a win-lose type of mentality.

If I am trying to sell a client on myself or my firm, it is easy to fall into the trap of making it a win-lose scenario where you either win by getting the new business or lose by not getting the business. Taking this approach can also create a win-lose perception for the client or prospect. None of us like to be sold anything, but all of us like to buy. Therefore, our goal should always be to educate and move our clients and prospects (and even referral sources) to a buying decision. Our goal is to help them to see the value of us, our services, our advice, and our "difference" so that they decide to allow us to work with them. This is a win-win approach to selling and relationship building and it requires a commitment to a different way of helping our clients.

In the previous chapter we talked about the most powerful question—"What do you need?"—which is an integral part of the "selling by connecting" method of selling legal services (or any products or services). Selling by connecting involves finding out how you can help your clients, prospects, and others and then connecting them with the people, information, or resources they need. "Selling by connecting" is all about the clients, prospects, and others (not about you), and it creates a pure win-win scenario for everyone. But it also takes away the discomfort with direct selling methods, since you are not there to sell them anything—you are there only to find out what they need help with and how you can help them. The key is that you must be totally committed and fully engaged toward helping them with whatever their needs are, even if they have nothing to do with you or your services.

This is a true form of investing in them, since you are committing to help without expecting anything in return. No direct benefit flows to you from your efforts. You are investing in the relationship by connecting them with people and resources to address their most important needs. What you are saying (directly or indirectly) is, "While I would love to share with you how I believe I can help you as your legal advisor, I am here to find out what you need help with and provide that help in any way I can."

This approach will require time to take root with the people you meet. Many people will be skeptical. Many are not used to this type of experience, and they may even hesitate to reveal their real needs, either because they are not certain of your motives or, frankly, they are not certain that you mean what you say. However, by being genuine and open with people you will be able to find out how you can help them and then you must follow through by doing what you have committed to do—help them.

Commit to Investing in People

We all know that the ultimate goal of building a relationship is to work together, but the road to getting there is all about focusing on other people. This requires that you be curious and genuine so that you can find out what is important to them, and then help them obtain it. If you are willing to listen, people will tell you what they need, giving you the opportunity to help them get it. In working with people we need to be consistent and have integrity so that we can demonstrate that we are worth having a relationship with. One great way is to give away good ideas before we do business with someone. When I meet with people, my goal is to have them leave the meeting feeling that they gained something of value simply from our conversation. Whether it is in a direct sales meeting, a relationship meeting, or even an introductory meeting to a potential client, I want people to feel that time invested with me was time well spent.

This is a powerful way of doing business. Not only does it differentiate you from nearly everyone else, but it takes all of the pressure off. There is no win-lose (get the business or not) mentality, but rather every meeting has the potential to end well with either a problem being solved or at least a need being identified. Admittedly, this approach requires a significant investment and commitment by both you and your firm. It will require you to invest time (not billable time) helping your clients without being paid for those efforts. However, it is a worthwhile investment. Consider the time you spend on other activities versus the value that this investment can deliver for your business development goals. You may not get an opportunity today for your legal services and counseling, but you can be fairly confident

> I read an article that quoted the president of a national company: "Every time I meet somebody, if I don't give them something educational that they can use, whether they buy from me or not, then I have not done my job."

that having proven yourself as a resource, you will be called on when a need for your services arises.

Even by simply asking "How can I help you?" you are communicating to the other person that you are more than a lawyer. Most lawyers talk to people about their legal needs, but advisors and counselors find out about all of their needs and how they can be of service. This is a unique model for lawyers, as well as anyone in business. You want to create an impression that you are available to help them with anything, whether it is personal or business. You want to be the person that people call whenever they have a question or a need. You want to be their "go to" person who solves problems, enhances success, and helps them to get wherever they need to go, personally or professionally. You can only be that person if you take the first steps toward being that person. Anyone can claim to be a "trusted advisor," but we prove it by what we commit to do and then following up and doing it.

Think about it yourself. When you consider all the people you have done business with, personally or professionally, how many have offered to help you outside of what they deliver? My guess is none, or at best, a very small number. Everyone in service businesses talks a good game about selling solutions, but the problem is that all of their solutions are about them (the seller). We have to make it about our clients, rather than just about us, and the only way to do that is to actually put their needs first.

Help People in Some Tangible Way

Although there are myriad ways to help clients and others, some key categories are helping them to make money or save money, being their advocate, promoting their business, and helping with any personal or family needs. Nearly everyone is looking for help in these areas. We should not necessarily talk about how our services can help them to make more money or to save money, but rather try to understand their goals and then help them achieve those goals. If our services can help them make money, save money, or minimize risk, then we must clearly articulate these benefits. That is why it is so important to be familiar with a variety of available resources and how they can help others.

The most obvious way to help people make more money is to refer business to them. Therefore, we need to ask people whom they do business with and whom they would like to do business with. We need to keep them in mind as we are going about our business so that we can spot opportunities for them, or even better, create specific opportunities. It all comes down to knowing the needs of our clients, and being proactive, even aggressive, in finding opportunities for them to make money or save money.

Another great way to support people is to support their businesses and their causes in tangible ways. First and foremost, it is important that we are "in touch" enough with people that we know what is going on in their lives. Second, we need to take it upon ourselves to at least find out whether we can help with any challenges. It is a rare person who offers support in tangible ways and by doing so you demonstrate very clearly your commitment to others and to their success. For example, if legislation is pending or passed that has a detrimental impact on your client or your client's industry, why not write a letter on his behalf to the appropriate agency or official? It requires very little time investment, but it goes a long way toward sending a clear message that you are much more than a lawyer and that you are genuinely concerned with the client's overall success.

Obviously, helping our clients and prospective clients (and others) to make more money or to save money is a great way to build and enhance relationships.

I once read of someone's idea to find a "common enemy" with your clients and business associates. In other words, you figure out who or what could potentially harm people and then support them against these "common enemies." For example, it could be insurance companies, the IRS, lawsuits, foreign imports, deadbeat dads, abusive spouses, competitors, and so on. No matter what the cause or "common enemy," identify it and help your clients fight or overcome it.

Another great way to support your clients is with their nonprofit or community projects. Anyone involved in these types of efforts always has some need, whether it is for direct dollars or donations, assistance with fund raising or sponsorships, or even support in the form of people and time. No matter what the cause, there are always needs, and if you are willing to help, you will enhance and build a relationship that will be part of the foundation for your ultimate business development results.

Everyone and every business has periodic challenges from outside influences such as legislation, economic conditions, legal issues (that may be outside your scope of services), or even public opinion.

Be aware of opportunities to help your clients with personal needs. It may be something as simple as finding a reputable contractor for a project at home, but providing this information makes that person's life easier and simpler. This is a great contribution to make to anyone. Sometimes people have needs, issues, or challenges with respect to their children. If you can be a resource to help them minimize, address, or eliminate these challenges, you can be a hero. It starts with being more than just a lawyer and engaging in open and honest discussions so that you can learn how you can help. These are opportunities for you to demonstrate in tangible ways that you are the type of person that people will want to do business with on many levels.

The key is to make this sales methodology—the trusted advisor or selling by connecting method—a part of your routine, your habits, and your overall mindset, so that you can engage in it naturally and easily. You will do it so often that at some point you will not have to even think about it. You will become that valuable resource and your phone will start ringing when clients and others are looking for help. That is the ultimate goal for all of us—to have the phone ring—whether they are calling to hire us or to ask for our help. In either case, we want the phone to ring, but people will call lawyers for help only if they believe that their lawyer can help them in ways far beyond legal services.

In the past year I have experienced several great examples of how "selling by connecting" can be a win-win for everyone. I was meeting with a prospective client and he shared with me a fairly long list of business needs or challenges. Fortunately, I was in a position to help him directly with three or four of those challenges, but another three or four were outside the scope of my expertise. Many people would have dismissed those other challenges, but I told this business owner that I would work on finding the resources and people he needed to address them. At the end of our next meeting I gave him a list of names, all of whom could help with specific challenges he faced. I had invested several hours in identifying the people on this list. Some of them I knew already, and based on my personal experience I knew they could help address his specific challenges. In a couple of cases, however, I needed to make several phone calls to find just the right person for his unique situation.

When I handed him the list, he looked at me and said, "Thanks, this is exactly what I need." The interesting thing is that he had not asked for help in these areas, but I had provided it voluntarily without expecting anything in return. Several of those resources proved to be exactly what he needed, and he repeatedly expressed his gratitude to me. The greatest thing is that I helped him because I really enjoy solving problems. I did not do it simply to build a relationship or to enhance the probability of

▼▼▼▼▼

This investment of my time (and of my energy and focus) did a great deal to build a terrific relationship with this business owner.

gaining a new client (or additional business), but rather out of a genuine interest in making a difference and in being the type of resource people will rely on. That was the win for me. The win for the client is that he got the resources he needed to address some significant challenges and issues. Yes, I am confident that there will be more and better opportunities to do business with this client in the future, but my focus was on helping him with immediate concerns, nothing more.

Another great example of this relationship-building approach came shortly thereafter. A new client called and said his recollection was that I had told him "we do everything." I told him I was sure I did not say that, but rather that I "could help him with anything." That is my commitment to the people I work with and have relationships with. He then explained that he had a need, but I was not sure I could help him directly with it. However, I committed to investigate the matter and to get back to him with an answer. Ultimately, it turned out that I could help him directly with his problem, but I also provided a couple of other options so he could select the best one for his particular need.

In addition, I shared my own thoughts on how to approach the situation, and later he told me he had followed my advice, with a very favorable result. What I told him in the original meeting is that I was available to help with whatever needs he had. What I did in the follow up was confirm that he could call on me with a challenge or a problem, and that I would be a valued resource committed to following through on my promises.

Admittedly, doing business this way is not the norm. Anyone can simply sell products or services, but it is a rare person who works hard at being a true value-added resource for their clients and others. When it comes to people, it is all about investing in them, so stop selling and start helping, and your business development opportunities will grow along with your results.

40 What Does Your Success Team Look Like?

Unfortunately, most of our training and even work experience has been more about individual achievement and self-sufficiency than teamwork. With the exception of study groups, law school was all about individual performance, particularly our beloved Socratic method, which called for you to be put on the spot (alone) among your peers and then expected to perform on demand. As many of you remember, your time spent working in a law firm too often involved a similar experience. Despite much conversation on the topic, many firms have been slow to implement a practical training and mentoring program. Most of your efforts were directed to doing what you needed to do individually to achieve the firm's goals and/or to support the other lawyers you worked for. In fact, your words often reveal the individual nature of your work as a lawyer—you talk about who you worked "for" in the firm, rather than who you worked "with."

Of course, this changed a little bit when you became a partner and you were theoretically on an even plane with your fellow partners, but it was still mostly about your own individual performance. Rarely do we hear talk of teamwork in a law firm. We may talk about working together on a specific project, but it never really seems to get to the point of talking about how much better we can be, how much better the firm can be, and how much better our clients can be served if we all work as a team. Unfortunately, this lack of teamwork also causes business development efforts to suffer.

A Team Approach to Business Development

Business owners know that success in business requires a team effort. For law firms this means that lawyers need to develop a team approach to everything, including business development. Rather than just arbitrarily meeting people and hoping that results follow, we need to work together with our fellow lawyers in the firm so that our efforts are consistent and integrated. Rather than pulling in a number of different directions, with better communication and a team approach to business development, the firm as a whole (and the individual lawyers) can start to focus their business development and relationship-building efforts on the right people and the right opportunities. Perhaps a better word would be the best opportunities for you, individually, and for the firm. As with investing in our clients and other relationships, this requires that we be selfless when it comes to our fellow lawyers.

While we all may have our individual goals, we need to focus on the end game (the firm's goals) recognizing that a team approach will help everyone achieve success. We should adopt an abundance mentality versus a scarcity mentality. We should view fellow lawyers in our firm as people who can help us achieve better results for ourselves and for the firm by working with us, rather than adopting a scarcity mentality that says there is only a limited amount of business and I want to bring it in myself.

▼▼▼▼▼

An abundance mentality means that we not only see the glass as half full, but we see the opportunities in working with, rather than against, the firm's other lawyers.

By now we should recognize and understand that people are different, which means that the people we talk to as clients, prospective clients, and even as business acquaintances have varying personalities. Since we are all different, it is naïve to believe that we are always the best person to pursue a given opportunity or relationship. By working together, we can make sure (or at least improve our odds) that the best people are pursuing the best opportunities.

Another great benefit of working together in a "team selling" environment is that it allows for much more effective listening and observing by one or both participants. We have already talked about how important listening skills are when it comes to business development and sales efforts, but it is true that being a good listener and a good observer is a challenge when you are being called on to participate in an active discussion in some way. However, if you have one person "leading" a meeting, the other participants can sit back and take it all in. They can listen carefully to the answers, they can look at body language, and they can carefully observe the client or prospect to better judge reactions, what is said or perhaps what is unsaid. You may be able to better anticipate and respond to those "unstated" questions simply because you are able to focus your energy on listening and observing. Team selling is a great way to approach business development, particularly in professional services, but it is an area that is often overlooked in law firms, primarily because of the emphasis on individual performance.

A great benefit of doubling up or "team selling" with clients and prospects is the ability to share valuable information. Each of us may know a great deal, but combining the knowledge of an entire team creates a formidable and powerful knowledge base. This is essentially the concept of building a law firm from the legal services side—you hire and train skilled lawyers to create a strong foundation for the firm's ability to deliver expert legal services. However, we forget about the power of sharing knowledge and information when it comes to business development. Each person in your firm usually has different information about the market, clients, prospective clients, and other relationships. With a little bit of enhanced communication, that knowledge and information base can be shared with everyone, thereby improving everyone's opportunities and results. This is also true of working with your team outside of the firm. You should be building a team of resources and advisors who can help you to better market and sell yourself and your services. By being specific, purposeful, and intentional in these relationships you can individually and collectively be better and more productive in your various business development efforts.

One often overlooked aspect of sharing information is the "who do you know" question. Each of us knows a different group of people and, if we rely solely on our own group, we are missing all of the opportunities to improve our results based on who the people around us know, whether it is inside or outside the firm. Let's take a look at this from a mathematical perspective. Let's assume that you have done a pretty good job of networking and that you know to some reasonable degree of personalization approximately 200 people. Let's also assume that of that number you have approximately 40 to 50 very strong relationships. By the way, most people who work in this area would say that these are pretty realistic numbers—that it is difficult to have strong relationships with more than 40 or 50 people and that the maximum number of people you could really know to the point of having

▼▼▼▼▼

Unfortunately, we have been taught (personally and professionally) that success is measured by what we can do on our own, when our goal should be to achieve the greatest potential from working together.

any effectiveness is somewhere between 150 to 200. If you would like to learn a little bit more about this concept, I encourage you to read the book titled *The Turning Point* by Malcolm Gladwell (Back Bay Books, 2002). Now let us assume that one of your fellow lawyers (either in the same practice area or in a different practice area) knows the same number of people. There may be a little bit of overlap (let us assume 10 percent), but your combined resources are 90 key relationships and 360 people known. Without even coming close to doubling your effort, you can easily double the number of relationships and people with whom you are connected.

Most of us are familiar with the concept of "six degrees of separation" which was made famous in a game related to Kevin Bacon. The "six degrees of separation" theory says that every person is connected to every other person by no more than six people. For example, I may not know you personally, but if you know a good friend of mine, then we are separated by one degree. The "six degrees of separation" concept is based on pure numbers and they are very real, but most of us have failed to take advantage of the opportunity presented by this reality. By partnering in our business development efforts, we can proactively take leaps and bounds across the various degrees of separation and get immediate contacts, introductions, and opportunities with the people we target. This is a powerful engine if we can only work together.

As we all know, one of the biggest challenges of business development for lawyers is lack of time. Many of the things we have talked about in this book relate to developing processes and systems to support our business development efforts, but one of the best systems is "team selling," which allows us to then share some of the business development duties and efforts, thereby leveraging our time and making everyone more efficient and more productive. We can work together on developing targets, niches, and business development plans. We can do team networking where we go to events together (and immediately separate), which gives us a support mechanism while enhancing our ability to "work the room" at such an event. This aspect of business development can be time-consuming, but imagine how much time could be saved if you and others in your firm (or even outside of your firm) were working together on these efforts.

▼▼▼▼▼

As with everything in life, there is strength in numbers when it comes to business development.

Unfortunately, and despite the claims that the American work ethic is diminishing, most lawyers have been trained to work hard, rather than work smart. It is not just a cliché. Doing it yourself is hard work and almost always less effective. Frankly, one of the biggest impediments to working together in business development is our egos. We want it to be all about us, and we want to be able to take all of the credit, but if we are willing to share the efforts and share the credit, everyone wins. As lawyers we often talk about win-win scenarios, but rarely do we actually implement strategies that can deliver win-win results. Team selling and partnering in business development efforts is a great way to create win-win scenarios for yourself, for the people you work with, and for the firm itself. The opportunities are there, but it is up to us to turn them into new business.

Spheres of Influence

One other area we need to cover relating to business development is the concept of a sphere of influence. Everyone has one. You have one. I have one. Your spouse has one. Your kids have one. Your sphere of influence is nothing more than the people who are part of your life in some way. In your personal life, it would be your spouse, your children, your family, your friends, your neighbors, your co-workers, the members of your church, and the people or businesses that you rely on for the things that you need. On a personal level, that sphere of influence could include everyone from your spouse (probably your closest relationship) to your mail carrier (whom you may not even know by name). These are all people you depend on in some way and to whom you are connected at some level. The same is true in business. For you this would include your fellow partners or associates, the resource people you rely on to help your clients in other areas, your mentors or advisors, your referral sources, and so on. These are all people you depend on in some way for your success.

Oh my, we forgot one—your clients. We certainly depend on them for our success, yet do we ever stop to think that they are really part of our sphere of influence and do we evaluate where they are in that sphere? Ideally, we should want to have clients who are very close to the inner circle within our sphere of influence, because that is where relationships exist and flourish, rather than having them on the outer loops of our sphere of influence, where they are merely a client or a necessary evil. How often have we heard lawyers say, “The practice of law wouldn't be so bad if it wasn't for the clients.” That tells us that we are not where we need to be in our relationships with some of our clients, and it also probably means that we need to fire some clients, but it is important to actually give some thought to where our various clients fit within our spheres of influence.

Our clients and prospects also have spheres of influence. These are the people they work with, depend on, rely on, and in some cases, look to for advice and counseling. As lawyers, most of us want to be in the inner circle for our clients and prospects, but too often we do not take any affirmative steps to move to that inner circle. We want it, but we do not do what we should to get there.

Shown below is a typical sphere of influence for a business owner.

The Spheres of Influence of a Business Owner

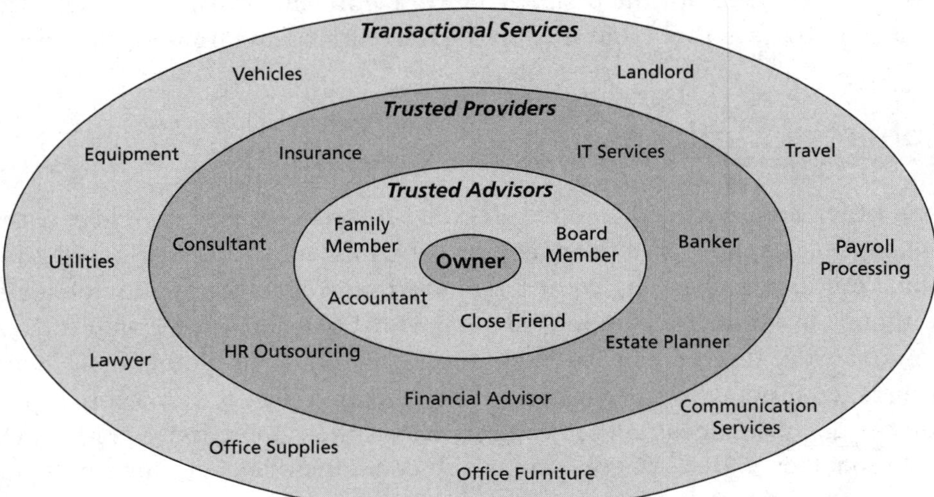

Whom do we see? We see typical vendors on the outer circle. These are the necessary evils. Obviously, some of these vendors have done the right things to achieve a higher level of relationship with a business owner, which allows them to move closer to, if not within, the inner circle. As you move closer to the middle, you find increasingly personal and confidential relationships where the business owner is likely more dependent on these service providers. They may still be only service providers, but there exists an element of a closer relationship. The closer you get to the inner circle, the closer the relationship and, most importantly, the greater dependence by the business owner on that person to be a resource and advisor.

Our goal as lawyers should always be to be part of our clients' inner circle. Unfortunately, many of us as lawyers are in that outside circle where we are merely necessary evils—merely service providers who do a job that needs to be done—and we are not depended on or sought after to provide other valuable input and help to our clients. We cannot wait to be asked. We need to start being that advisor and that resource now, which is the means by which we can ultimately move closer and closer to the business owner's inner circle. Too many of us are waiting for this to happen, but it will not happen without affirmative efforts on our part. Ultimately, the path to success in nearly all business development efforts is through people. It is not only the people we are seeking as clients, but also those that we can identify and target as key people who can help us to achieve our goals, both individually and as a firm.

To better evaluate (now and in the future) your relationship team, Appendix D contains a worksheet you can use to help you identify your current business relationship team, as well as to help you review and assess that team on a consistent basis in the future. On this worksheet list your top 40 business relationships (in order of value). The top 20 should be listed on the "big league" roster, and the second 20 should be listed on the "minor league" roster. Do not worry if you cannot come up with 40 business relationships—if you have only 20, then list 20. However, make sure to spend plenty of time thinking about the relationships you have. As of today, these are your key resources for growing your business and this is where you should be investing your time.

Individualism and self-reliance may be great character traits for a skilled lawyer, but success in business development is most often achieved by those who are willing to work with others as a team so that everyone achieves greater and better results.

Here are some thoughts and ideas for putting together these lists, but the ultimate goal is to have strong relationships that will help you achieve greater success in your business. List people who are already contributing to your success, as well as people who have the potential to do so. Be specific whenever possible (e.g., rather than list another law firm, individually list the lawyers in that firm), but you can list key associations or organizations.

- Clients
- Lawyer referral sources
- Business referral sources
- Business resources
- Family, friends, and neighbors
- Mentors and advisors
- Consultants
- Trade associations, business organizations, and nonprofits

Continually review and assess your relationship roster with a view toward improving your relationship lineup.

Too many of us not only fail to really identify who is part of our relationship team, but we also fail to evaluate the people we have included on our roster in order to either take steps to improve the relationships or the results obtained from it or to seek out replacements for our relationship roster. We should be constantly upgrading and improving our relationship rosters so we can always make the best and most effective use of our valuable time.

Fishing with a Net

We have talked many times about the concept of leverage, but business development is the area where leverage can be our greatest asset. When I am talking about leverage in business development I always like to share this picture with people. I have found this picture to be one of the greatest illustrations of the concept of leverage. As you can see, two professionals are sitting on the dock with fishing poles in their hands and a single line in the water. We will assume for purposes of this picture that these two professionals are fishing in the right pond and have the right bait and equipment to reel in the clients they are seeking to catch, but the problem is they are fishing with a single line. Their best-case scenario for the time that they invest is catching one new client at a time or one new piece of business at a time.

In contrast, look at the professional with the giant net. We can also assume that he is fishing in the right pond, but he does not want to settle for only one new client, one new matter, or one new piece of business at a time. Instead, he has built a business development net that he is using to sweep through the water with the goal of obtaining many new clients and many new matters all at once. You not only need to build the net, but you need to adopt a "fishing with a net" mentality so that you focus your valuable time and energy on the business development activities and efforts that will deliver the most opportunities and the most new business.

By focusing on building quality relationships, developing strong referral relationships, working hard at creating consistent referrals, having others selling for you, and continually expanding your sphere of influence, you too can begin to fish with a net. We need to stop marketing for one new client at a time, and direct our time, energy, and efforts toward activities that have the potential to deliver multiple rather than individual opportunities.

> Fishing for new business and clients with a net can only occur by using relationships and referrals. Having others selling for you allows you to move beyond the "one new sale at a time" approach to business development.

Ideally, we should not only be "fishing with a net" but building relationships around us where all of our contacts are also fishing with a net. Imagine the power of a business development team where everyone is fishing with a net. With time at such a premium, leveraged business development efforts—or "fishing with a net"—are the most important way for us to dramatically improve our business development results. As you put together your business development plan and your business development team remember this illustration. I encourage you to "decide" to fish with a net rather than use one line at a time, and one of the best ways to "fish with a net" is to view business development as a team sport.

As we said at the outset, it is unfortunate that law firms as a whole have not embraced the concept of teamwork the way most businesses have. Admittedly, there are many businesses that talk about teamwork, but don't walk the talk, but at least teamwork is part of the vocabulary, much more so than in many law firms. Even at the most senior level in your firm, how often have you talked about the concept of "working together"? How often have you developed specific initiatives around lawyers working together? Many years ago I heard about a highly paid outside consultant who came to a law firm to work on business development. The sum and substance of his advice was as follows:

1. The firm should focus most of its business development efforts and energy on cross-selling and up-selling with existing clients—in other words, look to achieve new business from existing clients first and foremost; and
2. To achieve this cross-selling and up-selling, the lawyers should be introducing other lawyers from the firm to their clients.

This is certainly simple and straightforward advice, but it is very powerful and effective if implemented. Unfortunately, the results were minimal because the lawyers who held most of the key relationships were not only reluctant, but in many cases refused, to make the introductions. Why? Because in their minds it was "their client" and "their relationship," which is a mindset that holds back many firms.

There may certainly be a personal and professional relationship between the primary relationship holder and the client, but it is the firm's client. Under no circumstances is it acceptable to refuse to introduce other lawyers to clients of the firm. In fact, that approach is really saying that we are not looking out for the client's best interests. If the firm has a solution, a service, or practice area that can benefit the client, yet we fail to introduce that solution or service, then we are doing that client a disservice and we should be fired for not making the introduction. It is a rainmaker's mentality to make sure that the client has access to the types of advice and expertise that will benefit the client. It should be all about the client, and nothing about the individual lawyers.

When you start to rank priorities, it should be clients first, firm second, and everyone else last. Without this mindset, it is difficult to deliver truly great performance and experiences for your clients, and it also makes it very challenging to achieve any sustainable and predictable business development results. As the well-known business saying goes, "Together everyone achieves more," and this applies to law firms as well as other businesses.

Appendix D: Relationship Team Worksheet

YOUR RELATIONSHIP TEAM

"Big League" Roster

1. ______________________________
2. ______________________________
3. ______________________________
4. ______________________________
5. ______________________________
6. ______________________________
7. ______________________________
8. ______________________________
9. ______________________________
10. ______________________________
11. ______________________________
12. ______________________________
13. ______________________________
14. ______________________________
15. ______________________________
16. ______________________________
17. ______________________________
18. ______________________________
19. ______________________________
20. ______________________________

"Minor League" Roster

1. __________
2. __________
3. __________
4. __________
5. __________
6. __________
7. __________
8. __________
9. __________
10. __________
11. __________
12. __________
13. __________
14. __________
15. __________
16. __________
17. __________
18. __________
19. __________
20. __________

The Future of Law Firms

41

Is the law industry in crisis? Probably not right now, but it may very well be in the near future. Law firms in many ways have been very lucky over the years. Despite a lack of real focus and commitment to client service, many firms have continued to not only survive, but flourish. Despite being one of the few industries that fails to deliver much, if any, predictability regarding costs, law firms have been able to maintain and sustain a reasonable client base and revenue stream. Despite high turnover and escalating salaries, law firms have not only survived, but many have shown significant revenue growth. For this reason many lawyers would say that the law firm model is not broken and, therefore, it does not need to be fixed. While the crisis has not yet hit, certainly we know that the pressures are building in many different ways. Many lawyers see that doing things the same old way under the same old law firm model will not work forever. The time will come when changes have to be made because they will be forced on lawyers and law firms, perhaps without sufficient notice.

The question is what type of lawyer and law firm do you want to represent? Do you want to be known as the law firm that continues to do things the old-fashioned way, or do you want to be the law firm and the lawyer who *decides* to be more business-like—to make decisions like a business, to operate like a business, to build a team like a business, and to grow like a business? Do you just want to "hope" to be a trusted advisor, or do you want to do all the right things so that you can truly be a trusted and valued resource for your clients? Are you satisfied with the status quo or do you want to build a firm that thrives and grows regularly, consistently, and predictably? Do you want to depend on market conditions for your future and for the future of your firm, or do you want to build a model law business that delivers the results that you want, rather than simply settling for the results that occur?

To move to a true business model for a law firm, we must first get past any thought that a law firm is unlike other businesses. We need to accept the reality that a law business is like any other service business so that we can move past the mental roadblocks holding us back from becoming better leaders. We also need to think and act like businesspeople, to make more businesslike decisions, and to develop more businesslike systems within our firm. We need to not only talk about the value of our people (professional and staff), but we also need to treat them as the valued resources that they are, and we need to establish hiring, training, and development programs that support and nurture them as integral parts of our law business team. We also need to get back to basics when it comes to clients and to build a truly client-centric organization, including client service systems that will support a "clients are first and foremost" model.

▼▼▼▼▼

Clients and new business are the lifeblood of any law firm, and we need to do things differently in terms of how we work with clients, communicate with clients, and service clients.

We know what clients want, but most of us have been unwilling to really deliver it, and the time has come to communicate clearly to our clients and prospective clients that we mean what we say when it comes to client service. The only way to do that is to take different actions and to follow through on commitments that we have made or should be making to our clients and prospective clients. Most important, we need to focus our client-related efforts on great performance and great experiences, and forget about merely providing excellent legal services, which will never be enough to build the types of client relationships that we need as a foundation of our law business.

Finally, when it comes to business development we must think and act according to the premise that it is all about people and relationships. We need to not only talk about relationships, but we must also do the things we instinctively know are right to build those relationships on a consistent basis. We need to be prepared to work together with our fellow lawyers, our law firm team, our clients, and our various business associates to find solutions and become problem-solvers. We can no longer just talk about being trusted advisors, but we need to put our words to the test and start helping clients, prospects, and others. We need to make it clear to all the people we interact with that we are here to help them and that we are prepared to invest in them (heavily if necessary) to help them achieve their goals. That is truly the path to great success in relationship building and, ultimately, business development.

As lawyers, many of us know what we want, but our actions in support of those goals often fall short of the mark. I hope this book has presented some ideas, insights, and ways of thinking and doing things that you can use as a road map to take your own practice and your law firm business to never-imagined levels. The path is there, but we must be willing to put aside some of the old ways, to take some risks, and to really invest in our clients and our relationships. It may not be an easy path, but by working together I am confident you can find a way to take your own practice and your law firm to greater heights of success and prosperity. Admittedly, this path is not for everyone. Many do not believe that change is necessary. Many are not prepared to make the changes necessary or to take the risk (perceived or real) that accompanies any change. However, for those who genuinely believe that clients and relationships are important and who want to build a truly great business, the opportunities are there just waiting to be converted into new, different, and better results.

The entrepreneurial spirit can be alive and well with lawyers and law firms if we are only willing to let that spirit guide our decisions and our actions as businesspeople. The world is full of lawyers and there will always be excellent lawyers, but there is plenty of room for great businesspeople who are also great lawyers. Wouldn't it be great to have a law firm filled with both? Time will tell about the future of law firms, but for today, tomorrow, and the foreseeable future, you get to choose your own path. Enjoy the journey!

Index

Selected Books from . . .
THE ABA LAW PRACTICE MANAGEMENT SECTION

Women-at-Law: Lessons Learned Along the Pathways to Success
By Phyllis Horn Epstein
Discover how women lawyers in a wide variety of practice settings are meeting the challenges of competing in an often all-consuming profession without sacrificing their desire for a multidimensional life. Women-at-Law provides a wealth of practical guidance and direction from experienced women lawyers who share their life stories and advice to inspire and encourage others by offering solutions to the challenges—personal and professional. You'll learn that, with some effort, a motivated woman can redirect her career, her home life, and her interests, in the long journey that is a successful life. If you are a law student, a practicing lawyer, or simply a woman considering a career

The Legal Career Guide: From Law Student to Lawyer, Fourth Edition
By Gary A. Munneke
This book is a step-by-step guide for planning a law career, preparing and executing a job search, and moving into the market. Whether you're considering a solo career, examining government or corporate work, joining a medium or large firm, or focusing on an academic career—this book is filled with practical advice that will help you find your personal niche in the legal profession. This book will help law students make the right choices in building their resumes, making informed career decisions, and taking the first step toward career success.

Managing Partner 101: A Guide to Successful Law Firm Leadership, Second Edition
By Lawrence G. Green
This completely updated and expanded second edition of an ABA bestseller is designed to help managing partners, lawyers, and other legal professionals understand the role and responsibilities of a law firm's managing partner. The book will shorten the learning curve for mastering successful management techniques for the new or experienced managing partner, through helpful guidelines, tips, and examples presented throughout the text. Of particular value is the author's extensive experience and his discussion on the importance of leadership to the effective managing partner.

The Lawyer's Guide to Marketing Your Practice, Second Edition
Edited by James A. Durham and Deborah McMurray
This book is packed with practical ideas, innovative strategies, useful checklists, and sample marketing and action plans to help you implement a successful, multifaceted, and profit-enhancing marketing plan for your firm. Organized into four sections, this illuminating resource covers: Developing Your Approach; Enhancing Your Image; Implementing Marketing Strategies and Maintaining Your Program. Appendix materials include an instructive primer on market research to inform you on research methodologies that support the marketing of legal services. The accompanying CD-ROM contains a wealth of checklists, plans, questionnaires, and templates—all designed to make implementing your marketing strategy as easy as possible!

The Successful Lawyer: Powerful Strategies for Transforming Your Practice
By Gerald A. Riskin
Available as a Book, Audio-CD Set, or Combination Package!
Global management consultant and trusted advisor to many of the world's largest law firms, Gerry Riskin goes beyond simple concept or theory and delivers a book packed with practical advice that you can implement right away. By using the principles found in this book, you can live out your dreams, embrace success, and awaken your firm to its full potential. Large law firm or small, managing partners and associates in every area of practice—all can benefit from the information contained in this book. With this book, you can attract what you need and desire into your life, get more satisfaction from your practice and your clients, and do so in a systematic, achievable way.

Keeping Good Lawyers: Best Practices to Create Career Satisfaction
By M. Diane Vogt and Lori-Ann Rickard
Now that your firm has recruited top legal talent, do you know how to maximize it? This book is filled with easy-to-implement suggestions for building and maintaining high levels of motivation and career satisfaction within the work environment. Management will discover how to train and retain good lawyers and keep them emotionally engaged with their work, their career development, and the success of the firm. Lawyers will learn how to find the balance between personal and professional goals, avoid boredom and burnout, and truly enjoy life.

How to Build and Manage an Entertainment Law Practice
By Gary Greenberg
This book addresses a variety of issues critical to establishing a successful entertainment law practice including getting started, preparing a business plan, getting your foot in the door, creating the right image, and marketing your entertainment law practice. The book discusses the basic differences between entertainment law and other types of law practice and provides guidance for avoiding common pitfalls. In addition, an extensive appendix contains sample agreements, forms, letters, and checklists common to entertainment law practitioners. Includes a diskette containing the essential appendix templates, forms and checklists for easy implementation!

How to Build and Manage an Employment Law Practice
By Mindy Farber
This guide provides practical, real-world advice from an employment law veteran, covering situations ranging from the initial client consultation to the pros and cons of solo versus group practice. Plus, you'll find samples of the most common letters and agreement used in employment law as well as general practice, including demand letters, the EEOC charging document, age and race discrimination lawsuits, plaintiff's interrogatories, and much more.

How to Build and Manage an Environmental Law Practice
By Stuart L. Somach
Through practical examples and explanations, this book reveals how you can gain environmental experience, understand the specialized business aspects of the environmental law practice, develop and maintain the ideal clientele mix, and much more, including the tactics, technology, and tools needed to run your practice for maximum efficiency and profitability. Includes an invaluable resource section!

How to Start and Build a Law Practice, Platinum Fifth Edition
By Jay G Foonberg
This classic ABA bestseller has been used by tens of thousands of lawyers as the comprehensive guide to planning, launching, and growing a successful practice. It's packed with over 600 pages of guidance on identifying the right location, finding clients, setting fees, managing your office, maintaining an ethical and responsible practice, maximizing available resources, upholding your standards, and much more. If you're committed to starting—and growing—your own practice, this one book will give you the expert advice you need to make it succeed for years to come.

Making Partner: A Guide for Law Firm Associates, Second Edition
By John R. Sapp
Many factors come into play in achieving the goal of making partner: the quality of your work; how you relate to your superiors, fellow associates, and staff; how you entertain your clients; your choice of outside activities; even publications you read. It may take six to nine years, or more, to make partner from associate. Do you know what you should and should not be doing? Do you really know what your chances are at your firm? This concise, straightforward book looks at all these factors and provides detailed advice on how to create your own strategic plan for success. It's also the perfect primer to give to all new associates!

Flying Solo: A Survival Guide for Solo and Small Firm Lawyers, Fourth Edition
Edited by K. William Gibson
The new fourth edition of this comprehensive guide includes practical information gathered from a wide range of contributors, who share tips and advice that can be easily implemented in your solo or small-firm practice. This classic ABA book first walks you through a step-by-step analysis of the decision to start a solo practice, including choosing a practice focus. It then provides tools to help you with financial issues including banking and billing; operations issues such as staffing and office location and design decisions; technology for the small law office; and marketing and client relations. What's more, the final section on quality-of-life issues puts it all into perspective. Whether you're thinking of going solo, new to the solo life, or a seasoned practitioner, Flying Solo provides time-tested answers to real-life questions.

The Lawyer's Guide to Fact Finding on the Internet, Third Edition
By Carole A. Levitt and Mark E. Rosch
Written especially for legal professionals, this revised and expanded edition is a complete, hands-on guide to the best sites, secrets, and shortcuts for conducting efficient research on the Web. Containing over 600 pages of information, with over 100 screen shots of specific Web sites, this resource is filled with practical tips and advice on using specific sites, alerting readers to quirks or hard-to-find information. What's more, user-friendly icons immediately identify free sites, free-with-registration sites, and pay sites. An accompanying CD-ROM includes the links contained in the book, indexed, so you can easily navigate to these cream-of-the-crop Web sites without typing URLs into your browser.

30-Day Risk-Free Order Form

Call Today! 1-800-285-2221

Monday–Friday, 7:30 AM – 5:30 PM, Central Time

Qty	Title	LPM Price	Regular Price	Total
______	Flying Solo, Fourth Edition (5110527)	$ 79.95	$ 99.95	$________
______	How to Start and Build a Law Practice, Platinum Fifth Edition (5110508)	57.95	69.95	$________
______	How to Build and Manage an Entertainment Law Practice (5110389)	44.95	54.95	$________
______	How to Build and Manage an Environmental Law Practice (5350074)	44.95	54.95	$________
______	Keeping Good Lawyers (5110437)	49.95	59.95	$________
______	The Lawyer's Guide to Marketing Your Practice, Second Edition (5110500)	79.95	89.95	$________
______	The Legal Career Guide (5110479)	29.95	34.95	$________
______	The Lawyer's Guide to Fact Finding on the Internet, Third Edition (5110568)	99.95	84.95	$________
______	Making Partner, Third Edition (5110576)	49.95	59.95	$________
______	Managing Partner 101, Second Edition (5110576)	44.95	49.95	$________
______	The Successful Lawyer—Book Only (5110531)	64.95	84.95	$________
______	The Successful Lawyer—6 Audio CDs, Boxed Set (5110537)	129.95	149.95	$________
______	The Successful Lawyer—Audio CD and Book Combination Package (5110533)	174.95	209.95	$________
______	Women-at-Law (5110509)	39.95	49.95	$________

*Postage and Handling	
$10.00 to $24.99	$5.95
$25.00 to $49.99	$9.95
$50.00 to $99.99	$12.95
$100.00 to $349.99	$17.95
$350 to $499.99	$24.95

****Tax**
DC residents add 5.75%
IL residents add 9.00%

***Postage and Handling**	$________
****Tax**	$________
TOTAL	$________

PAYMENT

❑ Check enclosed (to the ABA)

❑ Visa ❑ MasterCard ❑ American Express

Account Number ______ Exp. Date ______ Signature ______

Name ______ Firm ______

Address ______

City ______ State ______ Zip ______

Phone Number ______ E-Mail Address ______

Guarantee

If—for any reason—you are not satisfied with your purchase, you may return it within 30 days of receipt for a complete refund of the price of the book(s). No questions asked!

Mail: ABA Publication Orders, P.O. Box 10892, Chicago, Illinois 60610-0892
♦ Phone: 1-800-285-2221 ♦ FAX: 312-988-5568

E-Mail: abasvcctr@abanet.org ♦ Internet: http://www.lawpractice.org/catalog